the latin american kitchen

elisabeth luard

Elisabeth Luard is an award-winning food writer who has written many books on Spanish and Latin American cuisine. Both this, *The Latin American Kitchen*, and her recent book for Kyle Cathie, *The Food of Spain and Portugal* were recognized with Gourmand International awards, for best Latin American cookbook, and best foreign cookbook respectively. She is a regular contributor to various magazines and newspapers, including the *Scotsman*, the *Sunday Telegraph*, *Waitrose Food Illustrated*, *Decanter*, and *Gourmet Magazine*.

the latin american kitchen

a book of essential ingredients
with over 200 authentic recipes

elisabeth luard

WITHDRAWN

photography by francine lawrence

kyle books

**For my New World granddaughter,
Sophie Francesca Patricia**

This edition published in 2006 by Kyle Books
An imprint of Kyle Cathie Limited
general.enquiries@kyle-cathie.com
www.kylecathie.com

Distributed by National Book Network
4501 Forbes Blvd., Suite 200
Lanham, MD 20706
Phone: (301) 459 3366   Fax: (301) 429 5746

This paperback edition published in 2006
ISBN (13-digit) 978 1 904920 46 5
ISBN (10-digit) 1 904920 46 2

10 9 8 7 6 5 4 3 2 1

Project editors: Helen Woodhall and Caroline Taggart
Design: Geoff Hayes
Text editor: Robina Pelham Burn
Editorial assistance and picture research: Esme West
Home economy: Elisabeth Luard
Styling: Susi Hoyle
Production: Lorraine Baird and Sha Huxtable

The Library of Congress Cataloguing-in-Publication Data is available on file.

Half-title page: Mayan girl, San Lorenzo, Chiapas, Mexico
Title page: 'Fruits of Brazil', Rio carnival
*This page: New Year's Day festival in Mexico – teenage boys re-enact
the story of Mary and Joseph*

contents

introduction

My earliest childhood memories are of a cool house shaded by mimosa trees on the shores of the River Plate, the broad river that takes its water from the Paraná, which drains southward from the Mato Grosso, the tropical highlands of Brazil.

I was seven years old when my family took passage on the HMS *Andes* for the month-long journey from England to the southern tip of South America. We steamed steadily across the Atlantic, docking at the Canary Isles, crossing the equator by way of Rio, and sailing on in stately splendor until we arrived at our destination, Montevideo, my stepfather's first diplomatic posting among the Latins. As the capital of Uruguay, Argentina's little sister—cattle country settled by Scots as well as Spaniards—Montevideo was held to be suitable for diplomats with families.

We—my brother, mother, stepfather, and I—waited on the quayside while mountains of luggage were unloaded. My mother, who had inherited a considerable fortune, saw no reason to economize on life's small comforts. Our family possessions included a car—a brand-new silver Jaguar, which, winched from the hold, dangled precariously over the waters of the harbor. Customs officers appeared. Money changed hands. Released, we made our way to our new home.

My brother and I rapidly discovered that life among the Latins was far more colorful than the somewhat dismal life we'd led in postwar London. Passersby admired our curly blond hair and gave us sugarcane to suck. We learned Spanish almost overnight. My brother acquired a fishing rod and a posse of urchin friends. Most of my time, when I wasn't at school, was spent in the kitchen, since my mother employed a cook and enough maids to staff a small hotel.

Every evening, after school, I would sit on the back porch sucking a maté gourd through a straw, accepting sweets from strangers, my nostrils filled with the delicious scent of vanilla-flavored cookies or roasting chickens or caramelizing garlic—all equally exquisite. Then, if there was a party to be catered for, Esperanza, the cook, would open the door and call me in. I was needed in the kitchen. Really needed.

Actually, it was probably the first time I'd ever been needed in my life. Certain tasks were mine: rolling out the meatballs until they were perfectly round and no bigger than marbles, each flecked with green parsley. Mine, too, to peel the shrimp and pack them into avocado boats. On ordinary days I'd be be allowed to sift through the lentils for tiny stones, or pick over the rice for insects, or allowed to use a small, sharp knife to scoop out the creamy hearts of zapallitos, small, round marrows perfect for stuffing. On weekends my presence was not much required in the household, as my mother was busy with her own affairs. Happily, as children often will, my brother and I took advantage of what was, to the outside world, a degree of neglect. My brother overnighted with the fisherboys, while I would go home with Esperanza to the *barrio*, a row of tumbledown shacks full of people, chickens, and flea-bitten cats where, after a supper of maté tea sweetened with condensed milk and spiked with brandy, curled up on an old mattress on the earth floor among the sleeping babies and mouse-hunting felines, I slept soundly.

Those were the good times. Less good came when I was sent "home" to boarding school in England, a cold and dreadful place on the Welsh border, where my strange foreign ways, ability to speak languages, and weird holiday destinations — my family continued on the Latino circuit, taking in Spain along the way, and the summer holidays were all I was permitted — ensured I remained an outsider. Later, as a young adult almost — though not quite — engaged to be married, I took employment in the embassy in Mexico City, a hardship post for my parents but not for me, since I took advantage of my stepfather's seniority to attach myself to expeditions organized by Mexico's Sociedad Indigenista — Society for Indigenous Peoples. We traveled by bus, bumping through badlands, the Chiapas, where the natives spoke no Spanish and everyone carried guns. On the river Uxumazintla I learned how to pluck and roast a parrot; on the plains of Guerrero I was shown how to ferment the juice of the maguey cactus by passing it through my mouth in a straw.

Sounds exotic? Indeed it was. And yet there was much that was familiar. Still more so when I made the decision that my own children should have the benefit of life among the Latins, though the land of my choice was Andalusia, Spain's southernmost province. Perhaps I chose it because it made me feel at home — certainly there was no other reason, only that I had an instinctive feeling that four children (I was a young mother, and all were at one time under six) would be happy where I was happy.

I did not know it at the time, but there was reason for me to feel at home. The culinary habit as well as the speech patterns of my Uruguayan childhood were unmistakable. It was from the impoverished rural populations of Andalusia that the early colonizers of the New World were drawn.

The glittering port of Seville, a day's donkey journey from our valley, held the great library of the Indies, and it was here, in the writings of Bernal Diaz and the companions of Columbus himself, that I found the written record of what I already knew by instinct.

The culinary habit of Latin America — a shotgun marriage, the result of the fusion of two entirely different cultures and pantries — dates from 1492, the year in which Christopher Columbus made landfall in what he declared to be the New Indies. That this voyage took place immediately after the fall of Granada — the final battle of the fight to regain the lands of southern Iberia held by the Moors for seven centuries — was no accident. The victory claimed by the combined might of the Catholic kings, Isabel of Castile and Ferdinand of

Aragon, closed the route to the Orient, the source of so much pleasure to the cooks who learned their trade from the Moors. Hunger might be appeased by the wheat fields of the Guadalquivir, but man cannot live by bread alone. With her population clamoring for spices, Isabella pawned her jewels to fund the wild dreams of a Genoese seaman who promised a new route to the East.

From the moment the Old World's fragile ships made landfall in the New, a two-way traffic began. This trade, a process known as the Columbian Exchange, was in men and women, in ideas and philosophies, in gold and silver, in spices and oddities valued for their rarity—but above all in food, the raw material of life. The process of integration was surprisingly rapid, leading to an interweaving of culinary habit that, through the use of unfamiliar ingredients in familiar ways and of familiar ingredients in unfamiliar ways, makes the gastronomy of Latin America an edible history lesson. By the time Granada fell to the

Catholic kings in 1492, the cooks of Spain and Portugal used spices liberally, had acquired pastry-making skills as well as learning the confectioner's art, and understood sophisticated culinary techniques such as the use of pounded nuts to thicken sauces, the art of rice cooking, the use of delicate flavorings such as saffron and cilantro. Along with these Moorish tastes, they had acquired a willingness to sample new and unfamiliar ingredients.

The early colonialists—Spanish and Portuguese, mainly from the south and therefore poorer and more Arab—imported the meat and milk animals of the Old World: pigs and chickens throughout, cattle to the Argentinian pampas, and sheep to Patagonia. They set about subduing the indigenous peoples—the Aztec and residual Mayan civilizations in Central America, the Inca empire of Peru, as well as other less well-organized tribal groups. Some, such as the Caribs of the Caribbean, defended their territories fiercely,

Colonial architecture in the historic district of Salvador, Brazil

Ploughing near Pucón, Chile

others treated the newcomers with more circumspection—indeed among those with an expectation of divine visitation, they were greeted as gods.

As the indigenous population declined or, less willing to take the consequences of defiance, retreated to the less hospitable interior, the European colonizers began to import slave labor from Africa, adding another layer to the culinary and social makeup. More recent gastronomic colonization has taken place for economic reasons: coffee grows well in Brazil, bananas thrive throughout the tropical and subtropical zones, while additional botanical riches—though scarcely needed to swell the indigenous coffers— include pineapples, mangoes, and all types of

citrus fruits, as well as grapevines for the wine makers of Chile and Argentina.

Although the ingredients themselves, both flora and fauna, can be clearly defined in naturalist's terms as being of native or alien origin, culinary habit is far less easy to distinguish. Who's to say if the seviches of Mexico are more closely related to the *escabeches* of Spain and Portugal than they are to the marinated fish dishes enjoyed by the Maya, whose taste for raw fish is shared by the inhabitants of the islands of the Pacific, including Japan? It would be a brave ethnologist indeed who could trace the descent of the dried-shrimp dishes of Bahia to the salt cod traditions of Portugal without acknowledging the use of dende oil as part of the conservation process, an ingredient and method of purely African origin. Or who could claim exclusivity for the use of the earth oven or pit barbecue, a method of cooking that, as it happens, is common throughout Southeast Asia as well as among the aboriginal shore-dwellers of Australasia?

To generalize (always a dangerous exercise), the basic culinary habit of the native peoples of the southern lands of the Americas was and remains vegetarian, with much attention paid to nutritional balance and digestibility. A little opportunist meat-eating was mainly confined to tribal gatherings— and even today, meat is considered festive food. There were exceptions, naturally. Coastal dwellers of Chile and Brazil depended on fish augmented by sea vegetables, while the jungle dwellers of Amazonia and the highlands of central America depended on river fish, berries, and roots.

By the time the Europeans appeared, the indigenous inhabitants—those who had settled down as farmers rather than those who had simply continued as nomadic hunter-gatherers— had already developed and refined the food plants on which they depended, exchanging and exporting between themselves. Tomatoes, for instance, are found in their wild and unpalatable form in Peru, but were cultivated in their modern form by the Aztecs of Mexico. Mexico, too, is the homeland of the avocado, a tree that remains sterile unless grafted with a fruit-bearing branch, indicating human intervention at an early stage in its food-supplying career. At the same time, a system of intensive cultivation was developed that suited the climate and the natural fertility of the soil. Some of the crops were simultaneous: rows of corn provided a climbing frame for a crop of

Decorated pig at La Taconga festival, Ecuador

beans—lima, pinto, black, or brown; winter and summer squash acted as a weed suppressant between the rows. These three vegetables are often cooked together, providing a perfectly balanced meal in a single pot.

The indigenous population quickly accepted Europe's domestic animals—the cow as a milk producer, egg-layers in the form of chickens, the mighty sty-pig as the principal meat animal, sheep and goats for cropping marginal lands—as useful additions to the New World's fauna. The Europeans had much to learn from those they colonized, including sophisticated skills in the preparation of ingredients that, in their untreated state, ranged from the indigestible to the inedible to the downright toxic. Ingredients as varied as cassava, corn, chocolate, and vanilla all fall within the categories of foodstuffs that need special preparation to achieve their potential. Added to these was an abundance of roots, tubers, fruits, and vegetables—among them potatoes, tomatoes, peppers, squash, dried beans, pineapples, avocados—whose taste and culinary virtues were completely unknown to the world beyond their native territory.

Although these unfamiliar foodstuffs were slow to gain acceptance in the Old World, it was not so among the early colonizers of the New, who, naturally enough, were rarely accompanied by their wives. Contemporary accounts of the Conquistadores as provided by the evangelizing monks who followed close behind describe the surprising palatability of the dishes prepared by their hosts. Once the colonizers brought their wives, the emphasis shifted. The ladies— women in their own kitchens being notoriously conservative—demanded the introduction of food plants and domestic animals of the Old World, establishing a process of overlay rather than outright replacement. Wheat was planted to

provide the raw material for yeast-raised breads (corn being relegated in many areas to animal fodder), which were served, and still are, in tandem with the corn flatbreads of the indigenous inhabitants.

In the gardens of the homesteads—*estancias* built to the Hispanic pattern—were planted familiar Mediterranean herbs, onions, carrots, brassicas, and leaf vegetables in the form of lettuce and spinach; in addition, citrus groves were established, and salt, vinegar, and sugar were introduced as methods of preserving fresh foodstuffs. Commercial interests established banana, sugar cane, and coffee plantations where the climate and soil were suitable. During this time, the missionaries had already planted vineyards and were busy replacing pagan hallucinogens with reliable Christian wine (as well as introducing the process of distilling in the form of brain-addling Christian brandy). Meanwhile, the Africans, transported as slave labor to work the new plantations in the Caribbean and Brazil, took advantage of the parts of the animal discarded by the white man by developing a sophisticated repertoire of variety meat dishes.

Pioneers, whether intrepid explorers or ironclad armies, must live off the land or die—a necessity that can be turned to good account when the sun shines and the land is fertile. A culinary habit that is born of hardship—hammered out in response to the need for the taste of home, not simply to satisfy hunger but to render the exotic not only familiar but pleasurable—becomes doubly precious. When this is allied to the desire, once the colonial yoke is removed, to reconcile two alien cultures, culinary habit can be transformed into a declaration of national identity, an expression of

something that might not find outlet in any other way. The exile not only longs for the taste of home, but is sure of exactly what he longs for—seasonings and all.

The territory is vast, the climate and geography bewilderingly diverse: all these factors contributed to the development of a sophisticated regional cuisine long before the imposition of colonial power.

Officially, there are twenty-six sovereign nations in Latin America, more if you include the islands of the Caribbean, which—though some are French-, English-, or Dutch-speaking—nevertheless can be said, culinarily speaking, to belong to the Latino tradition. In the United States, the official Latin American roll call, according to the U.S. Board of Census, which uses the term "roll call" to identify its immigrant citizens, is, in rough geographical order starting in the north: Mexico, El Salvador, Nicaragua, Costa Rica, Guatemala, Belize, Honduras, Panama, Venezuela, Colombia, Ecuador, Peru, Bolivia, Chile, Argentina, Uruguay, Paraguay, Brazil, the three Guianas (Suriname, French Guiana, Guyana), Cuba, Puerto Rico, the Dominican Republic, Jamaica, and Haiti.

Although all these nations share the New World larder, there are differences of climate and geography that allow one foodstuff to thrive in one place and not in another. Of the staples, maize—Indian corn, corn on the cob— is grown throughout Central America (including Mexico) and by the Andean nations, Colombia, Chile, Peru, and Ecuador. In the Caribbean and the lands of Amazonia, the staple is cassava root, a tuber whose most important characteristic is its rib-sticking starchiness. The potato is widely grown throughout, although it achieves the status of a staple only in the Peruvian highlands, where its cultivation ensured the survival of the Inca Empire in a region that yielded no alternative crops.

Old world meets New: a woman offers fabric for sale in front of the highly decorated facade of La Merced church, Antigua, Guatemala

Quiche Maya Indian market in Guatemala

In addition, it's possible to divide the culinary habit of the territory into groups that reflect the way in which food is prepared and served. The nations of the Pacific coast prefer spoon foods—soupy combinations that can be eaten from a bowl; the tortilla-eaters of Mexico and Central America have a preference for scooping foods—salsas, bean purées, meat and vegetables chopped small so that they may easily be conveyed to the mouth without cutting. The gaucho nations—Argentinians and their neighbors of southern Chile, Uruguayans, Paraguayans, and the cowpokes of southern Brazil—are meat-eaters: they like their meat on the bone and roasted over an open fire; they don't care much if it comes with bread or vegetables, and they like plenty of it.

Brazilians and Caribbeans of African origin developed a taste for variety meats not simply because it was the cheapest meat in the market. Innards and lungs—oxfoot, pig's tripe, and all the other odds and ends the butcher might otherwise be unable to sell or that make up what's left from the salters and barrelers who stocked ships for the Atlantic crossing—can be subjected to long, slow cooking in a closed pot, the method used to tenderize wild-gathered game of uncertain age. Pepperpot, the Caribbean's famous stew, is a collaboration between the hunters of the New World who used cassareep, an extract of bitter cassava, to tenderize their game, and the home cooks of the sugar plantations. They were searching for a way to feed their families and found in the pepperpot method and flavorings a little of the taste of home.

Of the Latino nations that can claim a distinctive culinary identity, that of Mexico is probably the most widely recognized—though not necessarily for the right reasons. Much of what is believed to be Mexican is actually northern borderlands cooking, Tex-Mex, chili con carne, and the wrap, a simplification of what is, in reality, a highly sophisticated culinary tradition traceable back to the Mayas, the civilization that predated the Aztecs. The staple foodstuffs are dried beans and lye-treated corn flour, with avocados and tomatoes providing a nutritional balance; the chile is the most important flavoring; chocolate and vanilla, both prepared by a complicated process of fermentation and sun-drying, are the luxuries. The presentation puts the emphasis on choice: chiles and salsas are presented separately, the diner being left to make his or her own decisions on how to eat the various elements and the degree of pepperiness or sweetness to be added.

Three distinct traditions combine in Brazil: indigenous, Portuguese, and African. Among these, the indigenous inhabitants had, and continue to maintain, a sophisticated understanding of what might be done with forest foods and a preference for earth ovens and barbecues. The Africans brought ingredients from their homeland—black-eyed peas, dende oil, okra, coconuts—to add to a natural willingness to eat what nature provided, however unpalatable or unfamiliar it might seem. The Portuguese brought a taste for sailors' one-pot stews and saltfish and an appetite for meat expressed in the churrascos—barbecue pits—of Bahia and Rio. Their wives were blessed with a light hand with the frying pan and that peculiarly Catholic taste for egg-and-sugar confections acquired from the Moors. Add to all this the traditional Mediterranean skills of cheese-making, ham-salting, and the art of spicing dried sausages, and the result is a distinctive gastronomic tradition as inventive as it is exuberant.

Throughout the region, a distinction can be made between the food of the towns and country cooking. While rural households make little distinction between mistress and maid—both consume the same foods cooked in the same way; the master simply eats more than the servant—the food of the urban poor consists of what the rich man leaves behind, variety meats and the cheaper cuts of meat that must be tenderized by chopping or grinding. For this reason, and because country people are more resistant to change, it's among the pots and pans of the old haciendas that the conservative cooks of the old tradition can still be found. Among the

A couple perform the quintessential South American dance, the tango, in Plaza Dorrego, Buenos Aires.

specialties of these rural kitchens are rich bean stews fortified with salt-cured sausages; roast meats made fiery with chile; egg custards made with pineapple juice; ices perfumed with vanilla and chocolate; desserts made to Old World recipes with New World fruits—papaya, pineapples, guava, passionfruit; cakes and cookies made with cassava-meal or corn ground

Macaws—the most colorful of South American birds—photographed in the Amazon region of Brazil

to a fine polenta flour (instead of using wheat flour). As soon as the Hispanic housewife had access to milk beasts—cows or goats—she made cheeses of the homey sort, treats for children, milk porridges for invalids; in addition she stocked her cellar with homemade wines, jams, jellies—all the good things that any rural housewife took pride in putting by against the changing seasons.

The tradition is practical, the rules flexible— frontiersmen must adapt or die. There's little of what might be described as *haute cuisine*. Elaborate presentation is left to commercial confectioners—caramel and cream fantasies are strictly for bakeries, to be sampled Spanish-style, held in the hand in a scrap of paper, consumed at the counter as the high point of the morning's marketing. The everyday cooking, the salsas and sauces of the Latino kitchen, require a subtleness of palate but very little in the way of culinary tricks. There's no mystery—unless it's in the skill with which the tortilla-maker pats out her circular flatbreads in a Mexican market, or the swiftness with which a Chilean fisherman shucks an oyster or slips the top off a prickly sea urchin to expose the sunny corals.

This is not a cuisine of trickery—you'll find no low-fat solutions to compensate for your willingness to come to the table. To eat without appetite, or consume good food in the expectation that it won't do what it's meant to do—satisfy and fortify—is to insult the cook or, worse, make mockery of the gods. The food itself—flavors, scents, textures, colors, the pleasure of profusion—is what matters in the Hispanic tradition, in the New World as well as the Old. That's not to say it's dull. The Latino temperament is famously contrary: fiery and earthy, romantic and homey, conservative as well as inventive. Domestic traditions that evolved from necessity rather than choice—exile, captivity, isolation—are a product of compromise. Latin America—the phrase itself a marriage of old and new—is exactly that.

An understanding of the spirit of the recipe matters more than the correctness of the ingredients—some of which may be hard to find, or even when available, not in perfect condition. This is true of any culinary tradition whose integrity is based on limitations—season, geography, a common wellspring of inherited knowledge. Few of us these days keep a household cow, or have the possibility to walk down the road and buy fresh fish directly from the fisherman or even catch our own fish, or pull vegetables straight from the earth, or pick fruit from the tree, or—even rarer—slaughter and salt down the family pig for winter storing.

Yet Latin Americans who have settled elsewhere—and the United States has a huge population of immigrant Latinos—don't throw up their hands in despair if they can't find the right ingredient. If what they need is not available at the right price and quality, they find something else. That's easy enough if you know what you're trying to substitute, less so if you've never tasted the original. With this in mind, I have suggested ingredient alternatives throughout: it helps to know that the small, plump Mediterranean cucumbers make an acceptable substitute for chayote; shredded celery root has the look and texture of jicama; chili flakes plus a handful of raisins deliver a fair copy of the sweet syrupy flavor of *chile pasilla*. In addition, botanical information makes it easier to select fruits or vegetables that, though they may only be available locally, have close relatives commercially grown elsewhere.

Lifestyle largely dictates what we will and won't cook, with time being the most important factor in our busy, modern lives. The everyday recipes of the region are usually quickly prepared—even the

Garlic offered for sale in typical Brazilian wrapping

slow-cooked bean dishes need little preparation. Admittedly, festive dishes such as the mighty Brazilian *feijoada,* black beans and pickled pork, are labor-intensive—but that's because at family gatherings, the preparation is part of the pleasure. While few of us can call on an extended family to share the labor of pounding and grinding the chiles and spices that make the Mexican *mole negro* one of the world's great dishes, such tasks can be performed in minutes by modern machinery. The food processor has revolutionized home cooking: recipes that would otherwise be dauntingly time-consuming—particularly salsas and sauces that depend on the chopping knife— are easy and quick.

While no special equipment is required, some of the techniques and cooking processes can be startlingly unfamiliar. For example, the use of lye as a preparation process, the earthenware comal used

Something for everyone—flowers and beer on the same Brazilian stall

A few of the processes might seem too exotic to be considered at all. Where's the sense in recommending, to someone cooking on a single burner in a small apartment, say, the exquisite fragrance imparted to the meat of a wild turkey when it's wrapped in banana leaves and buried in an earth oven? Then again, why not? The earth oven is simply a response to the same culinary restrictions: a single heat source, limited ingredients, and the need to cook food economically without losing any of its goodness. A chicken, when slow-roasted in a covered pot on a single flame and seasoned with aromatics from the corner store—while not quite up to the romantic standards of the Brazilian rain forest—delivers the right stuff to the taste buds, and without having to dig a hole in the ground. And if the alternative to a pot-roasted fowl is burger made from unidentifiable meat basted with a chemical copy of hickory smoke—ancestor-nostalgia gone crazy—how much more delicious is a casserole of creamy white beans gently cooked on the lowest possible flame, finished with squash, corn, and a flavoring of sweet basil?

The Latin American kitchen, in a nutshell, is reactive rather than recipe-led: what's right for the dish matters more than a slavish attention to authenticity. It's the spirit that counts—and just as well, since no recipe, however detailed, is infallible. No two cooks, provided with the same ingredients and identical cooking instructions, produce exactly the same dish, not even in a professional kitchen. The way food reacts to the application of heat depends on more variables than there are parrots in the Guatemalan jungle: among these, fuel source; shape and construction of the cooking implement—whether the pan's made of iron or earthenware or teflon-coated steel; the raw materials—freshness, ripeness, sweetness, sourness, juiciness, wateriness; the temperament of the cook, even the weather. When it rains, cornmeal needs

as a bakestone, and the meticulous attention paid to the blending of dried chiles. While culinary manners vary from culture to culture, even from kitchen to kitchen, it takes confidence to step outside a familiar cultural framework—doing things like refraining from frying the meat before adding the liquid to make a stew, or learning to pat an arepa rather than roll it, or adding a colored oil or aromatic lard as a finishing flavoring.

less liquid to make a tortilla dough. When the sun shines, ripe tomatoes need no more than a sunny windowsill to melt into a salsa; a raw-fish seviche is made in minutes rather than hours.

While cooking can never be an exact science, the culinary habit of this diverse region is more inexact than most. It has no secrets—unless it be a light hand and an open heart. What it does have, and in abundance, is soul. Beyond this, no special equipment is required. Bring your favorite pan, the pot of your choice, and your sharpest knife. The reward, as I hope you'll discover for yourself, is a cuisine that is simple yet sophisticated, robust but subtle, and that reflects the beauty of the land, the sunny nature of the people, and the profligacy of a fertile earth. This—as the Incas explained to their disbelieving conquerors—is a treasure far more valuable than gold, the gift of the gods, the food of the sun.

Festive masks on sale in Chichicabtenango, Guatemala

vegetables

The geography of this vast continent—a landmass that stretches from the Arctic to the Antarctic—combined with the relatively late appearance of man there, has led to an astonishing diversity of habitats. This diversity—from the most inhospitable rocky uplands to the lushest of tropical floodplains, thousands of miles of coastline, innumerable islands—allowed the development of a vegetable kingdom without equal anywhere else on earth. Not all its secrets are yet revealed: the flora of the equatorial forests of Amazonia have yet to be fully explored, as have parts of the Andean uplands and riverine landscape of Central America. Nevertheless, long before the arrival of chemists and botanists, the indigenous inhabitants of the Americas were already cultivating sophisticated strains of edible plant foods totally unknown anywhere else, developing ways of processing foodstuffs that, in their untreated state, were at best unpalatable, at worst, deadly.

While the most useful and easy to prepare—corn, beans, potatoes—quickly became staples to fill the world's pantry, others—chiles (modified to produce the mild sweet pepper), tomatoes, avocados, the mighty family of squashes—became widely popular because they tasted good, filled a need, and were remarkably easy to grow. Many of the vegetable foods of the region remain relatively unexploited—though appreciated in their land of origin—sometimes because they occupy a specific botanical niche that cannot be reproduced elsewhere, but more often because their preparation and usefulness is little understood.

tomato

or tomate, jitomate (Mexico, from the Nahuatl xitomatl)
(*Lycopersicon esculentum*)

A vine fruit native to the Americas, the tomato is a member of the nightshade family. Slow to gain acceptance in the Old World where it was initially classed as a fruit, the tomato found what can be considered its spiritual home in the Mediterranean vegetable patch. It is in this new form, often combined with garlic and olive oil, that it reappeared in Mediterranean recipes.

How it grows

Small-fruited and hardy in the wild, the form in which it's still found in the Andean uplands, the tomato was described by a botanist who traveled with Pissaro in Peru as a weedy, aggressive little plant of minor gastronomic interest. The Aztecs of Mexico thought otherwise, cultivating the vines in the irrigated gardens of their holy city and offering the fruits in their temples as food for the gods: blood-red juices to satisfy blood-hungry deities.

Appearance and taste

Modern tomato hybrids come in every shape and size, from the fragrant little cherry to the rich-juiced plum to the big meaty beefsteak. While most varieties ripen to scarlet, some produce fruits that ripen to cream, yellow, orange, a deep crimson, all the way to almost black.

Buying and storing

Look for firm fruits with a plump unwrinkled skin and strong fragrance (the best pointer to flavor). Color is not necessarily a guide to sweetness and ripeness: some varieties are deliciously sweet when still streaked with green. Field tomatoes that have been allowed to ripen on the stem are always superior to any other. While the tomato takes well to the greenhouse—hence its popularity as a year-round salad fruit—tomatoes grown under glass, unless left to mature in their own time, are watery and tasteless, particularly if grown for looks rather than flavor. When buying fresh, store at room temperature—never in the refrigerator. To preserve for longer, cook them down to a concentrate and bottle under oil. In cooked sauces (mostly of Mediterranean origin) canned plum tomatoes are preferable to out-of-season fresh fruits.

Medicinal and other uses

Tomatoes are a good source of vitamin C, most of which is found in the jelly around the seeds; vine-ripened tomatoes have twice as much vitamin C as fruits picked green and left to ripen. Naturally antiseptic, tomatoes are useful in the treatment of cirrhosis of the liver, hepatitis, and other complaints of the digestive organs. The tomato is reputed to be a neutralizer for skunk spray—invaluable when you need it, no doubt.

Culinary uses

Plum tomatoes are meatier and less juicy than the round varieties—good in sauces and for oven-drying. To prepare, cut in half vertically, sprinkle with salt, and lay out to dry in the lowest possible oven temperature (it should be roughly the warmth of a summer's day in Acapulco). Cherry tomatoes have a concentrated sweetness perfect for salsas; beefsteak tomatoes are good for stuffing and baking. Latin American recipes concentrate on presenting the tomato in its raw form—sliced, chopped, or pulped as a salad or salsa. To separate the flesh from the rest of the tomato, cut off the top and scoop out the seeds; holding the body of the fruit firmly in your palm, rub the cut surface down the coarse holes of a grater, peeling the skin back as you go, until you're left with nothing in your hand but a flattened circle of skin.

Tomates rellenos con granos tiernos

(Tomatoes stuffed with corn)
Serves 4

An Ecuadorian dish of tomatoes filled with a delicate stuffing of fresh corn, finely diced zucchini, and Andean yellow carrot—*zanahoría amarilla*—whose replacement is parsnip or celeriac.

4–8 tomatoes (depending on size), ripe but firm
1 cup fresh corn kernels, sliced off the cob
1 parsnip or thickly sliced celeriac, diced
  small
1–2 zucchinis, diced small
¼ cup olive oil
Juice of ½ lemon
1 garlic clove, crushed
1 teaspoon salt
Pinch sugar
1 tablespoon chopped cilantro
1–2 fresh chiles, seeded and finely sliced

Blanch the tomatoes for 30 seconds and then skin them. With a small spoon, hollow out the interior, saving the pulp and discarding the seeds. Dice the pulp.

In a small pan with the lid on, cook the corn along with the diced parsnip and zucchini in very little water (no salt) until tender—about 10 minutes—and drain.

Meanwhile, use a fork to mix the oil with the lemon juice, garlic, salt, and a little sugar. Toss the drained vegetables with the dressing. Let cool a little before you fold in the reserved tomato flesh, cilantro, and chile. Spoon the filling into the tomato shells and finish each with a curl of lemon zest.

Tomatoes stuffed with corn, dressed with chile and cilantro

Mermelada de tomate

(Spiced tomato marmalade)
Makes about 3 pounds

A Cuban way with a fruit that hasn't quite decided if it's a vegetable or a dessert— here, it's neither a jam nor a relish, but something in between. Served in Old Havana as a membrillo, a fruit-paste eaten with cheese.

2 pounds ripe but firm tomatoes, chopped small
6 allspice berries
Short piece cinnamon stick
3–4 cloves
1 lemon, peel and juice
About 4 cups granulated sugar

Put the chopped tomatoes in a pan with the allspice, cinnamon, cloves, and lemon peel, add half a cup of water, bring to a boil, turn down the heat, put the lid on loosely, and simmer for 20–30 minutes, stirring occasionally, until completely pulped.

Push the pulp through a strainer. Stir in the same weight of sugar as pulp, add the lemon juice, and bring gently to a boil, stirring until the sugar dissolves. Let it bubble, stirring to avoid sticking, until it sets—it's ready when a drop on a cold saucer wrinkles when you push it with your finger. Bottle in warm, sterilized jars.

tomatillo

or tomate verde, miltomate, tomate de capote (Mexico), green tomato (*Physalis ixocarpa*)

A smallish tomato-like vine fruit, about the size of a small egg, the tomatillo is native to Mexico and Guatemala and belongs to the same family as the physalis or cape gooseberry (see page 216 for the other members). Used in the recipes of the Aztecs, it is much valued in Mexico as a sauce ingredient—essential in green sauces, to which it imparts a gluey texture and lemony flavor; it is also used, although to a lesser extent, in Guatemala.

Buying and storing

Choose firm, hard, dry fruits whose calyx shows no sign of mold or blackening, and with a clean, sweet, well-developed gooseberry scent. They can be stored unhusked in a single layer in a cool place for several months.

Medicinal and other uses

The tomatillo is high in fiber with plenty of vitamin C. In its land of origin, a tea brewed from the calyces is said to cure diabetes.

Culinary uses

To prepare, remove the papery covering, rinse (don't worry about scrubbing off the sticky substance around the stalk-end), and chop. It is usually eaten cooked, though in Central Mexico it is sometimes used in a raw salsa as a dip for barbecued meat. The skin is very fine—no need to remove it.

How it grows

A bushy perennial with tomato-like leaves, usually grown as an annual, the tomatillo has downward-pointing, lanternlike fruits enclosed in the mildly toxic, green exterior husk or calyx, which are common to all *Physalis* species. As the fruit swells, the husk becomes brittle and papery, and bursts.

Appearance and taste

The fruit is green even when ripe, though it can progress to yellow or purple. The flesh—crisp and juicy when raw, soft and glutinous when cooked—is solid all the way through, sprinkled with seeds tender enough to crunch between the teeth. The flavor is that of gooseberry and apple sauce, with a touch of lemon zest.

Marketplace, Mexico

Salsa verde de tomatillo, Mexico's favorite dipping sauce

Salsa verde de tomatillo

(Green tomato salsa)
Serves 4

A deliciously fragrant, rather gluey-textured salsa—one of the truly nostalgic flavors of the Mexican kitchen.

8 tomatillos (green tomatoes), hulled and
*   wiped*
2 green chiles (jalapeño or serrano),
*   seeded and chopped*
1 garlic clove, finely chopped
1 teaspoon sugar
Salt
1 tablespoon chopped cilantro

Cut the tomatillos into chunks and put them in a small pan with just enough salted water to cover. Bring to a boil and simmer for about 10 minutes until perfectly soft. Stir in the chopped chile and garlic, mash to soften, season with sugar and salt, and let cool before stirring in the cilantro. Serve warm or cool with anything with which you would serve a red tomato sauce. Delicious spooned over a fried egg, excellent with cold chicken.

Tomatillos gratinados

(Gratin of green tomatoes)
Serves 4

A Mexican specialty, very rich and delicious. Serve as a party dish, with freshly baked bolillos: bubble-shaped rolls no bigger than can comfortably be held in the hand, slow-risen to give a dense-textured crumb, baked in a wood-fired oven to give a thick golden crust, and sold fresh in the bakery every morning.

2 pounds ripe tomatillos
1¼ cups cream
2 tablespoons olive oil
1 garlic clove, peeled and chopped finely
3 tablespoons fresh bread crumbs
1 tablespoon chopped parsley
1 teaspoon crumbled oregano
1 tablespoon grated white cheese
Salt and pepper

Preheat the oven to 425°F. Slice the tomatillos thickly and overlap them in a single layer in a gratin dish. Pour the cream over them and sprinkle with salt and pepper. Bake for about 15 minutes, until the cream is boiling. Meanwhile, warm the oil in a small frying pan, add the garlic, and fry gently until it softens. Sprinkle in the bread crumbs and let them brown in the hot oil. Stir in the herbs and pour the contents of the pan over the tomatoes. Finish with a sprinkle of grated cheese.

avocado

or acuacate (Mexico), abacate (Brazil), palta (Chile), and formerly known in the U.S. as alligator pear (*Persea americana*)

Technically a fruit but treated as a vegetable, the avocado is pear-shaped to perfectly spherical, ranging in size from as small as an egg to as large as a cantaloupe.

Sorting recently picked avocados beside Lake Atitlán, Guatemala

How it grows

A magnificent, glossy-leaved, semitropical tree native to Mexico, the avocado is infertile unless grafted with a fruit-bearing branch. The fruits don't begin to ripen until they drop (or are harvested) from the branch.

Appearance and taste

Hundreds of different varieties are grown. Skin color varies from frog-green to purple-bronze; the skin texture varies from tender, smooth, and fine, to pockmarked, tough, and woody. The flesh when ripe is buttery and soft, varying in color from pale green to cream—when hopelessly overripe, it becomes fibrous and dark. In Mexico, only the superior large, round, thick-skinned, creamy-fleshed fruits are considered suitable for eating whole, either sliced or scooped directly from the shell; the inferior, smaller, thin-skinned varieties are considered more suitable for guacamole—the Aztec word for pulp.

Buying and storing

The larger the avocado, the better the ratio of seed to flesh. Look for an unblemished exterior. If you buy hard avocados, you won't know if they've been bruised or not until they ripen. Once ripe, keep them in the refrigerator: being very rich in oil, they go rancid.

Medicinal and other uses

The avocado is as close as any fruit gets to the perfect food: remarkably high in protein, rich in fiber and carbohydrates, endowed with all essential vitamins and minerals, and easily digested; it is good for babies, the elderly, and all stages between. High levels of copper and iron in easily assimilable form make it ideal for the treatment of anemia, and invalids and convalescents will find it improves hair and skin quality. It is not recommended for anyone with liver trouble since its high fat content (largely monounsaturated) makes it hard to digest. An infusion of the leaves is used as a diuretic in Brazil.

Culinary uses

Don't prepare ahead of time. Once cut, the flesh quickly discolors, a process that also affects the flavor: if you have no choice but to prepare ahead, leave the pit in the hole or, if mashing, pop the pit in the middle of the mashed avocado and keep covered with plastic wrap—there's no logical explanation, but the presence of the pit does delay the darkening. An unripe avocado can be ripened by popping it in a paper bag and leaving at room temperature for 2–3 days—less if you include a ripe banana. Avocado oil—bland and odorless, qualities that make it sought-after by the cosmetics industry—has a remarkably high burn point: 520°F.

Crema de palta

(Iced avocado soup)
Serves 4

A sophisticated green soup in which the rich flesh of the avocados provides the thickening as well as the flavor. To serve hot, blend with boiling broth and serve immediately—it goes brown very quickly. The smooth-skinned green avocados are best for this dish: the flesh is creamier and smoother than the rough-skinned Hass avocados.

2 perfectly ripe avocados, skinned, pitted,
  and diced
2¹/₂ cups cold chicken broth
2 tablespoons lime or lemon juice
Salt

To finish:
1 tablespoon diced cucumber
1 fresh green chile, seeded and sliced
 A few fresh cilantro leaves

Blend all the ingredients thoroughly to a smooth purée. Dilute with water if too thick. Taste and salt lightly. Ladle into bowls and finish with cucumber, slivers of green chile, and a few cilantro leaves.

Guacamole

(Avocado dip)
Serves 4 as an appetizer

A chopped salad in which all the ingredients are separately identifiable—a preparation known to the Aztecs. To serve as a sweet relish, combine with pomegranate seeds and dress with honey and lemon juice.

2 large ripe avocados, diced
3 tablespoons diced mild onion
3 tablespoons diced tomato
2 tablespoons chopped green bell pepper
1 small green chile, seeded and chopped
  small
2 tablespoons chopped fresh cilantro
Juice of 1–2 limes
Salt

Mix everything together lightly with a spoon, adding lime juice and salt, to taste. If you don't mean to serve it immediately, to prevent browning, pop one of the avocado pits in the middle to fool the avocado it's still in the shell. Serve with romaine lettuce leaves and crisp tortilla chips for scooping—fry your own chips, the commercial ones are very salty.

Dolce de abacate

(Avocado whip with rum)
Serves 6

The Brazilian housewife treats the avocado as a dessert fruit, serving it with cream and sugar. Here, it's finished with pomegranate seeds, tart and crunchy. All the ingredients should be cold before you start.

2 small, perfectly ripe avocados
2 tablespoons lime juice
4–6 tablespoons superfine sugar
1 tablespoon rum
About 1¹/₄ cups light cream

To finish:
Seeds of 1 ripe pomegranate

Skin and pit the avocados, put them in the blender along with the rest of the ingredients, and blend to a purée, adding the cream gradually until the mixture has the consistency of thick yogurt. It'll keep in the refrigerator for a day or two—or you can freeze it and serve as an ice cream. Pile in individual glasses and finish with pomegranate seeds.

Clockwise from top: avocado soup, avocado and pomegranate relish, guacamole

jicama

or yam bean, Mexican potato
(*Pachyrhizus erosus, P. tuberosus*)

The tuberous root of a member of the pea family, the jicama is a native of Central America and the lands of Amazonia. The name comes from the Nahuatl *xicama*, meaning "storable root."

How it grows

The jicama is a garden plant, grown for the beauty of its trumpet-shaped flowers that turn themselves into inedible pods. The edible part is the subterranean tuber, storage system for the plant in winter, which looks rather like a large brown turnip.

Appearance and taste

When young and fresh, the skin is fine, almost translucent, and the flesh is snowy white and a little sweet, very much like a water chestnut in flavor and texture—crisp and delicate. Older specimens develop a flavor rather like raw potato, so are best cooked when they become starchy and bland but retain much of their crispness.

Buying and storing

Pick medium-sized tubers that are firm and free of blemish, with fine, tan-colored, smooth skin; elderly tubers are rough-skinned and dry looking, with fibrous and starchy flesh, only suitable for cooking. Store in a plastic bag in the refrigerator for up to three weeks. To prepare, just peel off the fine potato-like skin and the fibrous layer immediately beneath, and slice or dice. Once peeled, keep in cold water with a squeeze of lemon.

Medicinal and other uses

Low in fat, high in fiber: perfect for dieters.

Culinary uses

The jicama can be eaten raw when young: cut into chips or slivers and dressed with citrus juices, the form in which it's sold as a quick snack in Mexican marketplaces. When included in a fruit salad, it can be mistaken for apple. Mature roots are suitable for inclusion in spicy stews or for cooking in combination with other root vegetables.

Pico de gallo

(Rooster's-beak salad)
Serves 4 as an appetizer or side salad

This salad takes its name from the dressing: pico de gallo or rooster's beak—the sharpness of the citrus juices balancing the blandness of the raw root, while the softness of the fruit complements the vegetable's crispness.

1 jicama, about 1 pound, peeled and cut into matchsticks or ribbons

The dressing:
Juice and finely grated peel of 2–3 bitter (Seville) oranges or lemons or limes
Salt

To finish:
2 sweet green oranges in segments (or 1 large eating orange in segments)
1 tablespoon pine nuts, toasted
Chili flakes or finely chopped fresh red chile

Toss the prepared jicama with the orange juice and salt and leave for an hour or two in a cool place. Combine with the orange segments and finish with the pine nuts and the chile.

Fruit and vegetables on sale in Buenos Aires

Pico de gallo, a refreshing summer salad finished with pine nuts

Manchamantales con jicama

(Jicama and chicken hot-pot)

Serves 4–6

Food for the greedy—hence its reputation as a tablecloth-stainer. Wear a bib and eat with your fingers.

2 pounds jicama, peeled and cubed
1/4 cup oil
2–3 garlic cloves, slivered
1 large mild onion, finely sliced in half moons
4 chicken wings or 1 pound cubed pork
4 chile poblanos or 2 green bell peppers, seeded and cut in strips
4–5 large ripe tomatoes, chopped
A handful dried apricots, chopped

A handful prunes, pitted
1 tablespoon raisins
2–3 chile pasillas, soaked and torn
2–3 dried chiles, seeded
1 short stick cinnamon
1 teaspoon powdered cumin
1 tablespoon dried oregano
Salt and pepper

To finish:
1 tablespoon powdered sugar mixed with powdered cinnamon

Put the jicama to soak in lightly salted water. Heat the oil in a roomy pan and fry the garlic and onion. Push them aside as soon as they soften and add the chicken or pork and the poblano or green pepper strips. Fry until it all browns a little. Add the tomato pulp, fruits, chiles, spices, oregano, salt and pepper. Add enough water to cover, boil, put the lid on, and let it simmer until the meat is tender and the juices well-reduced—an hour or so.

Halfway through the cooking, add the jicama—you'll need more water.

To finish, take off the lid, turn up the heat, and let the sauce boil fiercely for a few minutes to evaporate extra moisture and thicken the sauce. Pile into a big bowl and finish with cinnamon sugar. Serve with thick slices of fried plantain and green papaya dressed with lime juice.

winter squash

or calabaza, abóbara (Brazil)
(*Cucurbita* spp.)

Edible gourds of the storable varieties—in varying sizes, shapes, and colors—are among the most venerable of the continent's cultivars. Ethnobotanists suggest it was the first of what has been called the American Triad: beans, squash, and corn—food plants still grown in association and prepared in recipes that feature all three.

How it grows

A vine-fruit, storable once harvested, winter squash swell through their long, slow, growing season, accumulating sweetness as the vine withers.

Appearance and taste

A very variable bunch—spherical, squashed-oval, or pear-shaped—winter squash have hollow hearts that contain a great many small, edible seeds. Most develop hard, warty, inedible outer skins, though the butternuts and some of the green-skinned winter squashes are exceptions.

   The texture is hard when raw, soft and melting when cooked. The flesh varies from pale gold to a deep orange and is very sweet, though some squash are sweeter than others.

Buying and storing

Pick healthy gourds with no sign of bruising. Buy whole for storage, or cut into chunks or in pieces for immediate consumption, in which case it will need to be wrapped in plastic and kept in the refrigerator for no more than 3–4 days. Whole squash can be stored over winter on top of a cupboard, even in a heated kitchen. Varieties popular in the region include the bottle-shaped butternut, which has a fine, tender, almost translucent gold-to-ivory skin and dense orange flesh, very sweet and almost spicy. Largest is the mighty pumpkin—tough-skinned, with rather watery flesh, but making up in quantity what it lacks in quality—which is particularly popular in the Caribbean, where it can be spherical or squashed, and the skin can be any shade between pale ivory to deep orange, to speckled ivory to deep green. The Brazilian pumpkin is more fibrous and denser-fleshed than the Caribbean variety.

Medicinal and other uses

Winter squash are packed with easily assimilable sugars and carbohydrates, and are low in calories and high in vitamin A and potassium. The juices are highly alkaline—useful in the treatment of acidosis of the liver and blood, and recommended as an anti-inflammatory. The raw seeds are eaten to get rid of tapeworm.

Culinary uses

The denser-fleshed squashes—butternut and other small- to medium-sized varieties—are delicious in desserts or cut into chunks and roasted, or baked with cream. The larger, watery-fleshed pumpkins make excellent soups and stews; as a pie-filling, they need to be cooked down to evaporate excess moisture. The flowers are also eaten, particularly the males that can be picked without damaging the fruits. Related ingredients include *pepitas*—toasted pumpkin seeds—and pumpkin-seed oil (nutty and delicate but it goes rancid rapidly.)

Sopa de calabaza

(Dominican squash and orange soup)
Serves 4–6

Spiced with ginger and sharpened with orange, this is the most delicious of the Caribbean's many squash soups. It is best made with one of the dense-fleshed squash such as butternut or banana squash. If you are using one of the large watery-fleshed Halloween-type pumpkins, you'll need a little sugar and a squeeze of lemon.

1 butternut squash, or a wedge of pumpkin, weighing 2 pounds
A pat of butter
1 yellow or white onion, finely chopped
1/2 teaspoon ground ginger
1/2 teaspoon nutmeg
4 cups chicken broth
1 1/4 cups freshly squeezed orange juice
Salt and pepper

To finish:
Pumpkin seeds, lightly toasted

Preheat the oven to 400°F. If using a whole squash, slice it in half, scoop out the seeds, and place it face down on a baking sheet lined with foil. If using a wedge of pumpkin, seed it, cut into chunks, and arrange on the foil. Bake for 40 minutes or so, until perfectly soft and a little caramelized. Slip off the thin skin, but don't get rid of the little brown bits.

Meanwhile, melt the butter in a roomy pan and fry the chopped onion gently until it softens and takes a little color—don't let it burn. Sprinkle in the ginger and nutmeg and add the squash, chicken broth, and orange juice. Bring to a boil, turn down the heat, and simmer for 20 minutes to marry the flavors. Purée in a food processor or blender until perfectly smooth. Reheat when you're ready to serve. Finish with a sprinkle of toasted pumpkin seeds.

Sopa de calabaza, sweet and spicy

Dulce de calabacín

(Candied squash)

Very sweet, sticky preserves such as this are traditionally served as a welcome to visitors. They can be offered in little dishes with a glass of water; but are nicest served on a small spoon over a glass of chilled coconut-water or fresh orange juice.

3 pounds squash, peeled, seeded, and cut into large, chunky strips (about 1 x 1/2 x 4 in.)
1 cup sugar
6 tablespoons water (less if squash is watery)

Layer the squash and the sugar in a heavy saucepan. Add the water. Set the pan on a very low heat, cover tightly, and simmer for 50 minutes or so, until the squash is tender and the syrup thick and shiny. You may need more water, or you may need to boil the syrup down with the pan uncovered—it all depends on the squash. Let it cool in the pan in its syrup. Once cool, put in a serving dish, making sure the squash is completely submerged, and serve.

summer squash

or vegetable marrow, calabaza, courgette, zucchini, calabacín, zapallito (*Cucurbita* spp.)

This pepo—the name given to the fruit of a member of the gourd family—is grown to be harvested in spring and summer, and harvested green: hence, summer squash.

Marrow ready to be harvested

How it grows

A bushy, tendril-forming annual herb with yellow flowers, the zucchini has rough hairy stems and deeply pinnate leaves. It is often grown in association with corn and beans, when its rambling habit and broad, shady leaves serve both as a weed suppressant and moisture preserver. Traditional recipes reflect this association.

Appearance and taste

When young, it is bright green and shaped like a small cucumber, with creamy, yellow, mild-flavored flesh; when older and larger, the soft skin darkens and hardens, the roundness develops into flat planes, and the flesh becomes more watery and fibrous. There's also a round, pale green or speckled ivory-green variety, sapallito, specially grown for stuffing. It's the perfect size for eating when it sits comfortably in the palm of the hand.

Buying and storing

Young, immature fruits should feel firm and have no soft patches or flexibility. Store them in the salad compartment of the refrigerator and eat them as soon as possible. Mature marrows should also be clear-skinned with no bad patches. They keep well and can be stored at room temperature.

Medicinal and other uses

Digestible and easily assimilable, but, being 90 percent water, their nutritional value is limited.

Culinary uses

To prepare when tender and young, simply clean and slice; older specimens should be skinned, and the woolly middles and seeds scooped out and discarded. Quickly cooked when young or old, it is best steamed or cooked in a covered pan with as little liquid as possible. Young squashes are firmer and more delicate than older specimens, which need to be skinned and seeded before cooking. The flowers are also eaten: they are delicious shredded and included in a stuffing for an empanada, or stuffed, dipped in batter, and deep-fried.

Budín de zapallitos

(Zucchini cheese pudding)
Serves 4 as a main dish

A dish I remember from my Uruguayan childhood: rich, creamy, and flavored with lots of cheese.

3–4 large zucchinis, grated
2 tablespoons butter or oil
1 large mild onion, finely chopped
2 large eggs
1¼ cups milk
2 tablespoons grated parmesan

4–6 slices white bread, crusts removed
¼ cup freshly grated cheese—
  gruyère or cheddar
Salt and pepper

Preheat the oven to 375°F. Salt the grated zucchini and leave in a colander to drain for half an hour. Rinse and shake dry.

Heat the butter in a frying pan and fry the onion gently until it softens. Add the zucchini, put the lid on, and shake the pan over the heat until the flesh turns transparent. Mix the eggs in with the milk, stir in the parmesan, and season.

Lay half the bread in the bottom of a buttered gratin dish, cover with the vegetables, and top with the remaining bread. Pour in the egg–milk mixture, and sprinkle the top layer of bread with the grated cheese. Bake for 20–25 minutes, until deliciously golden and bubbly.

Tortillitas de calabacín

(Zucchini fritters)
Serves 4 as an appetizer

The crispness comes from the presalting—necessary to draw excess moisture—as well as the use of textured flours. Stone-ground is best.

6–8 zucchinis, sliced lengthwise
1 tablespoon fine salt

Batter:
3 tablespoons coarse bread flour
1 tablespoon roughly ground cornmeal
1 teaspoon coarse salt
1 tablespoon olive oil
1¼ cups water
1 large egg, separated

To cook:
Oil for deep frying

Salt the zucchini slices and leave in a colander to drain for half an hour. Whisk all the batter ingredients together, reserving the egg white.

Heat a panful of oil until you can see a faint blue haze rising.

Rinse the zucchini slices and pat dry. Whisk the egg white until firm, and fold it into the batter. Dip the zucchini slices—one at a time—into the batter and drop into the oil, only as many as will bob comfortably about on the surface. Let them brown, turning to fry the other side—they will take 3–4 minutes. Remove with a slotted spoon.

Eat them as they come out of the pan, with a squeeze of lemon.

Budín de zapallitos, a creamy gratin of grated zucchini

chayote

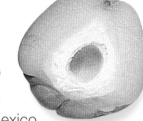

or christophene, chocho, custard marrow, mirlitón (*Sechium edule*)

A summer squash that looks like a large green pear, the custard marrow is marked from stem to stern with deep irregular ridges. Classed as a pepo —the name given to fruits of the cucumber type—it is native to Central America and was first cultivated in Mexico by the Aztecs, who gave it its name. The color varies from dark to pale green; the pale green flesh has more or less the texture and flavor of cucumber, with a touch of kohlrabi.

How it grows

A perennial vine that draws its nourishment from large, subterranean tubers, it is astonishingly prolific: a single seed planted in a pot in sunny conditions with plenty of water can produce enough leaves and fruits to shade a whole veranda.

Appearance and taste

When young, the skin is pale green and soft (only older specimens need be peeled) and the flesh is crisp and firm. The female fruits have smooth skins while the males are prickly—the former are fleshier and preferred to the latter. All parts of the plant are edible: leaves, shoots, tubers, and the nut that develops within the fruit.

Buying and storing

It is best eaten in its infancy—no bigger than an egg—when the flavor will be more concentrated and the flesh juicy rather than watery. Choose clean, clear-skinned chayotes that feel firm in the hand. Store them in the refrigerator and use while still fresh—they go moldy after a week.

Medicinal and other uses

Bland, delicate, and digestible, it is suitable for invalids and babies, particularly when given additional food value by being cooked in a broth or in combination with dairy foods.

Chayote for sale, Mexico

Culinary uses

The fruit is bland and almost tasteless—a blend of cucumber, kohlrabi, and zucchini—so it's perfect as a vehicle for other flavors. It can be grated and eaten raw in salads, stir-fried, steamed, or stuffed and baked (there is no need to skin it). To boil the chayote, rinse and remove the single seed before cooking. The kernel is edible and has a delicate, rather almondy flavor. The tuberous root looks and tastes like a yam, and young shoots are picked in the spring, to be eaten like asparagus or stirred into soups.

Buttered chocho

Serves 4 as a side dish

This is the Jamaican way with this most delicate of summer squashes—butter and mild sweet onion form the dressing, with a touch of chili to excite the taste buds.

2 pounds chayote, cut into small cubes
1 sweet yellow onion, finely sliced
A generous pat of butter
Salt

Buttered chocho—classic, simple, and delicious

Salt the chayote cubes lightly and leave in a colander to drain. Rinse and transfer to a saucepan along with the sliced onion. Add a splash of water—there's plenty of liquid in the vegetable—put the lid on tightly, and steam in its own juice over medium heat for about 10 minutes, until perfectly tender but not mushy. Pile it onto a dish and drop the pat of butter on top.

Chancletas

(Chayotes baked with cheese and cream)
Serves 3 as a main dish, 6 as an appetizer

A Puerto Rican dish, known as old slippers—no doubt as much for the delectable scent of the stuffing as the shape of the container. Pattypan squash is an acceptable substitute as a container.

3 chayotes—each weighing about 12 ounces
Small pat of butter
2/3 cup light cream
2 cups shredded white cheese such as
   mild cheddar or gruyère
3 tablespoons raisins
1 teaspoon vanilla extract or a knife-tip scrape
   from a vanilla bean
1 tablespoon sugar
Salt

To finish:
6 tablespoons fresh bread crumbs
2 tablespoons grated hard cheese—mature
   cheddar, parmesan

Cook the chayotes in enough boiling, lightly salted water to cover, until perfectly tender: 45–50 minutes. Drain, let cool a little, then cut in half lengthwise. Scrape out and discard the woolly middle and seeds. Scoop out most of the flesh, chop roughly, and set aside. Arrange the shells in a buttered baking dish.

Preheat the oven to 375°F. Drop the reserved flesh in the blender and blend to a purée along with the cream. Transfer to a bowl and mix in the cheese, raisins, vanilla, and sugar. Spoon into the shells and sprinkle with the bread crumbs mixed with the grated cheese. Bake for about 20 minutes, until the top is crisp and golden.

okra

or ladies' fingers, gumbo (West Indies), quiabo (Brazil) (*Hibiscus esculentus*)

A pod-vegetable, okra is an ancient cultivar of the hibiscus family, known to the ancient Egyptians, imported from Africa as part of slave culture, and established in the Caribbean and Brazil in the seventeenth century.

A small tree-like annual with pretty, yellow, trumpet-shaped flowers, it is a member of a family that includes the cotton plant and the roselle (raw material of sorrel, a refreshing drink popular at Christmas in the Caribbean).

Appearance and taste

The part of the plant of interest to the cook is the immature seed pods—ridged, finger-shaped, with one pointed end and one capped, about the length of a thumb—though the young leaves are also edible. Two varieties are grown, one longer than the other. In cross-section, it looks like a miniature wheel with tiny seeds sticking to the spokes. The flavor is pleasantly pea-like, while the juices are naturally gluey in texture (mucilaginous), its chief attraction as a soup-thickener.

Buying and storing

When fresh, the pods have a glow to them. To choose, look for bright green pods with no sign of browning or withering. Inside, the seeds should still be pale and pinkish—if dark and hard, the okra will be old and stringy. To store, treat as green beans: keep them in a paper bag in the refrigerator and use as soon as possible.

Bundles of okra in Castries market, St. Lucia

Medicinal and other uses

Although high in protein and well-endowed with vitamin C, okra is chiefly valued for its mucilaginous qualities, and is invaluable as a soothing lubricant for irritated intestinal membranes.

Culinary uses

Cook like green beans or in any recipe that suits the summer squash. To avoid bleeding out the mucilage, trim the stalk without cutting into the pod, and leave the tail in place. Some—not me—don't like the glueyness: to minimize this, cook the okra with a little lemon juice or vinegar; for the same reason, some cooks don't add salt during the cooking. To reduce the mucilaginousness still further, sprinkle with salt and leave in a warm place to dry for an hour. Okra flour, milled from dried okra pods, can be used to thicken and add nutritional value to soups and stews.

Okra and potato salad with green mango

Serves 4–6 as an appetizer or side dish

A West Indian salad that combines soft okra with the crisp, tart flesh of unripe mangoes. In the West Indies, green mangoes are eaten in the street, straight from the hand, like apples.

1 pound okra
1 pound small new potatoes, scrubbed
1/4 cup olive or sunflower oil
2 garlic cloves, finely chopped
1 small onion, finely chopped
1 small green chile, seeded and chopped
Juice of 1 lemon
2 tablespoons chopped fresh cilantro
Salt and freshly ground black pepper
*1 unripe green mango, chopped (skin on—but
    slice out the seed)*

Remove the hard caps and trim off any hard little tails from the okra. Rinse well and shake dry. Boil the potatoes until tender—start them in boiling salted water—and drain well.

Warm the oil in a shallow frying pan or wok. Toss in the chopped garlic and onion and let it sizzle gently until it softens—3–4 minutes. Don't let it brown. Turn up the heat, add the chile and the okra, and stir it over the heat for 5 minutes or so, until the okra has softened a little but is still fresh and green.

Turn down the heat and stir in the potatoes and lemon juice, turning to mix everything thoroughly. Add the cilantro, season with a little salt and plenty of pepper, put the lid on, and let it simmer gently for 5 minutes to marry the flavors. Let it cool before combining with the mango. Serve at room temperature, with plantain chips (see page 207).

Quiabo con tomate

(Okra with tomato)
Serves 4–6 as an appetizer or side dish

A Brazilian way with more mature okra pods, which require slow, gentle cooking.

1 1/2 pounds fresh okra pods
2 tablespoons oil
1 onion, chopped
2 garlic cloves, chopped
3 large tomatoes, chopped
1 chile pepper, seeded and chopped
1 teaspoon sugar
Salt

Prepare the okra by trimming the stalks close to the pod. If you don't enjoy their glueyness— though lots of people do—don't hull, just trim off the stems, toss the pods with salt and a little vinegar, and leave in a colander for an hour or two, by which time they will have yielded up their gloop; rinse well before using. Cut into chunks.

Warm the oil in a heavy pan or flameproof casserole dish and gently fry the onion and garlic until soft—don't let it brown. Add the tomato, chile, and sugar, and let them boil, squashing with a wooden spoon to encourage a rich little sauce. Stir in the okra, add a glass of water, and let it boil again. Turn down the heat, put the lid on loosely, and simmer for 30–40 minutes, until the pods are perfectly tender and the sauce deliciously rich and sticky. Or bake in the oven at 300°F. Serve at room temperature, with quartered limes and chili-pepper sauce on the side.

For a more substantial dish, include slivers of beef or pork tossed in the hot oil when you fry the onion and garlic, or finish with a handful of fresh shrimp.

Quiabo con tomate, okra pods cooked gently in a rich tomato sauce

hearts of palm

or palm-heart, palmito, pupunha (*Euterpe edulis*)

Hearts of palm refers to the growing tip of a young palm tree, which springs up with remarkable rapidity in the Amazonian rain forest whenever a clearing is made. A seven-year-old palmito produces a heart about 2 inches in diameter. Luxuriously large hearts—3 to 4 inches in width—are the product of a tree that has already been growing for twelve years or more.

How it grows

The removal of the heart kills the tree—a form of cropping perfectly acceptable when the jungle could renew itself virtually overnight, less so when there's not enough to go around. New plantations supply the canning factories, which satisfy the increasing demands of gourmets in other lands.

Appearance and taste

When sold fresh in the market, hearts of palm appear as a tightly packed bundle of leaf-bases, about the thickness and length of a man's arm. When canned, the hearts of palm is ivory-colored and tender, a little like a short length of bamboo, with layers of outer covering enclosing a soft inner heart. Very delicious, even when preserved in brine—like artichoke-flavored asparagus.

Buying and storing

Hearts of palm are hard to find fresh, but when available, choose pale, plump hearts with no sign of dehydration or browning. They are available in cans or bottled—find a brand that suits you.

Medicinal and other uses

The hearts of palm has all the virtues of young vegetables when fresh: it is a laxative, and well-endowed with vitamin C. When canned, it is of little nutritional or medicinal value.

Culinary uses

The hearts of palm can be eaten raw and fresh, and is also delicious roasted or as a creamy soup. When canned, it is best combined with seafood in a salad, to which it contributes texture as well as taste. Related palm-tree products include dende oil, a frying oil of African origin extracted from a relation of the coconut palm and much prized in Brazil. In its untreated form it is high in beta-carotenes and is almost 100 percent saturated fat. Palm sugar, known in Mexico as piloncillo, is the cooked-down sap produced by tapping one of the sugar palms—date or coconut.

Palmito asado

(Roasted hearts of palm with butter and honey)
Serves 4

Freshly roasted hearts of palm, drenched in butter and sweetened with honey, are served as an appetizer in the estancias of the farming districts of São Paolo: a rare delicacy, presented glistening on a banana leaf with justifiable pride.

2 large hearts of palm (about 1¹/₂ pounds each)
2 sticks (1 cup) unsalted butter, clarified
Salt and freshly ground pepper
Honey for a sauce

Preheat the oven to 325°F. Run a sharp knife down the length of the hearts of palm and remove the outer layer. Leave the next layer in place, even though it's a little tough. Place the hearts on foil, brush with butter, sprinkle with salt and pepper, seal tight, and place on a baking tray. Bake for an hour and a half, until perfectly tender, soft, and buttery. Unwrap and serve with its juices, with melted honey handed around separately.

Young palm trees in Peru, grown for their delicious hearts

Salata de palmito e cangreijo

(Hearts of palm salad with crab)

Serves 4

Shore crabs scuttle around among the palm trees that line Brazil's beautiful white beaches. The sweetness of the crabmeat provides a perfect counterpoint to the delicate flavor of the hearts of palm. To prepare canned hearts of palm (perfect for the dish), cut off any tough outside pieces and use a potato peeler to cut tagliatelle-like ribbons—also a good technique should you manage to lay your hands on fresh hearts of palm.

1 can hearts of palm, sliced into fine ribbons

The dressing:
6 tablespoons olive oil
2 tablespoons lime juice
Shake of malagueta pepper sauce (see page 51) or Tabasco
1 teaspoon coarse salt

To finish:
1 romaine lettuce, shredded
About 12 ounces crabmeat (save the carapace for serving)
Shredded fresh coconut

Combine the hearts of palm with the dressing ingredients, let them marinate for an hour or two, toss with the shredded lettuce and crabmeat, and finish by sprinkling on finely shredded coconut.

Salata de palmito e cangreijo, a delicate salad of crabmeat and ribbons of hearts of palm

sweet potato

or batata, boniato
(*Ipomoea batatas*)

A tuber-bearing member of the morning-glory family, a New World native grown by the Mayas in Mexico and the Incas in Peru, the sweet potato was brought back by Columbus from the West Indies. It was one of the first of the New World tubers to make the Atlantic crossing and is now established as a food plant in tropical parts of the world where the ordinary potato cannot thrive.

Appearance and taste

Literally hundreds of different varieties are grown, ranging from long and slender to short and globular; the skins vary from ivory to rose to russet to deep chestnut, the flesh from cream to a deep orange. Pale-skinned varieties are likely to have ivory-colored, dry, mealy, mildly honeyed flesh; those with dark skin are likely to have orange, very sweet, juicy flesh and are sometimes labeled yam—although the true yam is an entirely different species.

Buying and storing

Look for fresh, bright-skinned tubers with no sign of blemish or shrinkage. Store at room temperature for up to two weeks, or in a cool dry pantry for up to a month, but never in the refrigerator—as a tropical tuber, they hate frost and develop an oddly musty flavor.

How it grows

The sweet potato is planted out as shoots that develop into a rambling vine, producing a thick mass of heart-shaped leaves and a few trumpet-shaped purple flowers. The leaves are sometimes cooked and eaten in times of famine, since the tubers take about eight months to mature underground.

Inca ruins at Machu Picchu

Medicinal and other uses

Easy to digest and nutritious, the sweet potato is mainly a source of starch but also has protein; yellow-fleshed varieties are particularly high in vitamin A. Most of the nutritional value is stored in and near the skin. It is good for the diseases of the digestive tract—ulcers, inflammation of the colon—and is a good detoxifier, thanks to the presence of phytochelatins, which attract heavy metals. An old folk remedy dictates feeding mashed sweet potato to those who've swallowed a metal object, as the potato should stick to it and allow it to pass through the colon easily.

Culinary uses

The sweet potato can be roasted, steamed, baked, or fried. Cooked and mashed, it can replace up to one quarter of the weight of flour in cakes and bread. Some varieties are starchy and bland, some sweet and spicy: sweet is the most popular. The flesh is dense—a modest helping will satisfy even the heartiest appetite.

Boniatillo

(Sweet potato purée with orange and cinnamon)

Serves 6

This is usually made with the white-fleshed boniato which, though less sweet than the orange-fleshed varieties, is considered to have a finer flavor. Either will do. At Christmas, the same recipe, without the eggs, is prepared as a festive treat. The trick is to cook it right down to a paste.

1 pound boniato or sweet potato,
  peeled and sliced
1$^1/_2$ cups unrefined sugar
$^1/_2$ cup water
1 orange, juice and peel
$^1/_2$ lemon, juice and peel
1 short cinnamon stick
1 tablespoon butter
2 eggs, separated
Salt

To finish:
Cream
Powdered cinnamon (optional)
A few curls orange peel

Cook the potatoes until tender, in enough lightly salted water to cover—they'll take about 40 minutes. Drain, let cool a little, and peel. Or bake in the oven and skin. Mash the flesh to a purée.

Meanwhile, melt the sugar in the water, along with the orange and lemon peel and juice and cinnamon and bring to a boil. Simmer for 5 minutes and set aside. Remove the peel and cinnamon stick, and combine the hot syrup with the mashed boniato. Return the mixture to the heat and beat it with a wooden spoon until it thickens to a soft purée that holds its shape on the spoon.

Remove from the heat and beat in the butter. Let it cool a bit and beat in the egg yolks. Whisk the egg whites and fold them in. Let it cool and pile into glasses. Finish with a dollop of cream, an optional sprinkle of powdered cinnamon, and a few curls of orange peel.

Boniatillo, a delicious sweet potato dessert flavored with orange and cinnamon

Batata frita

(Sweet potato chips)

Serves 4

Perfect with a seviche, for dipping in a guacamole, or with a chilled soup—in fact, with anything that benefits from a touch of crispness and sweetness.

1 medium-sized sweet potato, peeled and
  thinly sliced
2–3 tablespoons cornstarch
Oil for deep-frying
Salt

Rinse the potato slices, drain, and pat dry. Spread the cornstarch on a flat plate. Heat the oil.

Dust each potato slice lightly with the cornstarch before dropping it in the hot oil. It should immediately acquire a jacket of small bubbles. Continue with dusting and dropping until the surface of the oil is covered.

Fry until crisp. Remove with a slotted spoon and transfer to paper towels to drain. Continue until all are done.

jerusalem artichoke

or sunchoke, topinambur (*Helianthus tuberosus*)

The tuberous root of a member of the sunflower family, the Jerusalem artichoke is a North American native, one of that vast store of edible roots and tubers well-known to the indigenous population, but that has never achieved the same popularity universally. Although rarely seen in the markets of Central America, it is popular in Chile and Peru.

Jerusalem artichoke foliage

How it grows

A tall leafy annual with yellow daisy-like flowers, its many creeping roots produce numerous tubers that, in unhybridized form, are about the size and appearance of a ginger root: long and slightly flattened. Many varieties are now grown.

Appearance and taste

Jerusalem artichokes are knobbly little tubers with pinkish to coffee-colored skin and crisp ivory-colored flesh; they look a bit like an exotic variety of potato. Their shape is against them: peeling is a bit awkward. The flavor is earthy, delicately sweet, with a hint of fennel.

Buying and storing

Choose tubers with firm, bright skins and no signs of withering or green patches. Store in a cool place away from the light, as you would with potatoes.

Medicinal and other uses

Fat-free, the Jerusalem artichoke is an excellent source of nutrients much valued by the Huron in its land of origin. It is an excellent source of iron—almost as good as meat. Its notoriety as a flatulence promoter is due to the form in which the root stores carbohydrates: as inulin, a form of sugar that can be eaten by diabetics.

Culinary uses

The Jerusalem artichoke can be eaten raw, grated, slivered in a salad, or served with a dip. It is good for boiling, steaming, mashing, and makes delicious pancakes: grate, mix with a little flour, bind with egg, and fry. The peel is edible, although it rather spoils the look when mashed. For ease of peeling, boil for 10 minutes in salted water and then drain under a cold faucet, when the skins can be rubbed off. The flesh remains firm and slightly translucent, even when perfectly tender.

Guiso de topinambures con champiñones y olivos

(Jerusalem artichokes casseroled with mushrooms and olives)
Serves 4–6 as an appetizer

An easy one-pot dish—all you need is a little patience.

2 pounds Jerusalem artichokes
1 lemon
$^{1}/_{4}$ cup olive oil
2 large onions, finely chopped
2 garlic cloves, finely chopped
$2^{1}/_{3}$ cups diced mushrooms
1 teaspoon dried thyme
1 cup white wine
2 tablespoons green olives, pitted and
   chopped
1 piece of stale bread, crumbled
1 hard-boiled egg, chopped
Salt and pepper
1 tablespoon chopped cilantro

For serving:
Crumbled white cheese or hard-boiled egg
Crisp lettuce leaves for scooping

Peel the knobby little root artichokes carefully and divide into bite-size pieces. As you peel each root, drop it into a bowlful of cold water into which you have squeezed a little lemon juice.

Heat the oil in a roomy flameproof casserole dish or cast iron pot and fry the chopped onion and garlic until soft and golden (don't let it brown). Push them aside and add the mushrooms. As soon as they yield up their juices, add the artichokes and the olives. Let them sizzle for a moment. Stir in the thyme, season with salt and pepper, pour in the wine and the same volume of water, and let everything boil.

Turn down the heat, cover loosely, and let it simmer very gently for an hour, until the roots are perfectly tender. Stir in the cilantro and the crumbs—they'll soak up all the aromatic juices, leaving the tubers bathed in a deliciously fragrant dressing. Top with hand-crumbled white cheese or chopped hard-boiled egg, and serve with crisp lettuce leaves for scooping.

Chupe de topinambures y elote

(Jerusalem artichoke and corn soup)
Serves 4

A Chilean way with the knobby tubers—convenient since you don't have to worry about removing all the skin. The fresh corn kernels underline the natural sweetness of the roots.

1 pound Jerusalem artichokes
1 onion, finely chopped
2 tablespoons butter or corn oil
4 cups chicken or vegetable stock
6 allspice berries
$1^{1}/_{4}$ cups corn kernels
Salt and pepper

To finish:
A handful basil leaves, shredded
1 garlic clove, finely chopped
1 yellow chile, seeded and chopped

Scrub and roughly chop the roots. In a big pan, fry the onion gently until it softens—don't let it brown. Add the chopped roots and let them feel the heat for a moment. Add the stock and the allspice, bring to a boil, turn down the heat, put the lid on loosely, and simmer for 20 minutes or so, until the roots are perfectly tender. Purée the contents of the pan, reheat, and stir in the corn. Let it boil, reduce to a simmer, replace the lid loosely, and cook gently for another 10 minutes. Taste and season. Ladle into bowls and finish with a sprinkle of shredded basil, chopped garlic, and chile.

Topinambures con champiñones, a fragrant artichoke and mushroom casserole

edible fungi

Many of the familiar marketplace fungi—chanterelle, boletus, oyster, russola—are found throughout Latin America, as well as a great many edible varieties unknown outside the territory. Less familiar cap mushrooms include the tecomate, a large, firm-fleshed mushroom with a brick-red cap and yellow gills. Most unusual, but acquiring a gourmet reputation, is the cuitlacoche or maize mushroom, a fungi that transforms its host into a fragrant mush.

How it grows

All the copraphiliacs—fruiting bodies that take their nourishment from decaying vegetable matter—acquire most of their flavor and their chemical composition from their host plant, making them an unpredictable bunch. Even if they look familiar, gather from new habitats only if accompanied by a knowledgeable local guide.

Appearance and taste

While the usual cultivated mushrooms are available throughout the year, members of many of the edible fungi families, including gill mushrooms, sponge caps, puffballs, and morels, are gathered when in season and eaten with relish. The maize mushroom has a powerful morel-cèpe fragrance allied with the sweetness of the corn. Notable exotics include the *huitlacoche*—an ink-black fungus that appears on corn kernels, turning them silver; and the Haitian black mushroom used in a rice and bean dish, *djon djon*, and found nowhere but in Haiti; the woody stalks produce a deep black dye used to color the water in which the rice is cooked; after draining, the stalks are discarded and the rice tossed with the sliced caps, along with an equal volume of cooked lima beans.

Buying and storing

When selecting fresh fungi, whether cultivated or wild, choose dry, unblemished specimens that smell fresh and are bug-free. While many of the wild varieties are available in dried form, the maize mushroom—actually, a mush made from the affected corn kernels—is exported in cans since it has a short shelf-life and cannot be preserved by dehydration.

Medicinal and other uses

In some countries, both pharmaceutical and hallucinogenic fungi are sold alongside the non-mind-altering varieties. Make sure you understand exactly what you're buying.

An autumn haul of wild fungi includes chanterelles, horn of plenty, and russolas.

Culinary uses

Fungi are usually cooked simply—grilled or roasted with a little oil. In a stuffing for an empanadilla or tamale, they're treated as a meat substitute, included for flavor rather than substance.

Salsa de cuitlacoche

(Maize mushroom purée)
Makes just under a quart

The basic method of preparing maize mushrooms and their host corn kernels—cuitlacoche—produces a dense, fragrant paste that can be used as a flavoring. It is particularly good as a sauce for chicken, stirred into boiling cream. It'll keep for three months in the freezer.

6 cups cuitlacoche
3–4 tablespoons oil
1 tablespoon chopped onion
1 chile poblano or green bell pepper, seeded and cut into ribbons
1 tablespoon chopped epasote or cilantro (optional)
Sea salt or kosher salt

In a large frying pan, heat the oil and fry the onion and chile poblano, stir in the cuitlacoche, season with salt, and cook gently for 15 to 20 minutes, then stir in a little epasote or cilantro for extra flavor. The mixture should be moist but not wet: if the crop was picked on a dry day, you may need to add water; if the weather was damp, you may have to boil rapidly for a minute or two to evaporate excess liquid.

Empanadas de hongos con maiz

(Maize mushroom turnovers)
Makes about a dozen fist-sized turnovers

Tortilla-dough turnovers stuffed with maize mushroom salsa is one of the great dishes of Mexico. Failing the real thing, substitute corn kernels processed thoroughly with powdered porcini mushrooms—4 tablespoons corn to 1 tablespoon mushroom. Or use fresh mushrooms, chopped, lightly fried, and mixed with their own volume of corn kernels.

Empanadas de hongos con maíz

*1 pound salsa de cuitlacoche or
   substitute as above*
1/4 cup sour cream
*3–4 poblano chiles or green pimiento (or bell)
   peppers, charred and cut into strips*
1 cup grated cheese
Salt and pepper
Oil for deep-frying

The casing:
12 5-inch tortillas

Warm the cuitlacoche in a small pan. Put the cream in the blender along with the peppers, blend to a purée, scoop it out, and stir it into the cuitlacoche. Let it boil for a moment to blend, stir in the cheese, season, remove from the heat, and let it cool.

Drop a tablespoonful of the mixture in the center of each tortilla. Dampen the edges and fold in half to make semicircular turnovers, pinching the edges together to seal.

Heat a deep-fat fryer or a panful of oil. When very hot, slip in the turnovers, a few at a time, and fry until golden and crisp—3 or 4 minutes. Transfer to paper towels to drain. Delicious with a green-tomato salsa.

exotics

Edible leaves and shoots

A remarkable variety of leaf vegetables and shoots, variously textured, and with different degrees of mildness and bitterness, are used throughout the region—many of them peculiar to the area in which they're gathered. The leaves of the edible roots, tubers, and gourds whose use is widespread are the most commonly encountered, including the Trinidadian callaloo, the name given both to the stew and the leaf with which it's cooked. As a general rule, any edible leaf (e.g., collard greens, turnip greens) can be substituted for any other—failing these, Swiss chard, spinach, and the more tender members of the cabbage family will do.

Couve con maní

(Wild greens with peanuts)

Serves 4

A Brazilian dish of African origin, this is made with a wide variety of edible greens including spinach of the tough evergreen variety, the young leaves of pumpkin, cassava, and sweet potato, Swiss chard, spring greens, and cabbage. Serve as a vegetarian dish with soft polenta or rice.

1 1/2 pounds spinach greens or other leaves
1/2 teaspoon salt
2 1/2 cups finely chopped tomatoes
6–8 scallions, finely chopped

To finish:
1/4 cup pounded roasted peanuts

Cook the spinach in a tightly covered pan, just in the water that clings to the leaves after washing. Sprinkle with salt to encourage the juices to run.

As soon as the leaves collapse and soften, remove the lid and add a layer of chopped tomatoes and chopped scallion. Sprinkle with the powdered peanuts, but do not stir. Turn down the heat, put the lid on loosely, and simmer for about 15 minutes, until the tomato flesh has softened. Stir, put the lid on loosely again, and simmer for another 15 minutes. Remove the lid and let it boil to evaporate any excess juices. Scoop the contents of the pan onto the serving dish, and finish with a sprinkle of whole-roasted peanuts.

Andean roots and tubers

Of the many root vegetables grown by Andean farmers, though largely unknown outside the territory, the most notable—already gaining popularity among the gourmets of North America—is the Peruvian white carrot, *zanahoria blanca*, a celery-flavored, parsniplike root that cooks like carrot and combines particularly well with seafood.

Two others waiting in the wings are the *melloco* or butter-potato, and the *oca*, a sweetish tuber similar to the Jerusalem artichoke. Both can be substituted for potatoes in any recipe, though the butter-potato is more suitable for savory dishes—include it in bean soups, as a side dish dressed with garlic and chile; while a purée of *oca*—the tubers steamed in their skins and pushed through a food mill—works well as the starchy element in cakes and desserts.

Couve con maní

Edible thistle

Edible thistles/
wild artichokes

Of the local varieties of wild artichokes available
in the markets of Chile's Alta Plana, two—
chagual and penca—are of particular interest.
Chagual is described by Ruth Gonzales in *The
Chilean Kitchen* as a cone-shaped rosette of
tightly packed leaves that can be served as a
salad. Penca is a long, juicy stem that has to
be stripped of its thorns before it can be
eaten—like the chagual, the penca should be
dressed with oil, lemon, and salt. The taste,
Ruth Gonzales says, is much like celery.

Seaweeds

Sea vegetables were important as a source of
protein to the indigenous inhabitants of Chile's
long coastline in pre-Columbian times. All
seaweeds are edible, though some are too
tough to be palatable, and some taste better
than others. A wide variety used to be gathered
by the shore-dwellers who lived mainly on the
prolific crops of razor-shells. People still
understand what to gather and when, and
know how to name the various stages of
development—evidence of a sophisticated
culinary vocabulary. The fresh roots are called
ulte, while the leafy parts are known as luche.
When dried, they are known as cochayuyo, the
name by which they are sold, tied up in neat
bundles, and offered in the markets as the poor
man's steak. To prepare in the Chilean way,
reconstitute in the same way as other
seaweeds by soaking; then chop finely and
include in the stuffing of an empanada instead
of fish or meat. Any edible seaweed can be
substituted. It is good in combination with
yellow chiles and fresh, crumbly, white cheese.

chiles

All the capsicums, the pepper of the New World, are descended from the same pair of ancestors, *Capsicum annuum* and *C. frutescens*. *C. annuum*, natives of Mexico, which are, as their names suggest, bushy annuals whose fleshy, lantern-shaped fruits hang down like Christmas ornaments. *C. frutescens*, a Peruvian native, is a perennial shrub with torpedo-shaped, upward-pointing, thinner-fleshed fruits. Both are fiery in their natural state, though the Peruvian is hotter than the Mexican. The two species are inextricably entangled through hybridization, deliberate or accidental, since the earliest times, making it impossible to untangle lineage.

The chile's heat, the peppery element, triggers the production of endorphins, excitement-inducing chemicals manufactured by racing drivers and mountaineers in response to danger. The substance that delivers the message is capsaicin, an alkaloid with all the characteristics of poison, which, though present in both flesh and seeds, is found mainly in the white membrane that attaches the seeds to the interior ribs. Test for fieriness with caution: cut off an end and lick rather than chew since the really hot ones are pretty explosive. Don't rub your eyes when handling, and rinse your fingers in cold water afterward.

Chiles—fiery or mild—are hard to slip into a culinary slot, falling somewhere between a condiment, a vegetable, and a spice. Nevertheless, for culinary purposes, they can be divided into three groups: fresh flavoring chiles (including pickled), frying chiles (including bell peppers), and dried or pantry-stored chiles (including powdered and flaked).

flavoring chiles

or chile picante, ají (Peru)
(*Capsicum annuum/C. frutescens*)

These small chiles are eaten fresh or pickled, in the form of a condiment or as flavoring, much as freshly milled pepper (although the inclusion of one by no means precludes the other). The chiles can be lantern- or torpedo-shaped, and are picked at any stage of maturity. All chiles mature from green to varying shades of scarlet; some varieties stop at yellow, others progress to a purple so dark it's almost black.

How it grows

The chile grows as a crouching annual or upstanding bushy perennial, depending on ancestry and habitat. Mexico alone accounts for more than a hundred named varieties, each with a different shape, fragrance, and degree of fieriness.

Appearance and taste

Flavoring chiles vary in appearance but are all small. Neither color nor shape is a reliable indication of heat, which varies within the species, even within fruits from the same plant. The flavor of green immature chiles is grassy, acidic, and lemony; as they ripen in sunshine, it matures to sweet and fruity. Two of the most popular Central American varieties for eating green are the thick-fleshed jalapeño, an elongated blunt triangle of middling fieriness, the chile of choice for a guacamole and to flavor cornfoods such as tamales; and the *chile serrano* or mountain-grown chile (the pickling chile), which is thinner-fleshed and very hot. The habanero or Scotch bonnet, a quadrangular thin-fleshed, lantern-shaped fruit, is the Caribbean favorite. Andean chiles—*ajíes*—are triangular, short or long, of varying degrees of fieriness, with yellow varieties the most esteemed. The Brazilian favorite is the long, thin malagueta pepper, which ripens to scarlet and is very fiery.

Capsicum annuum on the plant

Buying and storing

To choose fresh chiles, look for a shiny, firm, stretched-looking skin—once a chile wrinkles, it's past its best—and check there are no little black patches, particularly around the stem. A chile harvested when green and immature, though it will certainly change color, will wither and rot. But a chile harvested when fully ripe will progress, just as nature intended, to dehydration—the stage at which it can be kept in a clean dry jar and stored for later. Do remember that a chile will lose fragrance and color (though not its heat) if kept too long on the shelf.

Medicinal and other uses

Fresh green chiles are high in vitamins A, B, and have up to six times as much vitamin C as oranges (although this decreases as they ripen, and disappears completely as they dry). Chiles are antiscorbutic (prevents scurvy), disinfectant, insect-repellent, and fever-reducing—virtues that can be ascribed to capsaicin, the hot element in the chile, that promotes sweating. All these virtues were known to the ancient civilizations of the Aztecs and the Incas. To counteract chile-burn—that moment of truth when you know you've bitten off more than you can chew—take a glass of milk or a bowl of yogurt. Reaching for the water pitcher will just compound the problem since capsaicin, like oil, does not dissolve in water, and swamping it with water simply spreads the problem.

Culinary uses

Stimulating to the digestive juices, chiles make anything taste good. However, too much makes a dish inedible—hence the wisdom of serving raw or pickled chiles on the side. The hot element, capsaicin, is present in both flesh and seeds, but is concentrated in the white woolly fibers that attach the seeds to the ribs.

Pimenta malagueta

(Brazilian pepper sauce)

Makes a wine bottle full

The true flavor of Brazil, this seasoning sauce—condiment, pickle—is as fiery as the temperament of the ladies of Copacabana beach. The liquor is a little milder than the chiles, but both are relished.

Hanging bunches of chiles from a hook is an effective and eye-catching way of drying them in a current of air.

1 pound malagueta peppers or bird's-eye chiles
$1^{1}/_{4}$ cups white rum or vodka
$1^{1}/_{4}$ cups olive oil
$^{2}/_{3}$ cup wine vinegar

Pick over the chiles, discarding any that are blemished. Be careful not to touch your face or rub your eyes while you're working. Rinse the chiles with the rum or vodka—washing in water makes them rot—and shake them dry. Pack the chiles in a clean wine bottle and pour in enough oil and vinegar in proportions of 2:1 to submerge the peppers completely. Jam in the cork and store for a month. The preparation keeps indefinitely.

Ají de maní

(Chile peanut salsa)

Serves 4–6

Typical of Peruvian ají—the name given to the sauce as well as its main ingredient, chile—it rarely includes tomato. Peruvian ají are long, thin, torpedo-shaped, yellow or orange chiles, thin-fleshed and fiery, with a distinctively fruity flavor. Yellow bird's-eye chiles or habaneros will do instead.

$^{2}/_{3}$ cup beef broth (or any well-flavored stock)
1 cup roasted, pounded peanuts
  (coarse peanut butter will do)
Juice of 1 lemon
6 yellow chiles, seeded and finely chopped
3–4 scallions, finely chopped
$^{1}/_{2}$ red bell pepper, finely chopped
1 tablespoon chopped cilantro
1 hard-boiled egg, finely chopped
$^{1}/_{2}$ teaspoon salt

Heat the broth until just below boiling, stir in the peanuts and lemon juice, and blend thoroughly, until an emulsion forms. Stir in the remaining ingredients. Serve at room temperature as a dipping sauce for the little, yellow-fleshed, perfectly spherical criollo potatoes, the caviar of the crop. Or with Colombian empanadas or tamales stuffed with pipian potatoes: criollos mashed with a tomato, red pepper, and peanut sauce.

frying & stuffing chiles

or *chile para freír, para rellenar*

A frying chile can be any of the larger capsicums that, lacking the heat of their smaller sisters, can be treated like a vegetable: fried, stuffed, roasted, grilled, or included in rices and stews for color and flavor rather than fire.

Appearance and taste

The *poblano* is the most popular Mexican frying pepper: a long, torpedo-shaped, thin-fleshed pepper usually eaten green. The alternative is the thick-fleshed bell pepper: a mild, sweet hybrid developed during the nineteenth century in Hungary, exported to Spain, and later exported back again to its land of origin.

Buying and storing

The color should be bright and the skin shiny and stretched. Check for bad spots and signs of wrinkling: there should be no soft dimples— a sign of impending rot. Store in the salad compartment of the refrigerator for no longer than a week. Unripe fruits—picked green and immature—will probably ripen to red, but will become wrinkled and soft. It is best to buy at the stage of ripeness that you need.

Medicinal and other uses

There's no loss of vitamins when a pepper is bred for mildness, although its antiseptic properties will not be as strong. Fresh green chiles are higher in vitamin C, which boosts the body's immune system, than ripe red ones; both ripe and unripe chiles are rich in Vitamin A.

Culinary uses

Capsicums have a remarkably high sugar content when ripe, which is why they roast or fry so deliciously, caramelizing just before they burn. To peel fresh peppers, hold in a flame until the skin blisters black, then drop in a paper bag and let them steam for 10 minutes, after which the skin will peel off in neat little rolls.

Empanadillas colombianas

(Colombian chili turnovers)
Makes about 12

These bite-size turnovers, crisp and fragrant, are made with arepa dough stuffed with green chiles and white cheese. Street food, they are sold in every bar in town by spotlessly aproned, arepa sellers, wearing their magnificent hand-woven wraps, making the rounds with their baskets.

The dough:
1 pound masarepa or tortilla dough
  (see page 81)

The filling:

3–4 fresh ají (chiles), seeded and finely
  chopped

2 tablespoons chopped flat-leaf parsley

2 tablespoons chopped basil

1/4 cup crumbled white cheese (feta-
  type)

A little milk or egg to bind

For cooking:

Oil for deep-frying

For serving:

Pickled chiles, puréed with oil to make a
  dipping sauce

Knead the dough into a ball and cover with
plastic wrap. Mix the filling ingredients together.

Break off a small piece of dough about the size
of a walnut, roll it into a little ball, and flatten it
in the palm of your hand to make a small round
disk—the thinner the better. Use your hands
rather than a rolling pin or the dough will crack.
Drop a little of the stuffing in the middle of the
disk, paint the edge with water, and fold one
half over the other to enclose the filling.
Continue until all are ready.

Heat enough oil to submerge the turnovers
completely. Slip them into the hot oil one by
one—the edges should acquire a fringe of small
bubbles. Fry, turning once, until crisp and
golden. Cornmeal dough takes a little longer
than whole wheat dough. Drain on paper towels.

Chile poblano en nogado

(Stuffed frying chiles with walnut sauce)

Serves 6, with accompaniments

**Mexican wedding food, suitable for a
celebration because the preparation is
laborious—many hands make light work.
Very delicious and very Latin.**

6–12 chile poblanos or green bell peppers
  (depending on size)

The picadillo for stuffing:

11/2 pounds ground pork

1 onion, finely chopped

2 garlic cloves, finely chopped

Chile poblano en nogado, a celebration dish of stuffed peppers with a creamy walnut sauce

2 tablespoons oil

21/2 cups skinned and chopped tomatoes

2 tablespoons raisins, soaked in a little orange
  and lemon juice

1/4 cup diced papaya or peach

2 tablespoons slivered toasted almonds

1 teaspoon powdered cinnamon

Salt and pepper

The walnut sauce:

1 cup freshly crushed walnuts

1/4 cup cream cheese

11/2 cups sour cream

A pinch of sugar and a little powdered
  cinnamon

Toast the peppers by holding them on a long
fork over a naked flame or by placing them
under the fiercest broiler until the skin chars
and blisters. Drop them in a paper bag and
leave for 10 minutes to loosen the skins. Slip
off the skin, slit neatly lengthwise, and remove
the seeds. Reserve.

Prepare the picadillo: gently fry the meat,
onion, and garlic in the oil until all is soft. Add
the tomato and let it boil to evaporate excess
juices—the mixture should not be too wet. Add
the fruits and nuts. Season with salt, pepper,
and cinnamon, and set aside to cool.

Make the finishing sauce by whisking all the
ingredients together. Chill, and set aside to
serve separately.

Fry the peppers for 3–4 minutes, until soft.
Stuff the peppers with the picadillo and arrange
in a baking dish. Heat through in a low oven.

If serving at a betrothal—a family feast—dip
the peppers in egg-and-flour batter and deep-fry
to give a crisp coating: richness expresses hope
for future prosperity. For a wedding—a feast for
the whole community—prepare as for a betrothal
and finish with pomegranate seeds—for fertility,
of course, though no doubt you worked that out
for yourself.

dried & powdered chiles

or cayenne, chili powder, pimentón, paprika (*Capsicum* spp.)

Dried chiles, small and fiery, are the peppercorn of the New World. In their land of origin, fieriness is considered secondary to fragrance, flavor, and color. It is this variability, the subtle differences—that make this one of those rare ingredients that, in the hands of a skilled cook, is capable of gastronomic greatness.

Manufacture

Chiles of all varieties are picked when fully mature and are allowed to dry naturally, providing the raw material of all dried-chili preparations. Chile-blending is elevated to an art in Mexico, where cooks often make basic blends or pastes to recipes handed down since the days of the Mayas. It is on the sophisticated combinations of different chiles, each contributing to the balance of the finished dish, that much of Mexico's formidable culinary reputation rests.

Appearance and taste

There are hundreds of chiles, many of them place-specific, drawing not merely from genetic inheritance but from the soil itself. Differences between one kind and another are as evident to devotees as, say, to a Tuscan chef making a choice between olive oils or a coffee connoisseur judging the virtues of a bean.

Buying and storing

When choosing whole chiles, check for powderiness, a sign of insect-infestation; the color should be deep and rich with no sign of fading. If buying in powdered form, a clear bright color is the best indication. As for flaked chili, my own preference is for seedless flakes—the flesh has all the flavor. If these are unavailable, prepare your own from whole chiles. The *chile ancho—chile poblano* in dried form—is the most useful of all the dried chiles, providing the basic flavoring for stews and sauces such as Oaxaca's exquisite mole negro (see page 177). In dehydrated form, chiles and paprika peppers can be stored almost indefinitely, whether whole, powdered, or flaked, so long as you keep them in a cool dry place away from direct sunlight.

Medicinal and other uses

Curative when applied topically to wounds, dried chiles provide the active ingredient in many cold treatments, hangover remedies, and cure-alls—they are particularly good for clearing the sinuses. Stimulating, disinfecting, and antibacterial (bury a chile in the bean pot to keep insect predators at bay), chiles make one less prone to the digestive upsets that afflict travelers. The paprika-loving Hungarians discovered its antimalarial properties when they were employed to dig the Suez Canal: only the Hungarians were immune. Capsaicin, the hot element in the chile, is actually a defense mechanism against insect predators and is not destroyed by cooking, freezing, drying, or any other attentions including, to put it daintily, human digestive juices.

Culinary uses

Dried whole chiles of the larger bell-shaped varieties should be seeded, torn into pieces, then soaked to reconstitute the pulp so that this can be scraped off the tough skin. The pieces can also be lightly toasted in a dry pan before soaking, a process that caramelizes the sugars and deepens the color. When adding to slow-cooked stews, you can omit the preliminary soaking. Although recipes may stipulate certain chiles—sometimes three or four in the same recipe—once the principal of their inclusion is understood, variations are possible. *Chile pasilla*—raisin-chiles—add sweetness; if unavailable, add a handful of raisins to the blend. If you have only one or two chiles, a pinch of the "sweet" spices—cinnamon, cloves, allspice—will add complexity and depth. Dried sweet peppers of the newer, fleshier breeds—*pimentos dulces*—provide color and flavor as well as varying degrees of fieriness, and are milled for *pimentón dulce* (mild paprika) and *pimentón picante* (chili powder). In powdered form, capsicums burn very easily—they are best added to wet ingredients rather than dry. *Pimentón dulce* can also be used as a sauce-thickener—the ground-up vegetable swells and absorbs moisture when added to a liquid. Don't try it with *pimentón picante*: it's far too fiery to add in sufficient quantity.

Enchiladas de San Cristobal

(Stuffed tortillas with chile cream)
Serves 4

The enchilada is really an excuse for eating as much chile in as many ways as possible. This is how they make them in San Cristobal, a pretty colonial town in the Chiapas, Mexico's mountainous southern region, where the revolutionaries come from. Perhaps the fierceness of the inhabitants can be ascribed to their fondness for fiery foodstuffs.

Enchiladas de San Cristobal

1 pound cubed, boneless pork
2–3 mild frying peppers, seeded and cut
   into strips
1 small onion, finely chopped
1 garlic clove, sliced
Salt

The sauce:
4–5 chiles anchos (or your chosen blend of
   dried chiles)
2 cups cream

To finish:
8–12 corn tortillas
Oil for shallow frying
2 tablespoons grated or crumbled white
   cheese

Cook the pork in a tightly covered pan with very little water and a pinch of salt, for about 30 minutes, until perfectly tender. Let it cool in its own juices, then shred it with a couple of forks, and set aside. Gently fry the pepper strips, onion, and garlic in a little oil until soft but not browned; season, and combine with the shredded pork.

Prepare the sauce by opening up the dried chiles and shaking out the seeds. Tear into large pieces and toast lightly by placing, skin side down, on a heated griddle, pressing down for about 30 seconds until the upper surface is a rich brown. Remove and soak in a cupful of boiling water for 15 minutes to swell. Transfer to a blender along with the soaking water and blend until smooth. Add cream and blend again. Transfer to a small pan, let it boil, and simmer until the cream thickens a little, then taste and add salt.

To assemble the enchiladas: fry the tortillas briefly in pairs in shallow oil, flipping once, until the edges curl. Transfer to a paper towel to dry. Dip each tortilla in the cream sauce, inner side only, and roll it around a tablespoonful of the pork filling. Continue until all the tortillas have been filled. Finish with the remaining sauce. Serve with pickled or fresh green chiles.

Salsa picante mexicana

(Mexican hot sauce)
Makes about 5 cups

A sauce to waken the dead.

8 pounds tomatoes
1¹/₄ cups vinegar
¹/₄ cup brown sugar
1 tablespoon crushed allspice berries
1 teaspoon salt
1–3 tablespoons powdered or flaked chili

Wash and roughly chop the tomatoes. Put all the ingredients except the chili into a large saucepan and let it infuse for half an hour.

Bring the pan to a boil, turn down to a gentle simmer, and let it cook over low heat for at least an hour. It shouldn't need much attention as the tomatoes produce plenty of liquid at this stage, so there's little danger of sticking. Strain the tomato mixture through a wire mesh strainer, leaving skin, seeds, and spice debris behind. Return the purée to the pan. Unless the tomatoes are field-ripened in full sunshine, it'll probably be far too liquidy.

Return to a boil and simmer vigorously, stirring until the sauce is as thick as you like it—it may take 40 minutes. Stir in the chili—as much or as little as you like. Adjust the seasoning. Bottle in empty tequila bottles and cork tightly.

starches, legumes, & grains

Roots and tubers, known in the Caribbean as "ground provisions"—food that cannot escape the gatherer—are treated as soul food in Latin America, as elsewhere. The traditional diet of the indigenous peoples of the Americas was almost entirely vegetarian, based on the mighty trinity—corn, beans, and potatoes—with cassava (manioc) grown wherever none of these three could survive. This simple but nourishing diet was balanced by a wide variety of gourds and greens, usually cultivated in association with the main staple food, with fish and shellfish when available. Meat, barbecued or cooked in an earth oven as part of the celebrations, was only consumed at festivals and on days when offerings were made to the gods.

cassava

or manioc, mandioc, yuca
(*Manihot utilissima/M. esculenta*)

Cassava is an edible tuber of the euphorbia family, a group that includes the toxic milky-juiced spurges and the Christmas poinsettia. Native throughout the warmer zones of the Americas, it was cultivated by the Mayas in the Yucatan, and considered a staple in Brazil and the Caribbean, where its starchiness and blandness makes it ideal for mopping up spicy stews.

A basket manioc press in French Guiana

Cassava, sealed under wax to preserve freshness

How it grows

An herbaceous semitropical plant, the cassava is sun-loving, tall—as much as ten feet—with indented, fan-shaped, edible leaves, and a long, fiber-covered, dark brown, tuberous root, which can weigh several pounds. Actually a node, this looks like a large hairy yam.

Appearance and taste

Two types exist, one bitter, one sweet. Bitter cassava is toxic unless subjected to lengthy preparation during which two byproducts, tapioca and the meat-tenderizing agent, cassareep, are produced. Sweet manioc (the only one on sale fresh) has ivory-white flesh that, when boiled or steamed, becomes almost translucent, with a deliciously buttery taste. Be warned: it quickly becomes gluey if overcooked.

Buying and storing

Selecting fresh cassava is more important than how you store or cook it. The tuber should be covered in rough, patchy bark and never cracked, slimy, or sour smelling—nowadays, however, it's usually given a wax jacket for export. Inside, the flesh should be perfectly white without bruising or dark patches. Store in

Recently harvested cassava

a cool place and slice off a chunk when you need it—the rubbery white juices will seal the wound. The shelf life is short unless you cut it into chunks and boil it, in which case it will last for a week in the refrigerator. It freezes adequately: just peel it, cut it into chunks, and put it in the freezer.

Medicinal and other uses

Nourishing, filling, and an excellent source of carbohydrates, the cassava is gluten-free. It also has a dark side: cyanide-laden varieties are used by South American assassins. While lethal cassavas are not cultivated for consumption, it's wise to avoid any that taste bitter. The poison is removed through grating and squeezing, followed by heating and fermentation—a process familiar to the indigenous population, the ignorance of which proved fatal to some of the early European colonizers.

Culinary uses

The cassava is a versatile vegetable, though starchy, bland, and sorely in need of a dressing or sauce. Only the sweet variety can be eaten fresh. To prepare cassava for the pot: scrub, peel, and cut it into sections, removing the central fiber, and bake, chip, fry, boil, or steam it. Cassava discolors quickly after peeling, so cover with cold water until needed. To make cassava chips, boil until tender, slice thinly, dust with cornstarch, and deep-fry. Additional uses: cassava juice is fermented to make a beer; and in season, the young leaves are boiled and eaten as a vegetable (see edible leaves page 46).

Yuca con mojo, cassava with a garlic and cilantro dressing

Yuca con mojo

(Cassava with garlic and lime)
Serves 4

Plain boiled cassava is a dull dish on its own. In Cuba, it's given a lift with a sharp little dressing. In season, bitter orange juice—from Seville or "marmalade" oranges—takes the place of lime juice.

3 pounds cassava root, peeled and cut
  into chunks
1/4 cup olive oil
4 cloves of garlic, crushed
1/4 cup lemon or lime juice
Salt

To finish:
Fresh cilantro, chopped
Cassava chips

Boil the cassava chunks in salted water for about 30 minutes until soft—don't worry if they disintegrate at the edges. Drain thoroughly.

Meanwhile, in a small frying pan, heat the oil and lightly fry the garlic to soften. Add the citrus juice and let it boil. Pour the dressing over the cassava chunks and finish with a dusting of chopped cilantro. Yuca con mojo is traditionally served with fried plantains or cassava chips (see below).

Yuca frita

(Cassava chips)
Serves 4

A quick snack throughout the Caribbean, cassava chips are particularly popular in Cuba, where they are eaten with a fiery, green papaya salsa. Cassava cannot be made into chips without being boiled first—without this preliminary step, it tastes unacceptably starchy. The idea is to cook the peeled root in a shape that can be sliced into circles.

A piece of cassava, about twice as long as
  your hand
Vegetable oil for deep-frying
Salt

Peel the cassava—easiest done under running water—and cut into three pieces. Drop into boiling water and cook until just tender—15–20 minutes. Drain thoroughly and let it cool. Slice into circles about 1/4-inch thick.

Heat the oil in a heavy pan. When a faint haze rises above the oil, slip in the chips in small batches. Remove and drain on paper towels as soon as they become crisp and golden. Sprinkle with salt and serve hot.

cassava flour

or manioc meal, harina de yuca, farhina

Prepared from the processed cassava root, cassava flour is used throughout the region in flatbreads and cakes, particularly the Yucatán's *cassabe* cakes and Colombia's rich little *pan de yuca*. As an everyday foodstuff, cassava flour takes the place of cornmeal in the diet of those whose terrain is not suitable for the cultivation of corn.

Manufacture

Bitter cassava root is boiled and then mashed and strained, or peeled and grated and then thoroughly squeezed. The juice is then boiled to a sticky black foodstuff called cassareep; at the same time it creates a starchy sediment, the raw material for both cassava flour and tapioca.

Appearance and taste

White- to ivory-colored, the flour comes in fine and coarse millings. The first is used for cakes and breads, the last is preferred for farofa, the Brazilian sprinkling flour that is somewhere between a condiment and a foodstuff.

Making dough from cassava meal, Colombia

Cassava bread stall, Venezuela

Buying and storing

Cassava flour is available in West Indian and Latin American stores or in Indian supermarkets as *gari*. Find a brand that suits you and store it in an airtight container.

Medicinal and other uses

Very bland and digestible, cassava flour is suitable for babies and invalids. It is not advisable as a single food source, since it lacks protein.

Culinary uses

When used in baking, cassava flour is often combined with grated cheese for both substance and enrichment. As a pulp, it can be formed into

cakes and baked slowly on a griddle, another way of increasing its shelf life. When toasted to make farofa, it is added to soups and stews, or can be eaten straight from the bowl.

Farofa

(Brazilian toasted manioc meal)
Serves 6

In Amazonia, coarsely milled cassava flour is used for farofa—toasted meal rather like fine bread crumbs. Here, the basic farofa is enriched by frying with a little palm oil, an ingredient of African origin that adds a sunny golden tint. You can also stir in a handful of chopped onion, cilantro, dried shrimp, slivers of malgueta peppers—whatever's on hand.

2 cups cassava flour (manioc meal)
1 tablespoon dende or vegetable oil, plus a little achiote or paprika

Sift the flour. When your stew or soup is ready, heat the oil in a small pan and sprinkle in the flour. Fry gently, moving the mixture constantly with a wooden spoon so that it browns evenly. Serve as a finishing ingredient with a soup or stew. The Amazonians like to sprinkle it over shredded, steamed manioc leaves, *maniva*. Indispensable with black beans in a feijoada, Brazil's national dish (see page 127).

Pan de yuca

(Colombian cassava breads)

Makes 24 small rolls

Little horseshoe-shaped cookies held together with cheese, these are very rich and crumbly. They are sold in Colombia's marketplaces as a quick breakfast for busy housewives.

1 cup cassava flour
2 cups grated cheese (cheddar or crumbled feta)
2 egg yolks
1/2 stick (1/4 cup) softened butter

Preheat the oven to 400°F. Mix the ingredients together and knead until you have a softish dough—you may need a little water. Set aside for half an hour to let the dough rise. Wet your hands and divide the dough into walnut-size pieces, then roll and shape each into a little horseshoe.

Transfer to a baking tray (no need to grease it), and bake for about 20 minutes, until pale gold and crisp.

tapioca

(from the Tupi Indian word for cassava)

A manufactured grain, the product of processing the bitter cassava root, tapioca is the staple starch-food of the Amazonian nations in probably its most familiar form outside its home territory. Once popular as a milk pudding, tapioca has fallen out of favor in recent years, maybe because so many milky desserts now come in instant form.

Manufacture

Tapioca is made by pushing detoxified, precooked, mashed bitter cassava through a mesh. The result is dictated by the size of the holes and the manner in which the root is prepared.

Appearance and taste

In dried form, tapioca resembles little white pellets. When reconstituted by cooking as a porridge, it is shiny and transparent with a nutty little heart. The taste is bland, the texture a little glutinous—you either love it or hate it.

Buying and storing

Look for large pearly grains of an even size and perfectly white appearance. Store it like rice, in an airtight container, where it will keep for years.

Medicinal and other uses

Tapioca makes an easily digestible and fortifying porridge, perfect for invalids and babies.

Various grains—and avocados—on sale in a street market in Quito, Ecuador

Culinary uses

Tapioca is an alternative to rice in milk puddings and broths. By swelling to roughly four times its original volume, it takes on the characteristics of its cooking liquid, which means that the richer the broth or the creamier the milk, the more delicious the dish.

Caldo al minuto

(Ready-in-a-minute soup)
Serves 1

This, a bowl of very hot chicken soup fortified with tapioca, was the comfort food of my childhood. When I lived in Montevideo—I remember a low white house with a flat roof and a view of the sea—my mother's cook would make this for me when I was sick. Since this wasn't very often, it remained a treat.

A mugful of strong chicken broth
1 level tablespoon small-grain tapioca

To finish:
*1 teaspoon finely chopped serrano or prosciutto
  ham*
1 teaspoon chopped hard-boiled egg
1 teaspoon chopped parsley

Bring the soup to a boil, stir in the tapioca, and simmer for about 20 minutes, stirring occasionally, until the grains are swollen, tender, and transparent. Stir in the finishing ingredients and transfer to a bowl. Sit on the porch and drink it while you watch the sunset.

Postre de tapioca con coco

(Tapioca and coconut cream pudding)
Serves 4

Could anything be more soothing than a bowl of tapioca cooked gently like a rice pudding in coconut cream, sweetened with cane sugar and served cool?

¹/₄ cup pearl tapioca
5 cups milk
2 tablespoons sugar

Put the ingredients in a heavy pot and stir them up. Simmer gently for an hour, until thick, creamy, and soft. Chill. Spoon into a glass bowl or fresh coconut shells, if such should come your way, and enjoy.

Peruvian
black

waxy yellow

fingerling

criolla

floury red

potato

or patata, papa (*Solanum tuberosum*)

The potato is a tuber-forming herbaceous plant related to the
chile, a member of the nightshade family. It is a plant of the
Andean highlands, capable of surviving at high altitudes as
well as in more amiable terrain. The potato was the staple
foodstuff of the Andean nations, particularly valued by the
Mapuche, an ancient people who have managed to retain
many of their pre-Columbian customs and foodways, and
who cultivate potatoes along the edges of the rivers and in
the swamplands of southern Chile. A native of Peru and
cultivated since the earliest times, the potato is resistant to
cold and can be planted in poor soil—virtues that enabled
the building of Machu Picchu, where the Inca kings took
refuge from their enemies, surviving and thriving in
impossible terrain. The potato is easy to cultivate and
undemanding of labor. The planting of the potato in the Old
World can be held responsible for the remarkable population
increases of the eighteenth century, which culminated in the
two revolutions—social and economic—and which altered
the entire political life of Western civilization.

How it grows

The potato is a leafy annual whose stems
swell underground—these are the edible
tubers. It is more easily propagated by
budding than by sowing seed, since the pretty,
papery, little cream-colored flowers are
frequently infertile. Nevertheless, the
appearance of the flowers and the dying back
of the leaves is an indication the crop is ready
to be lifted. Certain Andean varieties are grown
especially for freeze-drying, a natural process
known to the Incas, which reduces the tubers
to what look like lumps of coal but can easily
be reconstituted to palatability.

Sicuani market, Peru

Appearance and taste

Potatoes are irregularly shaped, and their skin colors range from brown, yellow, or russet-skinned tubers; some potatoes have a distinctly pink tint, while a few varieties are a very deep violet—almost black, and some even have dark purple flesh. The more common varieties have ivory to cream flesh beneath thin caramel to dark brown skin. The flesh is crisp and juicy when raw, but soft and floury when cooked. The tuber ranges in size from as small as a marble to as big as a football. There are now more than a thousand varieties known, with many more in its land of origin as yet unexploited. The flavor is bland and starchy but with a distinctive earthiness and nuttiness that is more pronounced in some varieties than others. It is a vegetable that, possibly more than any other, responds directly to the environment in which it's grown. Varieties grown in a stony field on the south side of a hill, say, will not taste the same as the identical variety grown in rich soil on a northern slope.

Buying and storing

Choose firm tubers that show no sign of rotting, spotting, sprouting, or greening—a sign they have developed a potentially toxic chemical, solanine, which must be ruthlessly carved out before cooking. Store in a cool dark place, or the tubers will do what comes naturally: sprout.

Medicinal and other uses

The potato is a fine fuel food, well endowed with all the necessary vitamins, protein, and, famously, carbohydrates. It is rich in potassium, good for the liver and as a system-cleanser. Much of the vitamin and mineral content is concentrated immediately beneath the skin—you will get much less benefit if you skin it before you cook it. It is of far greater nutritional value if consumed raw (though this would certainly not be the gourmet's choice), partic-ularly the juice, which is reputed to have antibiotic properties as well as a liberal endowment of vitamin C and minerals.

Culinary uses

Steaming rather than boiling is the recommended method of preserving as many of the vitamins as possible, although this is not a problem when the potatoes are cooked in the traditional Andean earth oven. The Mapuche, who only go to the trouble of digging an earth oven at tribal gatherings, will tell you that they cook their staple foodstuff in a closed pot not only to preserve the goodness but as a reminder of the unity of all things. Modern recipes of the region either use a minimum of water—cooking the tubers down to complete dryness so that none of the juices are lost—or prepare the tubers as a soup, which allows the cooking water to be drunk as a broth.

Wide variety of potatoes in Cuenca, Ecuador

Papas a la huancaina
(Potatoes with cream and cheese)
Serves 4–6

This is Peru's national dish: nothing fancy, but when made with good ingredients, worth the attention of any gourmet. Plain-boiled potatoes are sauced with cheese, melted with cream, and flavored with ají—chile. Varieties of Peruvian bush-chile, the upward-pointing triangular variety, range from the tolerable and mild to the screaming scarlet rocota, the chile that put fire in the belly of the Incas.

4 pounds small, round, yellow-fleshed potatoes (criollas, for preference)
Sea or kosher salt

The sauce:
3 cups grated cheese
1 1/4 cups cream
1 teaspoon arrowroot or cornstarch mixed with a little water
1 teaspoon chili flakes or 2–3 medium-hot ajies (chiles), toasted to blister, and cut into ribbons

Wash the potatoes and put them in a heavy pot with just enough water to cover, add salt, bring to a boil, put the lid on tightly, turn down the heat, and cook for about 15 minutes. Remove the lid and let it boil to evaporate excess liquid, cover with a cloth, and cook over a very low heat for another 5 minutes or so, until the potatoes are tender and dry.

Meanwhile, in a saucepan, melt the cheese into the cream, whisk in the arrowroot or cornstarch, and stir in the aji. Simmer until it thickens—5 minutes or so. Pour the sauce over the potatoes.

Chapale chileno
(Chilean potato bread)
Serves 4

A dense-textured potato bread, this is traditionally baked in an earth oven, the chosen cooking implement of the Mapuche, the indigenous inhabitants of the cold uplands of southern Chile, whose way of life depends on cultivation of the potato.

4 large potatoes, scrubbed
1/4 cup chuchoca (cornmeal)
1/4 cup grated cheese
1–2 links fresh chorizo, skinned and crumbled
1 teaspoon chili powder
1 large egg, beaten with a fork
Salt
Butter or oil for greasing the baking pan

Preheat the oven to 350°F. In salted water, boil the potatoes in their skins until tender—about 20 minutes, more if they're very large. Drain, saving the water. Peel as soon as they're cool enough to handle and mash roughly with a fork. Using your hands, but without crushing out all the lumps, work in the cornmeal, cheese, chorizo, chili, egg, and enough of the potato water to make a soft dough.

Grease a roasting pan and spread in the dough, leveling off the top. Bake for 45–50 minutes, until brown and crisp. Cut into squares and eat with a modest shake of chili sauce—southern *chilenos* like their food less fiery than the northerners.

Ecuador potato market

Papas a la huancaina, bite-size criolla potatoes, richly sauced and fiery with chili

amaranth

*(Amaranthus caudatus, A. melancholicus,
A. hypocondriacus, A. cruentus)*

The amaranth is a broad-leaved plant, a member of the spinach family that grows wild throughout the region. In Europe, its usefulness as a food plant was well known to the Ancient Greeks, who esteemed it both for the leaves and seeds. In the Americas, it was highly valued as a cereal crop by both the Inca and Aztec civilizations, second only to corn. Montezuma, the Aztec emperor at the time of the Spanish conquest, received enormous quantities in tribute—almost as much as was received in corn. His priests used the seeds, mixed with honey or sacrificial blood, to make effigies of their gods, which were then eaten by the priests and their victims. The Christian missionaries, horrified by what appeared to make mockery of the sacrament of the Eucharist, banned the crop, punishing those who continued to harvest or trade in it by cutting off the offending right hand. This, as might be expected, discouraged its use, and amaranth effectively vanished as a foodstuff, although not from the landscape.

Amaranth seeds

How it grows

The amaranth is a broad-leaf plant rather than a grass, a botanical distinction that makes the crop a seed rather than a grain. Indigenous to both India and the Americas, more than five hundred species are known worldwide, and it has adapted to the widest possible range of habitats, from lush tropical to arid desert, from near-Arctic conditions to steaming jungle. A single plant produces dozens of seedheads, each a droopy, bushy tassel yielding up to five thousand tiny seeds.

Appearance and taste

The grain is very small, almost sandy, ivory in color, but the seedheads vary from snowy white to a deep reddish-brown to black; the taste is strong and nutty with a peppery aftertaste, rather like unskinned walnuts. As a porridge, it cooks to a texture much like grain-mustard, a little gluey, never losing its shape. The greens—the best-known variety is Chinese spinach—are gloriously variable in color. The wild varieties have rather tough and indigestible leaves, but those grown as greens are robust and chard-like, with a strong peppery flavor; the young stalks are also eaten (older stalks are tough and woody), tasting a little like artichoke.

Buying and storing

You'll find amaranth grains sold in packets in health food stores; they're highly valued for their high protein content. Store the packet in a cool dry place or decant into a lidded jar. The greens, particularly those of a dark green, red-tinged, slightly fuzzy variety, usually labeled Chinese spinach, can be also be found in season. Treat it like Swiss chard: cut off any dry ends and put the stems in water, or store them in a plastic bag in the fridge.

Medicinal and other uses

Gluten-free, rich in minerals and protein, higher in fiber than wheat, rice, or soybeans, amaranth was rediscovered by U.S. chemists in the 1970s and promoted as the ideal vegetarian foodstuff.

Paella de granos de paraíso, a delicate combination of amaranth grains and greens

First cook the amaranth. Bring the water to a boil, stir in the amaranth grains, put the lid on loosely, turn down the heat, and simmer for 30–35 minutes, until soft, swollen, and tender. Remove from the heat and let stand for 15 minutes, with the lid still on, to swell some more.

Meanwhile, in a large shallow pan, gently fry the garlic and diced peppers in the oil until the vegetables are soft—don't let them brown. Add the diced squash and a splash of water, put the lid on, and simmer for about 10 minutes, until the pumpkin is nearly tender but still holds its shape. Pop the shredded greens on top, season with salt and pepper, let it boil, put the lid on again, and shake over the heat for another 5 minutes, just long enough to wilt the leaves. Fork in the amaranth grains, reheat, and pile onto a warm serving dish.

Pastel de los ángeles
(Angel cake)
Serves 6

Angel food in every sense: light, nutty, easy to digest, and delicious. The amaranth keeps the cake moist.

6 eggs
1 1/2 cups sugar
1 3/4 cups plus 2 tablespoons ground almonds
6 ounces precooked amaranth grains
  (about 1 heaped cup)
1 lemon, peel and juice

Preheat the oven to 350°F.

Whisk the eggs with the sugar until frothy, light, and white, a process that takes twice as long as you think. Fold in the almonds and amaranth grains, lemon peel, and a tablespoonful of the juice, spoon into a 7-inch round cake pan, buttered and lined with parchment paper, and bake for 40–50 minutes, until puffed and brown. It'll shrink back to a thick soft pancake when it comes out of the oven—no matter. Save the remaining juice to melt with honey to make a little soaking-sauce for the cake. Delicious with a scoop of coconut parfait (see page 225).

Culinary uses

It is a very versatile grain that can be used to add food value to other grain foods: use it in breads, biscuits, cookies, cakes, and pancakes (remembering that it's gluten-free so it will not rise or hold together unless heavily blended with wheat flour). The grain can be quickly prepared as a porridge to be served savory or sweet (delicious with cream and honey), or popped like popcorn with a drop of oil in a tightly lidded pan. Treat the leaves as cabbage or spinach: shred and cook in very little water.

Paella de granos de paraíso
(Amaranth paella with peppers and greens)
Serves 4

A paella, the Spanish risotto, takes its name from the container in which it's cooked: a wide, shallow, double-handled, iron pan of a design known to the Romans, who got it from the Ancient Greeks. If you can't find amaranth leaves, substitute any member of the spinach or cabbage family. Cook double quantities of the basic grains and use the leftovers to bake an angel cake (see below).

7 ounces amaranth grains (about 1 1/3 cups)
2 1/4 cups water
7-ounce piece squash, diced (about 1 3/4 cups)
2 garlic cloves, finely chopped
4 poblano or 2 green bell peppers, seeded and
  diced
2 tablespoons oil
A large handful amaranth or cabbage leaves,
  shredded
Salt and pepper

chickpea

or garbanzo bean (*Cicer arietinum*)

A dried legume, cultivated for at least five thousand years, the chickpea was found in the middens of Mesopotamia, from where it spread throughout the temperate zones of Asia, Africa, and Europe, finally colonizing the Americas. Portable and easily reconstituted to make a nourishing soup, the chickpea is soldiers' fodder, the legume that fueled the Muslim armies when they invaded Andalusia, provisioned Columbus's ships and, finally and most disastrously for the indigenous inhabitants, enabled Cortés's conquistadores to reach the court of Montezuma. A European import, it is now naturalized throughout the region.

brown chickpeas

green chickpeas

How it grows

The chickpea is a small bushy annual easily propagated from seed (the chickpeas themselves). The pods are short and hairy and contain no more than one or two seeds that, when fresh, are about the size of a small hazelnut.

Appearance and taste

As a stored legume vegetable, the chickpea is coffee-colored with a patterned surface coming to a point at one end. The flavor is nutty and sweet: chestnuts with a bit of fresh hay. There's a short period in midsummer when chickpeas can be eaten green and raw: while the flavor is much like fresh peas, the juices are so acid they stain your fingers black. In Andalusia where I lived with my young family, we grew a crop every year just for drying and storing; our neighbors, frugal housewives, taught me to add the pinched-out shoots to the beanpot.

Buying and storing

Buy from a source with a high turnover—dry-goods stores that serve ethnic communities—as chickpeas that have been stored longer than a single season take twice as long to soften. Freshly dried chickpeas have a plump appearance, a slight give when squeezed, and an absence of any powdery deposit in the packet. Hispanic cooks choose the large, pale varieties, although Indian and Middle Eastern cooks appreciate black, red, and dark brown varieties. Chickpeas are also available in cans—not the cheapest way to buy them, but convenient, particularly when they are being used as a secondary ingredient.

Medicinal and other uses

High in protein and gluten-free, the chickpea is well endowed with fiber and the necessary vitamins and minerals to sustain an army on the march.

Culinary uses

The chickpea is best appreciated whole in a stew, preferably in combination with pork variety meats such as tripe and pigs' feet, since both take the same amount of time to soften. Pounded and soaked, it makes a crisp little fritter. Chickpea flour, the milled version of the dried legume, is used in breads and to thicken soups, giving a pleasantly nutty flavor as well as improving the food value. It makes an excellent tamale dough, and mixed with water and allowed to stand and ferment a little, it makes a remarkably light, crisp, frying batter (particularly good as fritters made with small shrimp, *tortillitas de camarón*). Chickpea flour can also do duty as the Brazilian sprinkling condiment farofa (see page 60), if manioc meal is unavailable.

Menudo colombiano

(Tripe and chickpeas)
Serves 6

The classic Colombian stew—fortifying on a cold winter's day in the Andean uplands. The combination of pork and chickpeas is a happy one, particularly when enlivened with ají—the Andean form of the fiery chile.

3 cups chickpeas, soaked overnight
2 onions, skinned and quartered
1 pound cleaned tripe
2 pigs feet or a smoked ham hock
Short stick of cinnamon
2–3 cloves
1 teaspoon cumin
1–2 chopped, seeded chiles
2^1/$_2$ cups tomato purée
1 teaspoon dried oregano
Salt

To finish:
1 pound potatoes, cut into bite-size
* chunks (about 3–3^1/$_2$ cups)*
2^1/$_2$ cups corn kernels
A handful macaroni or any tubular pasta
A handful fresh chickpeas or green beans,
* cut small*
4–5 tablespoons olive oil
2 tablespoons drained capers

Drain the soaked chickpeas and transfer to a roomy cooking pot along with the rest of the ingredients—don't add salt yet. Bring to a boil, turn down to simmer, put the lid on loosely, and let it bubble very gently for about two hours, until the chickpeas are perfectly tender and the meat is soft enough to eat with a spoon. Add more boiling water as necessary.

Add the potatoes and return to a boil. After 10 minutes, add the corn and pasta, taste, and add salt. Let bubble for another 10 minutes

and add the fresh chickpeas or green beans. Return to a boil and cook for another 10–15 minutes, until the pasta is tender. The dish should be soupy but thick enough to support the weight of a wooden spoon. Finish with a swirl of olive oil and a sprinkle of capers.

Acarajé de garbanzos

(Chickpea fritters)
Serves 4

These are crisp Brazilian fritters made with presoaked but uncooked chickpeas, an alternative to the shrimp-enhanced black-eyed pea fritters. The aim is a crisp shell enclosing a soft, floury interior. You can vary the flavorings—more or less chili or cumin, no cilantro—to suit your palate.

1^1/$_2$ cups presoaked chickpeas
2–3 garlic cloves, crushed
1 teaspoon chili powder
1 teaspoon ground cumin
1 teaspoon salt
^{1}/$_2$ teaspoon baking powder
^{1}/$_4$ cup finely chopped parsley and
* cilantro*
Oil for frying

Drain the chickpeas and dry thoroughly. Pound in a mortar or mix in the food processor until you have a very smooth paste—the chickpeas must be absolutely dry before the pounding or mixing, or the paste will fall apart in the frying. Add the remaining ingredients in the order given, blending between each addition, until well mixed. Let rest for an hour. Break off small pieces the size of a walnut and form into small patties about 1^1/$_2$ inches in diameter. Arrange on a plate ready to slip into the hot oil—they're too fragile to pick up in your fingers.

Heat the oil, and use a spatula to push the patties into the hot oil, a few at a time. Fry until crisp and brown. If they splutter and split, the oil is too hot. Turn once and transfer to paper towels to drain. Serve with a shake of malagueta pepper sauce (see page 51).

Menudo colombiano, a rich, spicy tripe and chickpea stew

rice

or arroz (*Oryza sativa*)

Although unknown in the Americas before the arrival of the Europeans (wild rice is unrelated), rice was enthusiastically naturalized in suitable estuary and swamplands, particularly those with populations of African origin such as the southern states of North America, the Caribbean, and Brazil, where it features among the indispensable accompaniments to feijoada, the national dish (see page 127).

medium-grain rice

How it grows

The seeds of a water-dependent grass of Asian origin, rice is the staple grain of much of the world's most densely populated areas. More than seven thousand varieties are grown, each with its own shape, color, flavor, and fragrance.

Appearance and taste

White rice—few Latin American cooks would thank you for brown or any other kind of rice—is prepared by stripping the grain of its outer layer or husk of bran, leaving a snow-white kernel with a delicate, almost flowery fragrance, which retains a seductively nutty flavor.

Buying and storing

A medium-grain rice—slender, absorbent, about twice as long as it is wide—is generally the most suitable for Latin American recipes. Keep it in an airtight container. Chile-growing countries pop a dried chile into the storage container to discourage creepy-crawlies.

Medicinal and other uses

White rice, extremely digestible and an excellent vehicle for other foods, is pure carbohydrate since most of the vitamins, minerals, and fiber are lost in the husk-stripping process. When it was discovered that the exposed kernels are vulnerable to mold and insects, a practice developed of dusting the grains with talc—a product derived from the same source as asbestos. Talc-dusted rices are mostly sold in California, Puerto Rico, and Hawaii, but only rarely appear elsewhere.

Culinary uses

Appreciated throughout the territory as a staple grain food, rice is usually plainly cooked in water and served as a side dish, or combined with one of the legumes of the indigenous bean family. Medium-grain rice takes up moisture

Rice thrives in swampy conditions

and retains it, remaining fluffy and absorbent—a virtue when served as an accompaniment. Long-grain rice never completely softens, and short-grain is inclined to stickiness, making both less suitable as a background grain for the region's soupy stews and sauces.

Arroz brasileiro

(Brazilian rice)
Serves 6 as an accompaniment

In Brazil, as in Portugal, rice is the obligatory accompaniment to all main dishes. Nothing to it, really. While Spain planted the Middle Eastern, medium-size round-grain rice in its dependencies, Portugal preferred a long-grain, the rice popular in its Far Eastern dependencies.

3–4 tablespoons olive oil
2 1/2 cups long-grain rice
6 1/4 cups water (2 1/2 times the volume of rice)
2 garlic cloves, peeled and very finely chopped
1–2 cloves
1 tablespoon coarse sea salt or kosher salt

Preheat the oven to 350°F.

Heat the oil gently in a flameproof casserole dish or other heavy flameproof and ovenproof pot. Add the rice to the hot (but not smoking) oil until the grains are transparent. Add the water, the chopped garlic, cloves, and salt, bring to a boil and let it cook for 15 minutes. Transfer the dish to the oven and bake for 15–20 minutes, until the rice is tender and lightly crisped on top.

Jamaican rice 'n' peas

Serves 6

Popular all over the Caribbean, this dish is best if made the day before. It varies throughout the territory since each community and household has its own special recipe. Some include meat—pork organ meat, usually; others a different legume-vegetable such as black-eyed peas, lentils, chickpeas. Only the rice and the philosophical approach—nothing wasted, the legume-broth used to cook the rice—never varies. In Jamaica, you can buy the combination cooked and vacuum-packed.

3 cups cooked red beans and
  their liquid (about 1 cup)
1 ripe coconut
2¹/₂ cups medium-grain rice
2–3 sprigs thyme
2 cloves garlic, crushed
Salt and cracked black pepper
Variety meats (optional)

Split the coconut by dropping it on a hard tabletop or a concrete floor. Discard the water (unless you're thirsty). Ease the white flesh off the brown husk with a knife and break the flesh into small pieces. Pack the pieces in the blender and cover with cold water. Blend until mushy, strain through a cloth, squeezing to extract all the liquid. Reserve the liquid and return the mush to the blender, repeating the process with more water. (Combine the liquid from the first extraction with the liquid from the second. The first extraction is coconut cream; when the second is added to the first, it becomes coconut milk.)

Put the rice in a large saucepan with enough coconut milk to cover. Bring to a boil, season with salt, add in the thyme, lower the heat, and simmer slowly until all the milk is absorbed.

Meanwhile, drain the beans, reserving a cup of their liquid, and set them aside. Dilute the liquid with a cup of boiling water. Add this to the rice as it dries. When the rice is perfectly soft, stir in the drained beans and the garlic. You can, if you wish, also stir in slices of blood sausage or precooked pig's tail, ears, and feet, suitably boned and shredded—easy if you have a pepperpot simmering slowly on the back of the stove. Taste and season. Reheat to serve.

quinoa

or quinua (*Chenopodium* spp.)

The quinoa is a member of the spinach family, whose leaves are eaten in much the same way. It is widespread throughout the world in various forms, happiest in the harshest conditions such as those of the Andean highland, and was known to the Incas as the mother-seed, the source of all life. As such it was one of the two grain foods—the other the Aztecs' amaranth—targeted as unacceptable by the Hispanic colonizers for religious as well as political reasons. It survived as a staple grain food only among the people of Bolivia's Altiplano, particularly in the Cordillera mountains where it thrives at altitudes above 9,850 feet. The quinoa has recently started to come back into favor thanks to its value in a vegetarian diet.

How it grows

The quinoa is a leafy member of the spinach family that comes in many colors—pink, red, orange, lavender, purple, black, yellow, and white—and grows to a height of three to ten feet, carrying its seedheads in large clusters at the end of the stalk. Prolific and hardy, it thrives in extreme conditions. The quinoa is harvested mainly for its seed, though its leaves are indistinguishable from spinach.

Appearance and taste

The quinoa cooks and tastes like a nutty couscous—the grains swell up to four times their own volume—speckled with little crescent-shaped corkscrews, the debris of the outer coverings. It is sometimes known as the vegetarian caviar for the crunchiness and translucence of the small, perfectly spherical grains that never lose their shine.

Buying and storing

The quinoa has small, disk-shaped seeds that look like sesame in the packet. Seeds sold commercially will have been well rinsed of their sticky coating of saponin, a bitter, soap-like resin that protects them from seed-eating birds and insects. Pay no attention to the few little black speckles. Wild quinoa, which neither soften nor burst, have a pleasantly peppery flavor. Buy from a shop with a high turnover— the grains are at their best when fresh—and store in an airtight container in a cool place. Bear in mind that in any recipe the flavor is enhanced by a light preliminary toasting. If milled into flour, this should be stored in the refrigerator since a high oil content quickly turns it rancid.

Medicinal and other uses

Gluten-free, digestible, rich in proteins and minerals (particularly iron), quinoa is suitable for convalescents and muscle-building athletes alike. Volume for volume, it has more calcium than milk—useful in the prevention of osteoporosis— and more natural fat than any other grain.

Quinoa crop in the Andes

Culinary uses

Quinoa is a versatile cereal, as useful to the pastry chef looking for a way to lighten his cakes and biscuits as to the domestic cook feeding a family on a budget. As a cereal, treat it as bulgar: cook it in twice its own volume of water and serve either as a porridge, delicious sweetened with honey and cream, or as a pilaf, flavored with fresh herbs. In Ecuador, quinoa is traditionally combined with lye-treated cornmeal when kneading tamales and tortillas. In cakes and pastries, use it either as a cooked grain or in the form of flour, bearing in mind that quinoa, although its lightness makes it suitable for the finest pastry making, lacks the gluten necessary to hold a dough together. For best results, mix it with wheat flour in the proportions of 4 parts wheat to 3 parts quinoa, and grind in the food processor to make a delicate, exquisitely hazelnut-flavored flour.

Chaulafán de quinua y naranja

(Ecuadorian quinoa and orange salad)
Serves 4–6

A simple salad served as an accompaniment—condiment—in which the nutty sweetness of the quinoa is balanced by the acidity of the citrus.

1 pound quinoa (about 2²/₃ cups)
1 chayote or a small cucumber, diced
6 scallions, chopped with their green ends
Small handful flat-leaf parsley
Small handful fresh mint
1–2 oranges, segments and finely grated peel
2 green or red jalapeño chiles, seeded and chopped
6 tablespoons olive oil
2 tablespoons lemon or bitter orange juice
Salt

Rinse the quinoa under a faucet until the water runs clear. In a large pan, cover the grains with double their own volume of water. Bring to a boil, reduce to a simmer, put the lid on loosely, and cook for about 20 minutes or so, until the grains are translucent and the water has all been absorbed.

Combine with all the remaining ingredients. Taste, and add whatever's needed: a little more salt, an extra squeeze of lemon, perhaps. Serve with thick slices of corn on the cob or (in winter) a fistful of arepas—thick tortillas made with the snowy white corn of the Andes—hot from the griddle.

Galletas de quinua

(Quinoa cookies)
Makes about 24 cookies

These crisp, nutty cookies made with quinoa flour are easy to make since the little seeds only take a moment or two to crush.

¹/₄ cup quinoa grains
³/₄ cup self-rising whole wheat flour
¹/₄ cup seed oil, e.g., sunflower seed oil

Chaulafán de quinua y naranja, a summer salad dressed with orange

¹/₄ cup smooth peanut butter
¹/₄ cup brown sugar or grated palm sugar
¹/₄ cup white sugar
1 large egg, lightly whisked
¹/₂ teaspoon vanilla seeds scraped from the pod
Milk or water
Butter for greasing

Butter a cookie sheet. Preheat the oven to 375°F. Put the quinoa and the flour in the processor and mix for a few minutes—it'll crush quickly and easily. In a mixing bowl, blend the oil with the peanut butter, then beat in the two sugars until light and fluffy. Beat in the egg and vanilla seeds. Fold in the quinoa flour and enough water or milk to make a soft dough that drops easily from the spoon.

Drop spoonfuls of the mixture onto the cookie sheet, leaving plenty of room for expansion. Bake for 8–10 minutes, until lightly browned. Transfer to a baking rack to cool and crisp.

black-eyed pea

or black-eyed bean, cowpea, fradinho (Brazil)
(*Vigna unguiculata* et spp.)

An annual legume, the black-eyed pea is a member of the pea family related to the Chinese mung bean but of a strain long naturalized in Africa, popular in Brazil and among Caribbean cooks. It is one of the traditional seed foods that, if eaten on the first day of the new year, is said to bring luck for the next twelve months.

How it grows

The black-eyed pea is a short, erect or trailing plant with pods about as long as a man's foot and no thicker than a pencil. It is fully mature and ready for shelling three months after planting.

Appearance and taste

The form popular in the region is a small, ivory-colored kidney shape with a deep purple to ebony-black "eye." The flavor of the mature pea is robust and earthy, with an underlying sweetness and a smooth buttery texture.

Buying and storing

Check for freshness—the color should be bright and the peas still have a little give when squeezed between the fingers—and the absence of a powdery deposit, which indicates the presence of uninvited guests. Store in an airtight container in a cool corner.

Medicinal and other uses

The black-eyed pea is fuel food for field workers, high in carbohydrates and protein-rich, as are all the legumes.

Culinary uses

Fast food for busy people, black-eyed peas, unlike most dried legumes, need no preliminary soaking, and cook to perfect tenderness in about 40 minutes. They can be eaten whole when tender and young, but are usually left to mature for storing.

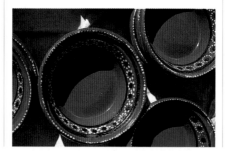

Soupe à Congo

(Black-eyed pea and pigeon-pea soup)
Serves 4–6

Martinique's contribution to the meal-in-a-bowl tradition is a mighty soup-stew in whose name can be traced its lineage. The pigeon peas—known as no-eye peas—are closely related to the black-eyed, but soften to a mush, thickening the broth.

2¹/₂ cups black-eyed peas
1 cup split pigeon peas (yellow dhal)
2 salted pigs' tails or 1 smoked ham hock
6 allspice berries, roughly crushed
1 sweet potato, peeled and diced
1–2 carrots, scraped and diced
2–3 garlic cloves, slivered
A generous handful okra, topped and tailed
Half a cabbage, shredded
Salt

To finish:
1 onion, finely sliced
1 eggplant, diced
3–4 tablespoons oil
1–2 fiery cayenne chile peppers, seeded and
* chopped*

Put the two kinds of peas in a large pan along with the pigs' tails or ham hock, and add enough water to cover to a depth of about 3¹/₂–4 inches. Bring to a boil, skim off any foam, and add the allspice berries. Turn down the heat, put the lid on loosely, and cook for half an hour, until the vegetables begin to soften. Add the potato, carrots, and garlic, and more boiling water if necessary to maintain the volume. Remove the ham hock, if using, strip the meat from the bone, and return it to the pot (the tails can stay as they are). Return to a boil and cook for 10 minutes, then add the okra and the cabbage. Cook for another 10 minutes, until all is perfectly tender and the juices are thick and fragrant. Add more water as needed.

Meanwhile, heat the oil in a frying pan, add the onion and the eggplant, and fry, adding the chile, and salting as the vegetables soften. When softened, stir the contents of the frying pan into the pot. Serve with white rice and sliced avocado dressed with lime juice.

Acarajé

(Black-eyed pea fritters with shrimp)
Serves 4–6

Exotic little fritters made with black-eyed peas and dried shrimp, acarajé are fried crisp in dende oil. A Brazilian dish of African origin and a specialty of the Bahia, the fritters are cooked to order on the street by women in the traditional flounced white dresses, spotlessly clean, and draped with colored necklaces. You'll find the same fritters sold on the streets of Ghana and Nigeria. The same mixture formed into dumplings, wrapped in banana leaves, and steamed, is called abara.

1¼ cups dried black-eyed peas, picked over, rinsed, and soaked overnight to loosen the skins
1 small yellow onion, finely chopped
2 tablespoons dried shrimp (look for them in Chinese markets)
Salt
Dende oil for deep frying (or any vegetable oil)

Drain the peas and peel off the skins—a bit time-consuming, but presoaking makes it easier. In the blender or food processor, purée the skinned peas, onion, shrimp, and a little salt—Brazilian dried shrimp are well salted. Keep going until you have a smooth purée, somewhere between a batter and a paste. If

using Chinese dried shrimp, you'll need extra salt.

Heat the oil in a deep-fat fryer or deep frying pan until very hot. To make small fritters, drop in walnut-size spoonfuls of the batter a few at a time, so the temperature doesn't drop. They will be ready in 3–4 minutes. Transfer with a slotted spoon to paper towels to drain.

To make larger fitters, form the purée into saucer-size patties and slide them gently into the hot oil. Flip them once, allowing 7–8 minutes in all. Serve with a shake of malagueta pepper sauce (see page 51).

fresh corn

or maíz tierno, choclo tierno, elote tierno, jojota tierno (*Zea mays*)

Corn is the preeminent grain crop of the Americas; prehistoric middens leave ethnobotanists in no doubt that it has been cultivated throughout the Americas for at least 7,000 years. Creation legends of both the Andean nations and the peoples of Central America present maize-corn as the raw material of life, much as Ancient Europeans attached mystical significance to wheat. The cob appears in depictions of elaborate ritual dishes; in Mexico, the Aztecs of Cortes's day planted the crop up and down their highways, so that no one would go hungry— generosity wasted on the conquistadores, who lost many of their number to starvation. Although of most practical use as a dried grain, valued for both man and his domestic animals, the tender young cobs are eaten fresh (*tierno*) in season. In tropical lands, where summer and winter are largely irrelevant, this can be three or even four times a year.

A corn co-op in Nicaragua

Buying and storing

Choose cobs still in their bright green husks— there should be no sign of drying or yellowing—and resist the temptation to open them even a crack: exposure to air begins the hardening and drying process. The shorter the distance from field to pot the better. After only a few hours, the sugar in the kernels begins to turn to starch.

Medicinal and other uses

One of the best balanced of the starch foods, corn is very easy to digest when fresh and steamed or grilled—but it is less digestible as a stored grain. Corn is good for building muscle and bone, and excellent for the brain and central nervous system. Said to reduce the likelihood of cancer and heart disease, it is recommended in the treatment of some skin diseases—either eaten or applied topically.

How it grows

Corn is a tall—13–16 feet high—bamboo-like grass whose fertile seed heads, the cobs, grow at intervals up the stem, allowing the neat rows of seeds to mature inside a protective sheath of modified leaves, the husk. The styles of the female flowers are the silky tassels that emerge from the tops of the husks, ready for pollination by the male flowers that appear as a spray of tiny blooms at the top of the stem. It is often grown in association with pumpkin or squash, which acts as a mulch and weed-inhibitor between the rows, and beans, for which the stalks provide a climbing pole. Fittingly, the three can be combined in the pot.

Appearance and taste

Many different varieties are grown, though two main strains can be identified: the sunny yellow corn of Central America and the larger, whiter, starchier corn of the Andean highlands. *Maíz morado*, a purple corn native to Peru, is the caviar of the crop, very sought after for its delicate, lemon-blossomy flavor.

Culinary uses

When the corn is perfectly fresh and tender at the beginning of the season, steam or grill it, and eat it with your hands. Later, scrape off the kernels from any leftover cobs to make a creamy soup (see *Crema de elote*, page 197), or include the kernels in one of the myriad multicolored stews, or cut the cobs into thick slices and serve with a seviche or a soup instead of bread.

Maíz tierno a la brasa

(Barbecued corn)

Serves 4

This is the Mexican way with fresh corn on the cob. Allow two per person, three if the cobs are small or appetites are large.

8–12 fresh ears of corn, unhusked

For serving:
Coarse salt
3–4 large dried chiles, seeded and
  crumbled or 4 teaspoons chili flakes
Quartered limes
Very cold tequila

Light the barbecue or heat the broiler. Pull back the husks and, leaving them attached as a handle, place the cobs on the barbecue and roast them over a high heat—the aim is to blister and blacken the tips for the shortest possible time. Don't salt yet, and avoid prolonged roasting or the tender kernels will dry out. Sprinkle with salt and chiles, and serve with lime quarters and a little glass of ice-cold tequila on the side.

Maíz tierno a la brasa, tender young ears of corn grilled on the barbecue

Humitas

(Fresh corn dumplings)

Serves 4–6

These are little corn dumplings steamed in the husk, as they like them in Chile and Ecuador, made with the large, milky, Andean corn kernels. Fresh corn is used in season, although humitas can be made with ground, lye-treated, dried corn, or a mixture of fresh and dried. The flavoring is albahaca, the fragrant Andean basil.

16 large, fresh ears of corn, still in the husk
A handful basil leaves, stripped from the stalks
1 small green serrano or jalapeño chile,
  seeded and finely chopped
2 tablespoons soft pork lard or oil
2 large onions, finely chopped
1/2 green bell pepper, finely chopped
1 egg (if necessary), lightly beaten with a fork
Salt

Carefully strip the husks from the corn without tearing them. With a sharp knife, slice off the kernels, and set aside. Using the back of the knife, scrape the milky residue from the empty cobs, and add to the kernels. Add the basil leaves and the chile. Either pound the ingredients or use the food processor to reduce all to a soft, smooth mush.

Meanwhile, heat the lard or oil in a small pan and gently fry the onions and green pepper, sprinkled with a little salt, until soft. Stir in the corn purée and simmer gently for another 10–15 minutes, until the mixture has lost most of its moisture. Taste, and adjust the seasoning. If the corn is not of the large-kerneled Andean variety, you'll need an egg to bind it.

Assemble the humitas: lay two of the inner leaves of the husk side by side, overlapping the edges by a finger's width. Drop 2 tablespoons of the corn mush in the center. Fold the bottom edge over the filling, then fold in the sides, finally folding over the top to make neat little wraps—don't wrap it too tightly as the mixture expands. Secure with a fine strip of husk or strong thread. Repeat until all the mixture is wrapped.

Bring a big pot of salted water to a boil. Pack in all the little wraps—they should be completely covered with water. Return to a boil, turn down the heat, and simmer for 40 minutes. Remove, drain, and let cool a little before serving. A little dipping salsa would be nice, though this is not essential or even traditional. To reheat, allow 20 minutes in the oven at 375°F. Or, for a delicious smoky flavor, roast them on the barbecue: Chile's rural housewives pop them straight on the coals.

masa harina

or tortilla flour, masarepa, arepa flour

masa harina

Masa harina and masarepa are prepared flours made from lye-treated, precooked, milled corn, the raw material of tortillas and arepas, the daily bread of the southern Americas. Both are griddle-baked flatbreads of varying thickness, which serve the same purpose as all other flatbreads: as food-wrapper, portable plate, spoon, fork, and edible scoop. Table implements are kept to a minimum in the heat of the tropics for practical reasons of hygiene.

Manufacture

To prepare your own masa for both tortillas and arepas, you'll need dried corn kernels stripped from the cob. Soak them in fresh water overnight with a pinch of lye, drain them, grind them to a soft mush by whatever means available, and knead with a little salt to make a smooth, soft dough.

Appearance and taste

Masa harina, tortilla flour, is yellow and a little speckled (variations in color are admired in an ear of corn), while masarepa, arepa flour, is prepared from the whiter, starchier corn of the Andes. The flavor of the tortilla flour is stronger and sweeter than the arepa flour, but both are satisfyingly nutty, with a honeyed aftertaste.

Buying and storing

Buy it in the form of all-purpose flour for the making of tortillas or arepas—pick a brand that suits you. Store in an airtight container in a dry place, as for other flours. Masa harina is not to be confused with cornmeal or polenta, because ordinary milled corn has not been subjected to the necessary processing.

Medicinal and other uses

Cornmeal that has been treated with lye has far greater food value than ordinary untreated milled corn. The method—originally a soaking with wood ash, replaced after the Spanish conquest with powdered lime (quicklime or whitewash)—was developed by both the Aztecs and Incas, who undoubtedly learned it from earlier civilizations. The need for these preliminaries was not understood by the Europeans, who brought what was seen as a miracle foodstuff back to the Old World and planted it in their fields, replacing more ancient crops. Too great a dependence on untreated cornmeal as a staple leads to pellagra, a vitamin-deficiency disease that can prove fatal—still a problem in Africa, where mealies are sometimes the sole foodstuff.

Preparing tortilla dough in a Mexico City restaurant

masarepa

Tortillas

(Mexican cornbread)
Makes about 24 tortillas

The daily bread of Central America—Guatemala and Nicaragua as well as Mexico—is lightly milled, patted out by hand, and baked on a *comal*, an earthenware griddle.

1 pound corn flour or masa harina
5 cups water
About 2 teaspoons quicklime (calcium oxide)

Soak the corn overnight in the water, bring to a boil, and cook for an hour—the skins will turn bright yellow and loosen. Rub off the skins, rinse thoroughly, and crush or grind the resultant mush, *nixtamal*, in a corn grinder or *metate*—the traditional stone mortar—until it forms a dense mass. Knead until you have a soft, smooth, flexible dough—not wet enough to be sticky, and not so dry that it cracks or crumbles. Divide into 16 walnut-size balls.

Now you're ready to make the tortillas. Flatten the dough balls lightly and cover with plastic wrap to keep them soft while you work. Pat or roll each piece out into a thin pancake about 5 inches in diameter. To pat out by hand, dip your hands in warm water before placing the flattened dough ball on the palm of one hand and patting it out with the other, reversing your hands between each pat (difficult), or roll out between 2 sheets of plastic (easy), or use a tortilla press (easiest).

Preheat a griddle or heavy frying pan and wipe with a piece of clean cloth dipped in lard. Cook each tortilla for one minute each side, until the edges start to curl (half that time if using the proper clay *comal*). Flip into a dishcloth to keep them warm and soft. Continue until all are done.

To soften by reheating in the oven, wrap in foil in piles of no more than six and allow 20 minutes in a medium oven (about 350°F). Alternatively, to reheat after storage, place them directly on an electric hot plate or on a very hot griddle and heat until the edges char a little; place another tortilla on top and flip the pair over to toast the other side; repeat until all are heated. Eat warm, spread with mashed avocado, affectionately known as Aztec butter.

Culinary uses

When the basic prepared flour is mixed with a little more than half its own volume of warm water, with or without enriching fat, it can be worked into a dough. This can be baked in the form of a flatbread, or used as an enclosing pastry for empanadillas, little turnovers. Prepared harina is also the raw material for tamales (see page 82). In its most digestible form, it can be taken as *atole*, either broth-based gruel, or made with milk, sweetened and flavored with cinnamon—drunk hot or chilled.

Arepas

(Andean cornbreads)

Andean corn, with its large, starchy, white kernels, is used for the making of arepas. These, being thicker and therefore easier to make at home than the Mexican tortilla, have a crisp crust, soft interior, and a remarkably short shelf life.

Arepas

3 cups masarepa
About 1¼ cups water

Thoroughly combine the flour and water. Dampen your hands and pat out the masarepa to make small, flat cakes, 3 inches in diameter and ¼ inch thick.

Bake on a very lightly greased griddle, like you would a pancake, flipping once to cook the other side. Remove as soon as the surface blisters black. Eat straight from the griddle. In Caracas, they like to eat them with the doughy interior pulled out and replaced with cream cheese or butter and honey—high luxury. What can you expect of city dwellers?

When stale—a few hours old—treat as a leftover. Soak in milk or broth to make a porridge. Or make eggy-bread: tear in pieces, dip in beaten egg, fry until crisp, and eat with chili sauce.

tamales

or dumplings, humitas

The tamale is a cornmeal dumpling usually (though not always) filled with something piquant or delicious, then steamed or boiled until firm. Unlike any other dumpling, it is designed for portability and is always eaten straight from the hand. The tamale is traditionally treated as festive food since it takes many cooks to prepare, and is open to as many variations as the imagination can devise. A feast of tamales—*tamalada*—is appropriate to a wedding, birthday, or christening, but above all, to be taken to the churchyard to share with the ancestors on All Souls, the Day of the Dead. The indigenous inhabitants of the Americas, gathering together for a tribal occasion, feasted on tamales baked in the barbecue pit along with any wild meat, such as peccary or turkey, that the hunters brought home.

Another use for a tamale basket

unbaked tamale dough

Manufacture

The basic material is farinaceous and the wrapper is any nontoxic foldable green leaf that will not disintegrate when heat is applied.

The dough can be anything that can be mashed and will hold together, including fresh corn (the Andean *humita*, see page 79), yuca, potato, yam, or plantain. A stuffing, sweet or savory, is usual, though not essential.

Appearance and taste

Variations in manufacture are many, as is only to be expected of so ancient a foodstuff. The most widely known ancient food is the Mexican tamale, a corn husk–wrapped dumpling made with masa harina—lye-treated precooked yellow cornmeal. Guatemala celebrates with sweet tamales colored with chocolate. In the province of Oaxaca in southern Mexico, tamales stuffed with *mole negro* (see page 177) are wrapped in banana leaves; in Peru, where banana leaves are also used, fresh white corn dumplings are called *humitas*—wet ones. The southern Brazilians like their tamale dough moistened with coconut milk, while the Amazonians make theirs with cassava meal. Each to his own— and it's as well not to argue.

Tamales rellenos

(Stuffed cornmeal dumplings)
Serves 4, allowing 3 per person

First choose your wrapper. Ready-prepared corn husks cut to size are available packaged, but these need soaking to soften. Fresh corn husks—outer leaves only, and you may need to overlap, must be trimmed at either end. Or use banana leaves cut into 12-inch squares. Failing these, squares of foil will do.

The filling:
2 tablespoons oil
1 small onion, finely chopped
2 large tomatoes, skinned and chopped
About 1 1/2 cups shredded turkey or
  chicken breast
1–2 squares dark chocolate
1/2 teaspoon ground allspice
1–2 teaspoons chili paste or flakes
Salt
Sugar (optional)

The dough:
3 cups masa harina, as above
1 teaspoon salt
3 tablespoons pork lard or oil
Warm water or broth

The wrappers:
Corn husks or banana leaves (or, if unavailable,
  use foil)
Lard or oil for greasing

Make the filling first. Warm the oil in a small frying pan and fry the onion gently until it softens. Let it cook and mash down to make a thick sauce. Season with salt and maybe a little sugar, and stir in the remaining ingredients except the meat. Let it bubble up for 10 minutes to marry the flavors, and then stir in the shredded meat. Let it bubble up again and then let it cool.

Meanwhile, work the masa harina with the salt and lard or oil, and knead in enough warm water or broth to make a smooth, slightly sticky dough; the flour swells as you work it. Set the steamer on a low heat—enough to bring the water to a slow boil.

Now assemble the tamales. Lay the wrappers on a clean cloth, laying them shiny-side up if using banana leaves; if using corn husks, brush lightly with oil. Dampen your hands and break off a piece of dough the size of a large walnut. Place it on a wrapper and spread with the heel of your hand as evenly as possible to make a rectangle the length and width of your hand. Drop a teaspoon of filling in the middle and bring the dough over to enclose, using a wet finger to seal the cracks. Continue until all are prepared. To wrap, fold one of the long sides of the wrapper over to enclose two thirds of the filling (the husk will bring the dough with it), fold over the other long side, then fold over the short sides to complete the enclosure. Secure with a strip of husk or string.

Bring the water in the lower part of the steamer to a boil—a strainer set over a large saucepan will do. Line the steaming implement with leaves and pack in the tamales in neat layers, seam-side down. Cover with another layer of wrapper, cover tightly with the lid, and steam for an hour, until the tamales are perfectly firm. Add more boiling water as necessary. As with any steamed pudding, the more even the cooking temperature, the lighter the dumplings.

Tamales rellenos

empanadas

or empanadillas (diminutive), empada, empadhinas, pastel
pies, pasties

Empanadas are street food, hot from the frying vat in the
market or from a kiosk by the roadside and eaten from the
hand. In Andean towns they are sold in every bar and gathering
place by empanadilla ladies, the makers themselves, spotlessly aproned and
wearing magnificent hand-woven wraps, making the rounds with their baskets.

empanada dough

Manufacture

A plain flour-and-water dough is rolled into a
disk, stuffed with something delicious, folded
over itself, and deep-fried. Sometimes, though

this is less usual, empanadas are baked, in which
case the dough will have been enriched with lard
or oil. It is the perfect way of making scarce or
expensive ingredients work for a living.

Quiche Maya Indian market in Guatemala

Empada de picadinho

(Pork and chile pie)
Serves 6–8

**The Brazilian version of the meat pie:
fragrant ground meat is enclosed in a
hot-water crust enriched with oil. Shrimp,
chicken, cheese, or hearts of palm can
replace the meat, and the same recipe
can be used to make fist-sized turnovers—
*empadinha*s.**

The filling:
2 tablespoons olive oil
2 garlic cloves, finely chopped
1 small onion, finely chopped
1–2 fresh chiles, seeded and chopped
2–3 tomatoes, finely chopped
1 tablespoon chopped oregano
1 1/2 cups finely chopped or ground pork
*2–3 tablespoons shredded greens or sliced
  okra*
Salt and ground allspice

The pastry dough:
2 1/2 cups self-rising flour
1/4 cup olive oil
2/3 cup boiling water
1/2 teaspoon salt

Heat the oil in a frying pan, add all the filling ingredients, and stir over gentle heat until most of the liquid has evaporated and the meat is tender. Taste, and add salt and a pinch of allspice. Set aside to cool while you make the pastry dough.

Preheat the oven to 350°F.

Sift the flour along with the salt into a bowl. Make a dip in the middle and pour in the oil and boiling water. Knead into a soft dough. Work it some more until it's smooth and elastic, then tip it onto a lightly floured board, form into a roll, and cut the dough in half.

Work each piece into a ball, roll out thinly to make two circles. Place the smaller one on an oiled and floured baking sheet and spoon the filling into the middle. Wet all around the edge and top with the other circle. Cut a small cross in the middle for the steam to escape, and mark around the edges with a fork to seal.

Bake for 30–35 minutes, until golden and crisp. Then transfer to a cooling rack and let it cool to room temperature. The hot-water crust won't absorb the juices, and will stay crisp for days.

Empanadillas de requesón

(Fresh cheese turnovers)

Makes about a dozen

These are little bite-size turnovers, crisp and fragrant, made with tortilla dough and stuffed with green chiles and cheese.

The dough:

3 cups masa harina or masarepa
1 teaspoon salt
Generous 1¹/₄ cups warm water

The filling:

3–4 fresh chiles, seeded and finely
* chopped*
2 tablespoons chopped flat-leaf parsley
2 tablespoons chopped basil
4 tablespoons white cheese (crumbled feta,
* ricotta, or cottage cheese)*
A little milk or egg to bind

Empanadillas de requesón

For cooking:

Oil for deep-frying

For serving:

Pickled chiles, puréed with oil to make a
* dipping sauce*

Mix the flour with the salt and work in enough water to make a softish dough—err on the side of dampness. Wrap in plastic wrap and set aside for 30 minutes to swell. Meanwhile, mix the filling ingredients together.

When you're ready to fry, break off small pieces of arepa dough about the size of a walnut, roll into a little ball, and flatten in the palm of your hand to make a small, round disk—the thinner the better. Use your hands rather than a rolling pin or the dough will crack. Drop a little of the stuffing in the middle of the disk, paint the edge with water, and fold one half over the other to enclose the filling. Continue until several are ready.

Heat enough oil to submerge the turnovers completely. Slip the turnovers into the hot oil one by one—the edges should acquire a fringe of small bubbles. Fry, turning once, until crisp and golden. This takes a little longer than you think. Drain on paper towels.

tortillas

The tortilla, a round flatbread made with yellow, white, or blue cornmeal, is the daily bread of the Central Americas and—just as in wheat-growing lands, bread and pasta is most often store-bought—it is usually bought ready-prepared. Even Mexican housewives buy their tortillas from the tortilla-maker in the market: when I lived in Mexico City, ours came to the door twice a day with her basket. When no longer perfectly fresh—a few hours old—the tortilla is treated as a ready-made ingredient, taking the place of pasta or serving as the basis for many of Mexico's put-together dishes—*platos combinados*—for which half a dozen separately presented items is not considered excessive.

Manufacture

Although the tortilla is now a widely available prepared foodstuff, in its precommercial form, a disk of lye-treated cornmeal dough was patted out by hand and baked on a *comal*, an earthenware griddle, which takes the heat of a charcoal fire evenly. Cornmeal tortillas are no larger than will comfortably sit on the spread fingers of one hand, and are baked fresh every day.

Appearance and taste

Tortillas are not always round. In Colina, central Mexico, they're boat-shaped and have an edge; in the Yucatán they make double-thickness tortillas—*panuchos*—especially for splitting and filling with frijoles and hard-boiled egg. Nor are they always made of cornmeal. Wheat flour tortillas are increasingly popular, though undeniably a post-Columbian preference: these are larger and paler, more pliable, and fry faster than the traditional tortilla.

Buying and storing

Choose a brand you like, failing your own personal trusty tortilla-maker. Keep the tortillas in their sealed package until needed and store them in a plastic bag in a cool place once opened; they will keep for up to a week. For longer storage, freeze.

Tortilla seller in Guatemala. Note the blue-corn tortillas at the bottom of the pile.

Culinary uses

The simplest way to use a tortilla is to serve it as a tostada: left whole and fried crisp in oil or lard, topped with meat or fish or cheese, and served with beans, lettuce, chopped avocado, and chile salsa; or cut into any shape you please—ribbons (*chilaquiles*), squares (*totopos*), triangles (*nachos*)—and fried crisp before sauce is added. There is no need for deep oil—a finger's width will do. Leftover tortillas can also be layered like a lasagne—with alternate layers of a creamy béchamel and chile-spiked tomato sauce is delicious—and slipped under the broiler until brown and bubbling. Then there's the *sopa seca*—"dry soup"—a clear broth fortified with strips of tortilla in much the same way as the Chinese include noodles, and the Italians add pasta.

Chilaquiles de requesón

(Chilaquiles with curd cheese)
Serves 4

This is Mexico's national breakfast. The easiest way with yesterday's tortillas is to cut them into bite-size pieces and reheat them in leftover sauce. Fresh tomato salsa and fresh curd cheese—the first stage in cheese-making—make this a particularly luscious version of the countryman's breakfast. Remember to snip up the tortillas the night before.

6–8 corn tortillas cut into small diamonds, dried overnight
Oil for shallow frying

The sauce:
2–3 fresh green serrano chiles, charred in a flame to blister and soften
3–4 ripe tomatoes, skinned and seeded
Sugar (optional)
Tomato paste (optional)
2 tablespoons finely chopped onion
2 tablespoons chopped epasote (or dill)
Salt

To finish:
Ricotta or any fresh curd cheese
Sour cream

Reheat the tortilla diamonds in small batches in a few tablespoons of oil until they crisp a little—don't let them brown. Remove and drain.

Put the chiles and tomatoes in the food processor and blend to a purée. Taste and season—you may need a little sugar or a squeeze of tomato paste.

Heat a tablespoonful of the frying oil and add the sauce. Let it boil, stir in the fried tortilla pieces, and let it boil again. Reduce the heat and sprinkle with the onion and epasote. Let it simmer gently for 8–10 minutes—shake the pan occasionally to avoid sticking.

Serve with a generous topping of ricotta and sour cream. Fortifying, particularly with refried beans (see page 94).

Totopos con huevos revueltos mexicanos

(Tortilla chips scrambled with eggs)
Serves 4

A fortifying snack enjoyed at any time, since in Mexico only one main meal is taken during the day, either at noon or at sunset, depending on the workday. Store-bought tortilla chips are a little on the salty side—it is best to prepare your own.

4 day-old tortillas
Oil for shallow frying
6 fresh eggs
1/4 cup lard or oil
3 tablespoons chopped onion
1/4 cup chopped, seeded ripe tomato
3–4 serrano chiles, seeded and chopped
Salt

Totopos con huevos revueltos mexicanos, eggs scrambled with crisp tortilla chips

Cut the tortillas into small squares—the quickest way is to stack them one on top of the other and slice right through, discarding the edges for elegance. Heat a panful of shallow oil and drop in the squares, a handful at a time. Fry until lightly browned and crisp, which takes just a couple of minutes. Remove with a slotted spoon and drain on paper towels.

Use a fork to mix the eggs together gently with a little salt. Heat the lard or oil in a frying pan and gently cook the onion to soften—don't let it brown. Add the chopped tomato and chile and let it boil for a few minutes to concentrate the juices—field-ripened tomatoes need less cooking to thicken. Stir the eggs and tortilla chips into the hot sauce, folding and stirring until the egg has set to soft curds.

cornmeal

or maizemeal, polenta, chuchoca (Chile)

Milled from corn, this is a meal that has not been treated with lye. It is mainly found in the southern parts of South America, where the staple starch vegetable is the potato, making the manufacturing process that produces bread or dumpling dough unnecessary.

Mayan tomb carving depicting an ancient maize god, Oaxaca, Mexico

Manufacture

To prepare your own cornmeal in the traditional way for breads and porridges, you'd need dried corn kernels stripped from the cob and some means of grinding the corn. Modern mills don't produce the right degree of roughness, so choose stone-ground if you can.

Appearance and taste

White, yellow, purple, brown, blue, red, and black corn is grown throughout the territory. Chuchoca can be any of these, each with its individual fragrance, or it can be a mixture of the above. The flavor is nutty, mild, and clean, with the honeyed aftertaste common to all corn products.

Buying and storing

Cornmeal is readily available packaged, sometimes sold as polenta. Polenta is usually a coarse milling, whereas cornmeal comes as fine, medium, or coarse. Choose stone-ground whole-grain corn whenever you can—it has all its vitamins and minerals intact, cooks well, and tastes exactly as it should. Store in an airtight container, as for other flours.

Medicinal and other uses

Corn is one of the most difficult of all grains to digest. When balanced with other foodstuffs, it's a good source of carbohydrate, minerals, and vitamins. Related products include the oil extracted from the kernels, around half of whose volume is fat, much of it "good" (i.e., polyunsaturated); corn oil is also high in linoleic acid, a substance useful in restoring the body's alkaline balance and recommended for the topical treatment of eczema.

Culinary uses

Corn lacks sufficient gluten for bread-making and is most useful in porridges and soups, or mixed with egg and milk as a pancake. On its own, cornmeal will not make a raised dough—bread, cake, or biscuit—unless blended with at least its own volume of wheat flour. Cornbread is a bit of a misnomer: it is not a true bread at all but a baked porridge of variable density, needing to be ladled out with a spoon—hence, spoonbread. Cornstarch, a powdery substance, is a by-product of the cornmeal industry; a thickening agent manufactured from the endosperm, it is used in desserts, particularly as an egg substitute in custards. Corn syrup, prepared by a process known to the Incas, is a popular replacement for maple syrup and honey. Most nutritious in the form of *posole*, a digestible porridge and a speciality of Mexico's northern borderlands, which is made with white corn and has a delicately sweet flavor, and can come as whole or cracked grains—i.e., grits.

Pan paraguayana

(Paraguayan spoonbread)

Serves 6

The festive food of Paraguay, this rich onion and cheese polenta-bake, quite soft and soupy, is served at weddings and homecomings—one of those nostalgic foodstuffs that remind expatriates of home.

1¹/2 cups yellow cornmeal (fine-ground polenta)
Scant 2 cups hot water
1 stick (¹/2 cup) softened butter
4 eggs, separated
¹/2 cup fresh curd cheese (ricotta or
*   cottage cheese)*
1 cup grated hard cheese (cheddar)
1 small onion, finely chopped, lightly fried
*   to soften*
²/3 cup milk
1 teaspoon baking powder
¹/2 teaspoon ground allspice
¹/2 teaspoon ground cumin
¹/2 teaspoon hot paprika or chili powder
¹/2 teaspoon salt

Preheat the oven to 400°F. Put the cornmeal in a bowl, stir in the hot water, and let it soak and swell for 20 minutes or so.

Butter a roomy roasting pan. In a warmed bowl, beat the butter until fluffy, then beat in the egg yolks and the curd cheese. Whisk the egg whites until they hold soft peaks. Stir the soaked cornmeal and all the remaining ingredients into the butter–egg mixture, and fold in the whisked whites. The batter will be soupy. Pour it into the pan and bake for 50–60 minutes, until firm and well-browned. Let it cool and set for 15 minutes before cutting into squares.

Chupe de papas con chuchoca

(Polenta and potato porridge)

Serves 4 as a main dish

A *chupe* is a Chilean soup or savory porridge—the word means "to slurp"—and can be as soupy or dry as you please. Here chuchoca, cornmeal or coarse-milled

Chupe de papas con chuchoca

polenta, is combined with potatoes to make a nourishing winter dish. Good with roast chicken.

2–3 large potatoes, peeled and cut into chunks
1 thick slice squash, skinned and cut into
*   chunks*
About 5 cups chicken or beef broth or
*   plain water*
1 onion, finely chopped
2–3 garlic cloves, finely chopped
¹/4 cup coarse-milled polenta
1 teaspoon chili flakes or finely chopped fresh
*   chile*
A handful fresh basil, leaves stripped from
*   the stalks*
Salt
2 hard-boiled eggs, peeled and quartered

Put the potatoes, squash, and broth or water in a roomy pan with the onions and garlic. Bring to a boil, stir in the polenta, add a little salt, and return to a boil. Put the lid on loosely, turn down the heat, and simmer for 30–40 minutes until the polenta is perfectly soft and the vegetables are tender. Finish with chili flakes, basil, and quartered hard-boiled eggs.

Corn muffins

The Mexican equivalent of the scone— quick, easy, and unbeatable for breakfast.

1¹/2 cups fine-milled yellow cornmeal
2 cups wheat flour
1 rounded teaspoon baking powder
1 egg
²/3 cup milk
²/3 cup vegetable oil

Preheat the oven to 375°F.

Mix the dry ingredients together in one bowl. Mix the wet ingredients together in another. Blend thoroughly and drop into muffin pans, well-greased (or lined with paper muffin cups). Don't fill them more than two-thirds full. Bake for 20–25 minutes, until well-puffed and beautifully brown.

These are best eaten straight from the pan, with a bowl of milky coffee or hot chocolate for dipping.

navy bean

or white bean, Great Northern bean, pea bean, haricot bean, white kidney bean, frijol blanco, frejol blanco, poroto (Chile), habichuela, canellini (*Phaseolus vulgaris*)

In all its shapes and sizes, the bean is a remarkable foodstuff—the perfect diet in storable, portable form. Its transportability made it invaluable as ship's store: hence navy beans. A member of the pea family native to the Americas, hundreds of different varieties had already been developed in pre-Columbian times, long before the arrival of the Europeans. Throughout its land of origin, taste in beans is astonishingly local; nevertheless, the white kidney-shaped bean is undeniably the universal bean: the bean that can take the place of all others, and does.

How it grows

The bean is easy to grow, undemanding of terrain, and simple to harvest and store—in short, the ideal legume for drying and storing. It is often grown in association with corn, which provides it with a convenient climbing pole, and also with squash, which keeps the weeds down between the rows. Easy when you've had a few thousand years to work it out.

Appearance and taste

Kidney-shaped, of varying size and multiple variations of color, the most commonly appreciated variety outside its land of origin is the white navy bean. Some five hundred bean varieties are now grown worldwide, each with its own distinctive shape, color, degree of flouriness, creaminess, butteriness, firmness, tenderness, and flavor. To generalize, the taste and texture is that of cooked chestnut: floury, earthy, and sweet.

Buying and storing

The fresher the bean, the better. This year's crop will feel a little springy under the pressure of your fingertips—so buy from a shop with a high turnover. Beans should not be stored from one year to another. Bury a few dried chiles or a garlic clove in the bean jar to keep the bugs at bay. To shorten preparation time, presoak, and store in the freezer until needed.

Medicinal and other uses

This is the perfect body-and-brain food: cholesterol-free, high in vegetable protein, rich in complex carbohydrates, and liberally endowed with vitamins, minerals, and fiber. The drawback? The bean-eaters' well-known propensity to flatulence, a phenomenon that can be explained by the presence of oligosaccharides that make even the best-cooked bean hard to digest. Whatever they may say, neither cooks nor chemists have come up with an infallible method of counteracting the problem. Discretion is the better part of valor. Follow local custom and eat your beanpot at noon, avoid it in the evening, and leave it strictly alone when in love.

Culinary uses

The quality of the beans dictates the length of time they take to soften—really fresh beans take no more than an hour. Don't add salt until the end, to avoid toughening the skins, and also wait until the end of the cooking to add acidic ingredients—tomato, vinegar, lemon juice—which, say those who know, can double the cooking time.

Bean market, Ecuador

Frijoles con morcilla, a creamy white bean stew with crisply fried blood sausage

Frijoles con morcilla

(Navy beans with blood sausage)
Serves 6–8

These are pre-Columbian beans given a Hispanic enrichment: there were no meat animals in the Americas before the arrival of the Spaniards, who brought in pigs as well as cows and chickens to remedy what they saw as a serious lack. Spanish blood sausages—*morcilla*—are deliciously spicy, garlicky, and flavored with oregano.

*2¹/₂ cups navy beans, soaked overnight
   and drained*
*A whole head of garlic, singed to blacken
   the covering*
*2 mild dried chiles (pasilla or pimentón),
   seeded and torn*
A short cinnamon stick
2–3 cloves
1 tablespoon crumbled oregano
*2 carrots or parsnips, scraped and cut into
   chunks*
1 tablespoon salt

To finish:
*1 pound small potatoes, rinsed and
   scrubbed (about 8 potatoes)*
A handful spinach, rinsed and shredded
*1 ring (about 8 ounces) morcilla (blood
   sausage), sliced*
A little olive oil
1 fresh red chile, seeded and finely chopped
3 tablespoons chopped cilantro
3 tablespoons chopped onion

Drain the beans and transfer them to a roomy pot along with the garlic, chile, cinnamon, cloves, oregano, and carrot or parsnip. Add enough water to cover generously, bring to a boil, turn down the heat, and simmer, with the lid on loosely, for 1–2 hours, until the beans are perfectly tender.

Remove the garlic head (squeeze the soft interior back into the pot) and add the potatoes and the salt. Let it boil again (you may need to add some boiling water), and simmer for another 20 minutes or so, until the potatoes are tender. Stir in the spinach and let it boil for

another 5 minutes, until the leaves wilt. Meanwhile, fry the morcilla slices in a little oil (some morcillas are quite fatty enough to fry without assistance). Or you can, if you wish to keep it simple, stir the morcilla slices directly into the beanpot—morcillas are precooked, as are all blood sausages, but frying gives a deliciously crisp texture and caramelized flavor.

Serve the beans in deep bowls, sprinkled with the fried morcilla, chile, cilantro, and onion. Eat with a spoon.

Porotos con acelgas

(Beans and greens)
Serves 4 as an appetizer

A simple appetizer, useful when you have leftover beans. Canned beans are fine. Although I suggest hard-boiled egg, the topping can be anything that excites the taste buds: crumbled chorizo crisped in a little oil, pine nuts or slivered almonds instead of peanuts—whatever you have in the cupboard.

2¹/₂ cups cooked white navy beans
*Generous handful Swiss chard or spinach,
   shredded*
Juice of 1 lemon
4 tablespoons olive oil
*1 dried chile (pasilla or ancho), seeded and
   cut into matchsticks*
*2 tablespoons toasted peanuts, roughly
   crushed*
1 tablespoon chopped scallion
2 hard-boiled eggs, peeled and chopped
Salt and pepper

Bring the beans and a little of their cooking liquor to a boil in a small pan, drain, and toss with the shredded greens—the heat will be just enough to wilt the leaves. Dress with the lemon juice and 3 tablespoons of the olive oil, as well as salt and pepper.

Heat the remaining oil and fry the chile strips—a moment, no more, just until they change color and become crisp. Tip the contents of the pan onto the beans. Finish with crushed peanuts, scallion, and chopped hard-boiled eggs.

black bean

or turtle bean, frijol negro (Mexico and other Spanish-speaking countries), feijao nero (Brazil) (*Phaseolus vulgaris*)

The black bean is a smallish, ebony-colored kidney bean. A staple of the cupboard throughout the territory, particularly in Mexico, the Caribbean, Venezuela, and northern Brazil, including Rio—where it's the star of the feijoada, Brazil's national dish (see page 127)—but in Colombia, it's relegated to cattle fodder.

How it grows

A very pretty plant, the flowers of the black bean are blush-pink, the pods a sunny yellow, and the seeds as black and shiny as onyx, the sacred stone of the Aztec priesthood—perhaps accounting for its esteem in the land of Montezuma.

Appearance and taste

The black bean is the gourmet bean. The flavor is subtly earthy with more than a hint of mushroom and an underlying chestnut sweetness. The flesh cooks to a creamy softness, while the skins, though long cooking makes them tender, never lose their shine. In Mexican cooking, the black bean often appears in mashed form, as *frijoles refritos* or refried beans (see page 94), a bean hash that also serves as a stuffing for tacos and tamales.

Buying and storing

Look for even-sized beans with a clean, shiny skin and no powderiness; check for dryness—a sign the beans are a little long in the tooth. They should still feel a little springy when pressed between the fingertips.

Medicinal and other uses

Look no further for the perfect diet in a pod, complete with protein, carbohydrate, vitamins, and all necessary minerals.

Culinary uses

Usually cooked on its own and only combined with other foodstuffs at the moment of serving, the black bean takes longer than most to soften, so a little forward planning is advisable. For convenience, cook in advance and freeze supplies for later.

Plato combinado mexicano

(Mexican mixed platter)
Serves 1

The combination platter is a way of eating rather than a specific recipe, since the composition is no more or less than exactly what pleases you within the limitations of your purse, with beans and tortillas the only immutable. Each additional element is presented separately and as appetizingly as possible, with attention paid to nutritional balance, digestibility, and visual drama. Colors are mingled for contrast or compatibility: white on black, green with green, red for drama, and so on. The care invariably taken in putting these simple basic foodstuffs together—some needing lengthy preparation, others virtually none, but making the most of each—says much about the Latino attitude to life.

Choose from:
Frijoles de olla (see opposite)
Tomato, cilantro, and chile salsa
*Rajas poblanos (ribbons of roasted green bell
    pepper dressed with oil and garlic)*
Sour cream
*Crumbled fresh white cheese (ricotta is a good
    approximation)*
*Sliced or mashed avocado dressed with
    lime juice*
Coarse salt
Fried eggs
Quartered hard-boiled eggs
Shredded chicken or pork
Shredded lettuce
*Onion slices soaked in salted water to soften,
    dressed with sugar*
Pickled chiles (jalapeños, naturally)

Arrange your choices on an oval platter. You will need tortillas for scooping. Eat with your fingers and be thankful.

Frijoles de olla
(Mexican black beanpot)
Serves 6–8

This is best prepared a day ahead to give time for the flavor to develop. In Mexico, plain-cooked pot beans are served on their own after the main course, with a soft tortilla for mopping, or during the main course, in a little bowl on the side, to be dipped into at will.

5 cups black beans
1 onion
2 tablespoons oil (the Mexicans use fresh pork lard)
About 2¹/₂ quarts hot water
Salt

Run the beans through your hands—it is therapeutic, like worry beads—and discard any tiny stones that sneak through, even in the best brands. Rinse twice: black beans are vulnerable to unwanted visitors. You can pre-soak them overnight to speed up the cooking process, but this is not essential.

Put the beans in a flameproof earthenware or enamel casserole dish along with the onion and oil or lard. Pour in enough hot water to cover the beans to a depth of at least 3 inches. Bring to simmering point, then turn down the heat, put the lid on tightly, and let it simmer (if you prefer in a moderate oven, set it at 325°F). Keep an eye on them, add hot water if necessary, and let cook for as long as it takes for the skins to soften completely—about

2 hours, sometimes 3. Then add salt. (Never salt beans until the skins have softened, or they will be tough.)

Continue to cook until perfectly tender. If you need to add water—check regularly—it should always be hot. Never drain the beans after cooking and throw away the liquid: evaporate the liquid by removing the lid from the pot if you want your beans dry rather than soupy. Those who use a pressure cooker should allow 40 minutes.

Serve with soft tortillas. For a Venezuelan version, add extra boiling water and finish with finely chopped chile, a sprinkle of cumin, and a swirl of oil colored bright red with achiote. For the Cuban version, stir in a dash of rum.

pinto bean

or speckled bean, frijol refrito, brown bean (*Phaseolus vulgaris*)

This is the everyday bean of the Mexican beanpot, the commonest of the tribe. The peasant's reliable field crop, it is to be found simmering on every stove throughout the region.

Appearance and taste

A highly hybridized medium-size bean, the pinto bean is caramel to chestnut in color. The flavor is earthy and robust and the texture mealy, softening to a mush.

Buying and storing

Look for the fresh pods in the autumn and buy from a reliable source with a high turnover. Test for freshness by squeezing gently between your finger and thumb—you're looking for a slight give.

Medicinal and other uses

Like other beans, it is high in protein, with the full complement of carbohydrate, vitamins, and minerals. The skin softens satisfactorily in the pot, allowing for easy digestion.

Culinary uses

The pinto bean is best eaten fresh in season, when it benefits from the inclusion of something sweet: a seasoning of corn syrup or a handful of fresh corn kernels. Dried beans are good for soups and for making baked beans, probably best known as the everyday refried beans, when they are first tenderized by boiling, then fried in lard or oil to form a soft, homogeneous mass that can be scooped up with a tortilla.

Sacks of beans on sale in Sicuani, Peru

Frijoles refritos

(Refried pinto beans)
Serves 4

A second cooking—*un refrito*—reduces the soupy contents of the beanpot to a thick, deliciously roasted paste. Once prepared, it can be frozen almost indefinitely. In Mexico, plain refried beans are eaten for breakfast with fried eggs, at noon after the meat, with tortilla chips for supper—in fact at any time a person might feel hungry.

5^1/$_2$ to 6 cups cooked beans
  (with their liquid, if home-cooked)
6 tablespoons good lard, drippings, or oil
2 garlic cloves or 1 small onion, finely chopped
Tortilla chips

Heat the lard or oil in a large, heavy frying pan. Add the garlic or onion and fry for a minute or two, until it softens—don't let it brown. Add a ladleful of the beans and their liquid and mash down over the heat until all the liquid has evaporated, scraping and turning to avoid sticking. Add the rest of the beans a ladleful at a time, until all is reduced to a thick aromatic paste that sits like a soft pancake in the pan. That's all. The same technique can be applied to any leftover bean dish. However soupy, sooner or later, it will dry and thicken.

Frijoles pintos con masa mora

(Pinto beans with mushy corn)
Serves 4–6

Robust and satisfying, this is the traditional summer Sunday lunch, made when the beans are still tender and the corn is young and sweet.

3 to 3 1/2 cups fresh, shelled beans
*1-pound piece squash, skinned and
 cut into chunks*
1 tablespoon soft pork-lard or oil
*1 link soft chorizo, crumbled (or 4 slices
 bacon, diced)*
2 large mild onions, finely chopped
1 red bell pepper, seeded and diced

1 carrot, scraped and coarsely grated
Salt
2 1/2 cups fresh corn kernels
*A handful epasote or fresh basil leaves,
 chopped*

To finish:
2 garlic cloves, skinned and roughly chopped
*1 tablespoon pimentón picante (or paprika with
 a pinch of powdered chili)*
1–2 tablespoons oil
Salt

Put the shelled beans and the squash in a roomy pot, add enough hot water to cover to a depth of two fingers, bring to a boil, reduce the heat, put the lid on and simmer until the squash has melted to a soupy sauce and the beans are perfectly tender: 40–60 minutes.

Meanwhile, heat the lard or oil gently in a small frying pan and fry the chorizo or diced bacon until it takes a little color. Add the onion, red pepper, and carrot, salt lightly, and fry until soft and a little caramelized. Stir into the beans and simmer for another 10 minutes.

Meanwhile, put the corn kernels in the blender along with a ladleful of the bean liquid and the epasote or basil leaves (reserve a few of the best). Blend to a purée, add to the beans and stir, and simmer for another 15 minutes—dilute with a little boiling water if it looks too thick.

To make the finishing oil, crush the garlic cloves along with a little salt, and work in the oil and pimentón. Serve in deep earthenware bowls, with a swirl of scarlet oil and an epasote or basil leaf to finish.

cranberry bean

or shell bean, shellouts, red bean, poroto pinto, borlotti, bolita (*Phaseolus vulgaris*)

A medium-size kidney-shaped bean, the color varies from the deep crimson of the poroto pinto (*pinto* means "colored") to the coffee-and-cream cranberry bean to the prettily speckled borlotti. The bolitas (little balls) are multicolored, small, and irregularly shaped beans—as unalike one another as pebbles on the beach.

Culinary uses

A word of warning: cranberry beans, if presoaked, accumulate toxins in the skin that must be neutralized. Rinse after soaking, bring to a boil in fresh water, boil for 10 minutes, then drain and add fresh boiling water before continuing cooking. This preliminary boiling is essential. To avoid toughening the skin, use soft water for the soaking and cooking broth—rainwater or bottled water with a low calcium content. This is because calcium slows down the cooking time to such an extent that the beans can fall apart without ever achieving tenderness.

Appearance and taste

The cranberry or red bean is a mealy bean with a deep red skin, pale creamy flesh, and a markedly robust, earthy flavor. Cranberry beans are particularly popular in Chile, the Caribbean, and southern Brazil. They are eaten in the Caribbean in combination with rice and coconut (see Jamaican rice 'n' peas, page 73).

Buying and storing

Choose beans with a clear, bright color that feel a little springy when pressed between the finger and thumb. To sidestep the problems outlined in Culinary uses, buy them ready-prepared in cans.

Medicinal and other uses

Cranberry beans—particularly the *bolita*—are higher in calcium and sodium than other beans.

Celebrating the gifts of the sun at Rio carnival

Ensalada de porotos pintos con pencas

(Cranberry bean salad with wild artichokes)
Serves 4 as an appetizer

Red beans are combined in a simple salad with *pencas*, the rosettes of a wild artichoke, a member of the thistle family and one of the first wild vegetables of spring—a successful combination of flavors. The wild thistle can be replaced by the cultivated: cardoons or artichokes.

3 cups cooked red beans
  (canned is fine)
4 pencas or 2 cardoon sticks or 6 artichoke
  hearts, sliced
Lemon juice
1–2 fresh chorizos, sliced
2–3 tablespoons olive oil
1 red onion, finely sliced into half-moons
1 tablespoon crumbled or chopped oregano
Salt

Scrape the thorny edges off the pencas and trim off any brown or stringy bits. If using cardoon or artichokes, trim, scrape, and slice. Cook in a little water for 10–15 minutes until the vegetables soften. Stir in the beans, reheat, and let cool.

When you're ready to serve, fry the chorizo slices in the oil until caramelized and crisp—don't let them burn. Pour the contents of the frying pan onto the beans, salt lightly, and finish with lemon juice, onion, and oregano.

Bolitas con jamón

(Chilean red beans with bacon)
Serves 4–6

This is the classic Chilean beanpot, fortified by a smoked ham hock, and finished with *color chileno*—pork lard flavored with garlic and colored a rosy red with achiote or pimentón (see page 186).

2¹/₂ cups bolita (or any other cranberry
  bean), soaked overnight
A smoked ham hock
¹/₂ whole head of garlic
1–2 onions, peeled and roughly chopped

3–4 cloves
1 large carrot, scraped and diced
1 short stick cinnamon
Scraping of nutmeg
1–2 dried chiles, seeded and torn

To finish:
1 pound small yellow potatoes, scraped
  (about 8 potatoes)
1 pound mild paprika peppers, roasted
  and cut into strips (about 2 to 2¹/₂ cups)
1–2 tablespoons color chileno (see page 186)
Salt

Drain the beans and rinse them in two changes of fresh water. Put them in a roomy pot with water to cover generously, bring to a boil, cook for 10 minutes, and drain. Tuck in the ham hock and enough fresh water to cover to a depth of two fingers.

Ensalada de porotos pintos con pencas, a sophisticated combination of cranberry beans, red onion, and artichokes

Bring the pot to a boil and skim off the gray foam that rises. Add the remaining ingredients (stick the cloves in an onion for ease of retrieval). Return to a boil, turn down the heat, cover, and cook for 2–3 hours, until the beans are quite soft. Keep the broth at a gentle boil—don't let the temperature drop or add salt or the skins won't soften. If you need to add more water, make sure it's boiling.

When the beans are floury and tender, add the finishing ingredients: first the potatoes, and then, after 15 minutes, the pepper strips. Let it boil each time. Allow another 10 minutes and stir in the color chileno. Serve with plantain fritters, *patacones* (see page 207).

lima bean

or butter beans, habas grandes, limeños,
(*Phaseolus limensis*)

Peru's native bean is a large, ivory-white bean, flattish and
kidney-shaped, first cultivated by the Incas on the Altiplano.
It is the largest of all the dried legumes.

Preparing lima beans by a Peruvian roadside

How it grows

The lima bean is a vigorous climber, prolific,
cropping over several months, and capable of
yielding two crops a year.

Appearance and taste

These are tender, creamy-fleshed beans that
hold their shape in the pot and have a delicate
flavor of freshly skinned walnuts: the aristocrat
of the bean family.

Buying and storing

They are worth seeking out fresh in the pod—
bright green—when they appear on the market
in the early winter. The variety known as the
Christmas lima (*limeño de navidad*) is
particularly large and plump, ivory-white
with a distinctive maroon streaking. It is
sometimes sold vacuum-packed, when
it can be surprisingly expensive. When
fresh and young, the skin should
be soft enough to pierce with a
fingernail. Lima beans are also
available in jars and cans—
useful for salads and as a side
dish, less so for a slow-simmered
stew.

Medicinal and other uses

When fresh, limas are easily digestible, high in
protein, and heavily alkaline: good for building
muscle. Dried beans are harder to digest and
the skins can irritate delicate internal organs.

Culinary uses

The lima contains toxins, potentially deadly
cyanide compounds, which must be removed
in the cooking process (not necessary if buying
ready-cooked). Boil the beans in an uncovered
pot so that the gases can escape with the
steam. This precaution is necessary for all lima
bean foodstuffs—fresh, dried, or sprouted.

Ensalada navideño

(Christmas salad)
Serves 4 as an appetizer or side dish

**A simple salad, good with roast meats or
on its own as an appetizer. While Peruvian
lemons are mild and sweet, the bitter
orange (Seville or "marmalade") gives the
dish its own special aroma.**

3 cups cooked lima beans
1 mild onion, finely sliced
*1 bitter orange or 1/2 lemon, juice and peel
    and 1/2 orange*
1/4 cup olive oil
*1 green or yellow chile, seeded and finely
    chopped*
2 tablespoons chopped parsley
Salt

For serving (optional):
Fresh corn, plain boiled

Combine all the ingredients, leave in a cool
place for a couple of hours to soften the
onion and marry the flavors, and serve at
room temperature, with slices of lightly
cooked fresh corn.

Cocido limeño
(Lima beans with pumpkin)
Serves 4–6

Peru's favorite Christmas dish: country woman's beanpot. When cooked on the doorstep over an open fire, the pots fill the narrow streets of the mountain villages with fragrant steam.

1¹/₄ cups lima beans, soaked overnight
1 pound yellow-fleshed potatoes, peeled and cubed in bite-size pieces (about 3 to 3¹/₂ cups)
1 pound pumpkin or any winter squash, cubed in bite-size pieces (about 4 cups)
2¹/₂ cups fresh or frozen corn kernels
Salt

Flavoring salsa:
3 yellow ají (chile), seeded and chopped
1 small yellow onion, finely chopped
2 scallions, finely chopped with their green
3 garlic cloves, finely chopped
2 tablespoons olive oil

To finish:
Chopped parsley
Crumbled white cheese such as feta

Cocido limeño, a cheerful winter beanpot

Cook the beans in a roomy pot with enough water to cover. Don't put the lid on. The water should tremble but never come to a boil. Allow 2 hours (1 hour if the beans are fresh) and cook until soft but not mushy. Add boiling water when necessary, but no salt.

Meanwhile, let the salsa ingredients boil in a small pan, and set aside to combine the flavors.

When the beans are tender, add the vegetables and extra boiling water, salt, and the prepared salsa, and cook for another half hour, until the vegetables are perfectly soft. The dish should be moist but not soupy. Finish with a handful of chopped parsley and crumbled white cheese—feta is the right texture.

eggs, dairy, & cheese

Eggs and dairy foods are relative newcomers to the New World kitchen. Since there were no barnyard animals in the pre-Columbian Americas, Europe's domesticated egg-layers and milk-producers—along with the pig, who cleans up the by-products of the dairy industry—were absorbed straight into an existing culinary habit. The welcome was enthusiastic, since both added not only variety and protein, but a touch of the exotic to everyday dishes, making them special. The appearance of a quartered hard-boiled egg poised elegantly on its bed of vegetables or a handful of crumbled white cheese sprinkled over a dish of black beans is greeted with pleasure and a festive sense of enjoyment, even today when eggs and dairy products are common culinary currency.

eggs

or huevos, oves

The eggs of wild birds, reptiles, and some insects were eaten by the indigenous peoples of the regions, but it was not until the arrival of the Europeans that the hen's egg became available.

Buying and storing

To tell if an egg is past its best, put it in water: if it lies flat on the bottom, it's fresh; if it tips up at the broad end and sits vertically, it's stale; if—heaven forbid—it bobs up to the surface and floats horizontally, it would be both unsafe and unpleasant to eat.

Medicinal and other uses

The egg is incomparably useful as a foodstuff. A quarter of the egg's volume delivers equal quantities of protein and fat, along with all the vitamins and minerals necessary to nourish a chick. Its admittedly high content of artery-clogging cholesterol is balanced by a pair of unclogging substances, lecithin and amino acids.

Culinary uses

Eggs are included in both sweet and savory recipes, though their functions are rather different. Hard-boiled eggs, quartered or sliced, are often popped on top of vegetarian dishes—particularly the traditional beans/corn/squash combinations—as a luxurious finishing touch. When used in desserts, it is in the form of sensationally sweet custards and cakes: Latin women have a great fondness for sugary treats.

Flan

(Caramel custard)
Serves 4

Flan—a baked egg custard—is Latin America's most popular pudding, as it is in Spain. You can buy it as a packaged mix, but it's easy and much more delicious if you make your own.

2 1/2 cups whole milk
3 tablespoons sugar
1 inch vanilla pod
1 whole egg plus 4 egg yolks

For the caramel:
3 heaped tablespoons sugar
3 tablespoons water

El Alto market, La Paz, Bolivia

Preheat the oven to 325°F. Combine the milk and the sugar to infuse with the vanilla over a very low heat—or in a double boiler if you're nervous—stirring gently until the sugar dissolves.

Make the caramel by melting the sugar and water together in a small pan and heating it until the sugar caramelizes. Take it off the heat as soon as it turns a rich beech-leaf bronze: once the color turns, it will be black in no time. Pour the caramel into the bottom of one large or several small molds or custard cups, and roll the caramel around the sides to coat.

Remove the vanilla pod from the milk, split it, and scrape all the sticky little black seeds back into the milk mixture. Use a fork to mix in the eggs, taking care not to incorporate air, and pour the mixture into the caramel-coated molds.

Set the molds in a roasting pan. Pour in enough boiling water to come halfway up the sides of the molds. Bake for 40–50 minutes, by which time the custard should be firm. If the temperature is too high, it'll bubble and acquire watery little air holes; if it's too low, it'll take longer to set. Don't unmold it until you're ready to serve, then reverse it onto a plate. The caramel provides its own sticky little pool of sauce.

Huevos rancheros

(Ranch hand's eggs)

Serves 4

The best breakfast in the world, as served in every Mexican truckstop from the cactus country of upstate Tijuana to the forests of the River Uxumazintla.

1/4 cup oil
4 corn tortillas
8 fresh eggs from free-range hens

The sauce:
1/2 mild onion, chopped small
1 garlic clove
1 green chile, seeded and diced
1 pound ripe tomatoes, diced (about 2 1/2 to 2 3/4 cups)
Salt

To finish:
2 tablespoons grated cheese
1/2 ripe avocado, roughly mashed with a little lime or lemon juice, salt, and chopped cilantro

Heat the oil in a frying pan and slip in the tortillas one by one to heat up—they should soften but not brown. Remove to warm plates. In the same pan, fry the eggs so that the edges of the whites are frilly and the yolks are just set, and pop each onto its tortilla.

Now make the sauce. Fry the onion and garlic in what's left of the oil (you may need a little more)—letting it sizzle and soften for a few minutes but not letting it brown. Add the chile and turn up the heat. Add the chopped tomato and let everything boil and reduce fiercely for a few minutes until you have a fragrant little sauce. Taste and season—a little sugar, perhaps?

Spoon the sauce over the eggs, finishing each plate with a little pile of grated cheese and a spoonful of the chopped, dressed avocado. Beats a Sunday morning hangover any day of the week.

Huevos rancheros, fried eggs with all the trimmings

milk & cream

Fresh, condensed, and evaporated goat and cow's milk are available throughout the region. Although Andean herdsmen sometimes milked their cameloids in the suckling season for local consumption, milk and cream were not known elsewhere until the arrival of the Hispanic colonizers.

Manufacture

Condensed and evaporated milk is often preferred to fresh, a taste acquired in the days when refrigeration was either unavailable or impractical. Condensed is the term applied to sweetened whole or skimmed milk reduced by two thirds. Evaporated is whole milk reduced by two thirds but unsweetened.

Buying and storing

Fresh milk is susceptible to adulteration and contamination, so care should always be taken when buying from unknown sources in a hot climate. If in doubt, boil to sterilize. Homogenized, pasteurized, and all forms of treated milk sold in sealed containers are a sensible alternative.

Medicinal and other uses

Milk is just about the perfect foodstuff for babies and seniors alike, equipped with protein, calcium, phosphorus, vitamins A and D, sugar in the form of lactose, and riboflavin. On the minus side, it's a bit high in sodium. Milk in all its forms is digestible and nourishing, although lactose intolerance—leading to digestive upsets—is to be found among those who regularly consume dairy products and those who do not. Goat's milk does not normally cause the same problems. Condensed and evaporated milk, when diluted according to instructions, is more easily digested than fresh.

Culinary uses

Fresh milk and cream, luxury items before refrigerators were available, are used in Latin America as in the North American kitchen—combined with fruits as a refreshing drink, included in fruit desserts, and used as an enrichment or cooking liquid in soups, sauces, milk puddings, and custards, both sweet and savory. Canned milk—condensed or evaporated—is stirred into drinks such as coffee and chocolate instead of cream. Peruvian fruit syrups are often topped with condensed milk.

Dulce de leche
(Caramelized milk)
Serves 4–6

This is unquestionably the best loved of all Latin American desserts. As a child, however, I hated it. I first tasted it as a schoolgirl in Montevideo, when it was the inevitable conclusion to school meals.

Llamas can provide milk for Andean herders

Dulce de leche with whipped cream

Perhaps my dislike was because as a war baby, I had little experience of sweet things—a peculiarity that made me popular at mealtimes, since my schoolmates were only too happy to mop up my helping. Nowadays I love it with whipped cream.

1 14-ounce can sweetened condensed milk
1 12-ounce can evaporated milk

Combine the two milks in a heavy saucepan and cook gently, stirring steadily, over medium heat for 20–30 minutes, until thick and lightly caramelized. The longer you cook it, the thicker and darker it becomes. It keeps for months in or out of the refrigerator, though after a few days, it gets grainy.

In Peru, it is used as a stuffing for churros—deep fried tubes of pastry dough—a street food much enjoyed by both adults and children. It is also used as a layering for cakes, to stuff cream puffs, and as a basis for ice creams.

Coajada con nuez moscada, soft milky curds dusted with grated nutmeg

Coajada con nuez moscada

(Junket with nutmeg)

Serves 4

Junket is the soft curds that form when fresh milk is "turned" with rennet.

2¹/₂ cups fresh whole milk
1 teaspoon rennet
1 tablespoon sugar
Freshly grated nutmeg

Warm the milk to lukewarm, reproducing the natural heat of the milk when fresh from the cow. Add the sugar, then stir in the rennet, pour into glasses or earthenware jars, and let set at room temperature—it'll take a couple of hours. Dust with nutmeg and serve with a crisp cookie.

butter & lard

or manteca, mantequilla

Butter—fresh or clarified—is used for cakes and cookies among the cooks of those Caribbean islands that came under the influence of the Celtic nations of Europe: Britain and France. Elsewhere, pork lard is the natural choice for shortening—although this is being replaced by margarine.

Manufacture

Butter is the fatty element in milk separated from the liquid by churning. Simply put fresh milk in a container and shake it: sooner or later you'll have butter. In this form it can either be heated and the fat further separated from the whey—a process called clarifying, which increases shelf life without refrigeration; or it can be salted (heavily or lightly) and kept cool. Pork lard—the enriching fat of choice throughout the Hispanic world—is used for shallow frying as well as in baking to shorten the dough for pies and pastries. Pure white lard, mild and sweet, is made by melting pork fat very, very slowly in the lowest possible oven with a little water to keep it from any possibility of browning—commercially prepared stuff won't do.

Buying and storing

The purer the product, the more delicious it is. Store it in the refrigerator; if kept cool and in the dark, it will last for months.

Medicinal and other uses

According to research, butter and lard soften the effects of too much red wine. Our ancestors knew they kept you warm in winter and made food more palatable and easier to digest. And anyway, a little of what you like does you good.

Culinary uses

In recipes for cookies and cakes, lard gives the lightest results, butter the most delicious flavor. Take your pick. As a frying medium, clarified butter and pure lard have a burn point only a little lower than oil, allowing you to cook at high temperatures. Cakes and cookies made with clarified butter or lard stay fresh for longer.

Beijos de cafezinho

(Coffee kisses)
Makes about 2 dozen little cookies

These Brazilian coffee cookies are delicious with *doce de banana* (see page 205) **and vanilla ice cream. Clarified butter, though not essential, gives a crispier result. To clarify butter, warm until it liquefies, then pour off the oil (the clarified butter), leaving the milky residue behind.**

3 cups all-purpose flour
1/2 cup clarified butter, softened
1/2 cup brown sugar
1 medium egg
2 tablespoons very strong black coffee
Coffee beans to decorate

Sift the flour with a pinch of salt. Beat the butter and sugar until light and fluffy, then beat in the egg and the coffee. Work in the flour to make a ball of soft dough—you may need a little more flour. Cover with plastic wrap and let rest in the refrigerator for an hour to firm up.

Heat the oven to 425°F. On a lightly floured board, roll out the dough. Punch out round cookies and arrange on a buttered baking sheet, allowing plenty of space for them to spread. Dampen the coffee beans and pop one on each cookie. Bake for 20–25 minutes until golden. Transfer to a cooling rack while still soft and warm—they crisp as they cool.

Cattle grazing in front of Osomo volcano in the Chilean lake district

Mantecados navideños
(Christmas cookies)

Makes about 2 dozen cookies

Literally translated: lardy cookies. Very soft and delicate, wrapped up in scraps of tissue paper for storage, this is the treat all good children hope to find in their shoes when the Three Kings bring them their presents on January 6th. This is a beaten dough—rather easier and quicker than the more familiar rubbing-in method.

2 cups all-purpose flour
$^1/_4$ cup roughly ground blanched almonds
1 tablespoon ground cinnamon
1 teaspoon ground cardamom
1 cup fresh white lard, softened
$^1/_4$ cup powdered sugar
1–2 tablespoons cold water

Sift the flour into the ground almonds and mix in the spices. Beat the lard with the sugar until light and fluffy—easiest in a food processor. Work in the flour and nut mixture until you have a soft ball of dough. Cover with a clean cloth, and let rest for an hour in a cool place to firm up.

Heat the oven to 350°F.

Roll the dough out to $^1/_4$ inch thick. Cut out neat little circles with a cookie cutter and transfer to a well-buttered cookie sheet. Press together the scraps with the tips of your fingers and cut out as many more circles as you can.

Bake for 15–20 minutes, until pale gold. Transfer gently to a cooling rack and let cool. The result is like very soft, crumbly shortbread. Wrap in scraps of tissue paper before storing in an airtight tin.

Beijos de cafezinho, crisp coffee cookies from Brazil

cheese

soft curd cheese

aged
cheese

fresh cheese

pressed
curd cheese

or queso fresco, queso maduro

In Latin America—which in cheese-related matters takes its lead from Spain and Portugal—pantry-stored cheeses are mostly nothing fancy, belonging to the familiar Mediterranean tradition of one-type-fits-all, cut-curd, basket-drained cheeses, which take their flavor from the milk—cow's, goat's, or sheep's—from which they're made. Mexico has a heat-treated mozzarella-type cheese, *queso asadero*, that melts in long strings, and a cheddar-type, *queso chihuahua*, much liked for quesadillas.

Medicinal and other uses

Cheese, a form of milk food that has been subjected to souring (the initial process of fermentation) or renneting (a form of pre-digestion), retains most of the virtues of the raw material but is more digestible.

Culinary uses

In many Latin American recipes, grated sharp or aged cheese is mixed with fresh cheese—hard cheese in its immature, soft, crumbly state—both in the form of *requesón* (naturally soured curds, drained) and *queso fresco*, the first stage of the aged cheese, for which feta is a convenient substitute. The Andean nations use grated cheese as a binder for farinaceous foods such as manioc (see Pan de yuca, page 61 and Cassava coconut cake, page 173). White sauces are often made without a thickening of flour and fat, simply by melting cheese into cream or milk—a surprisingly successful method of both enriching and thickening.

Manufacture

All cheese begins with a curd—the soft lumps that form when milk turns sour or when a curdling agent such as rennet is added. Rennet is a substance found in the stomach lining of all lactating mammals (ourselves included). Milk can also be "turned"—in essence, a process of digestion—with curdling agents found in a wide variety of plants, particularly the young buds of several members of the thistle family (including artichokes), fig tree sap, and an infusion of any member of the flytrap family (insectivorous little plants with glaucous leaves).

Appearance and taste

Traditionally, farm cheeses are round, since this is the most convenient shape both for cutting and storing, and small enough to be transportable. They are often rubbed with chili powder and popped on a beam to dry and mature.

Buying and storing

Hard cheese should be stored in a state that excludes air. It should not need refrigeration unless the climate is warm and damp—as in, say, a heated kitchen.

Cheese stall in the Mercado de la Abundancia, Montevideo

Bolinhos de queijo

(Brazilian cheese balls)

Serves 6–8 as an appetizer

The classic Brazilian appetizer—
salgadinho—**that makes a gathering of
friends into a party. Every cook has her
own recipe: some include potatoes, some
are rolled into little torpedo-shaped
croquettes instead of balls, some fried,
some baked. And every household has its
own preferences in the way of dipping
sauces. In Brazil, the cheese of choice
would be the hard, salty white cheese
made in Minas Gerais.**

*8 ounces grated parmesan (about 4 cups)
  or pecorino or dry cheddar*
*8 ounces fresh mozzarella, grated or
  finely chopped (about 2 cups)*
3 egg whites, whisked until stiff
2 heaped tablespoons flour
Oil for frying

Mix the two cheeses and fold into the egg whites.
Form into little balls or bolsters, roll in flour, and
deep-fry in shallow oil—no more than will
submerge the fritters.

Bolinhos de queijo al horno

(Oven-baked cheese croquettes)

Serves 6–8 as an appetizer

**Another version of Brazil's favorite finger-
food. The mixture can be fried, but baking
is considered more modern.**

1¹/₂ cups self-rising flour
3 cups grated parmesan
1¹/₂ sticks unsalted butter (³/₄ cup)
1 large egg, separated
About ¹/₄ cup fine, dry bread crumbs

Preheat the oven to 350°F. Mix the flour with
the cheese and butter and work to a paste with
the egg yolk. Form into balls or bolsters, dip
into the lightly beaten egg white and roll in the
bread crumbs.

Arrange the balls on a lightly buttered or
nonstick baking sheet and bake for 25–30
minutes, until puffed up and brown.

Quesadillas, crisp tortilla turnovers filled with
melted cheese

Quesadillas

(Mexican cheese turnovers)

Serves 4 as a light meal

**Wheat flour tortillas make the best and
lightest quesadillas. Use a combination of
cheeses—one crumbly, one melting.**

2 cups cheese—gruyère or cheddar, grated
*1¹/₂ cups fresh white requeson or feta-
  type cheese, crumbled*
8 flour tortillas
*1 large red bell pepper, roasted, skinned, and
  cut into ribbons*
1 teaspoon chili flakes or powder
1 tablespoon chopped cilantro
Oil for frying

Mix the cheeses together, lay out the tortillas,
and top each with a spoonful of cheese—drop
it off-center, leaving a wide margin around the
edge. Top each dab of cheese with a pepper
ribbon, a pinch of chili, and a few scraps of
cilantro. Dampen the edges and fold in half to
enclose the filling.

Heat about a ½ inch of oil in a large frying
pan. Fry the quesadillas for a few minutes on
each side, until the filling melts and the tortilla
crisps and browns. Alternatively, brush with oil,
sprinkle with chili flakes, and bake at 350°F for
6–7 minutes.

poultry & meat

All barnyard birds—chickens, geese, ducks, and guinea fowl—are post-Columbian except the turkey, which is indigenous to Mexico and the southern parts of the North American landmass. Recipes for barnyard birds are also suitable for feathered game; a pheasant or guinea fowl will give you a better idea of the flavor of the region's semiwild barnyard bird than the fat and flabby chickens of modern breeding.

Very little meat was available to the indigenous inhabitants of Central and South America until the arrival of the Europeans. Although the Andean nations herded camels, llamas, alpacas, and vicuñas that they kept mainly for wool but also for meat and milk in the breeding months, they had no knowledge of the domestic animals of the Old World: cattle, pigs, sheep, and goats. Once established, the herds had a dramatic effect on the landscape as well as the diet of the region.

chicken

Rural housewives of the region—and many a town dweller, given a backyard—keep poultry for their productive life as egg-layers. A young cockerel might be fattened up to be roasted for a festive meal or to fetch a price in the marketplace, but traditional recipes reflect the expectation that any table bird will be tough.

Buying and storing

In Hispanic cultures, killing poultry for the pot was always reckoned women's business; in outlying districts, the bird is still sold live, which, it goes without saying, makes refrigeration unnecessary. Otherwise, keep the chicken in the refrigerator and don't waste the little unborn eggs you might find in the cavity—gather them up and add them whole to the broth at the very end of the cooking.

Medicinal and other uses

Chicken soup, the cure-all—calming, restorative, fortifying—has lately been confirmed by medical scientists as doing what our grandmothers always said it did.

Culinary uses

The thrifty housewife turns an old hen into two meals: a nourishing broth with vegetables, and a filling for tortillas, empanadas, or tamales.

Pollo a la cubana

(Cuban chicken)
Serves 4–6

A fine way with a small, tender, free-range bird: chop it into small pieces and don't waste any of it, including the neck and gizzard. Four elements make the dish:

Grilling chicken over on open fire in an Argentinian estancia

crisply fried chicken, caramelized bananas, a fiery chili sauce, and a background of plain cooked rice.

1 small free-range chicken, cut up into bite-size pieces
2–3 tablespoons seasoned flour
Oil for shallow frying
4 large bananas, peeled, cut in half lengthwise

Chili sauce:
2¹/₂ cups chopped ripe tomatoes
1–2 garlic cloves, skinned and chopped
1–2 habanero chiles, seeded and chopped
1 tablespoon olive oil
1 teaspoon sugar

For serving:
White or saffron rice

Dredge the chicken pieces through the seasoned flour, shaking to remove any excess. Heat 3–4 tablespoons of oil in a roomy frying pan, lay the chicken pieces in it, and fry gently until perfectly cooked through and deliciously brown. Add more oil if you need it. Remove the chicken pieces and set aside.

Fry the bananas, turning them once and removing them carefully as soon as the surfaces are lightly caramelized. Meanwhile, attend to the chili sauce: put all the ingredients in the blender and blend to a purée, then transfer to a small pan, let it boil fiercely for a few minutes to concentrate the juices, then reduce the heat and let it simmer for 10 minutes to marry the flavors. Arrange the chicken, bananas, and rice on a serving dish and hand around the chili sauce separately.

Ajiaco santafereno

(Chicken stew)
Serves 6–8

Chicken-in-the-pot, as they like it in Colombia, is made with a sinewy old hen past her laying days, the best material for any broth. The three varieties of potato stipulated by the ladies of Santa Fe—*patuso*, *sabanero,* and *criollo*— each bring their own characteristics. *Patuso* are firm and waxy, providing body; *sabanero* are floury and crumbly, dissolving to thicken the broth, and *criollo* are little round yellow potatoes that hold their shape and add sweetness. The main flavoring herbs, huasca leaves, are occasionally available dried; failing these, use basil—much liked in Colombia in combination with corn.

The broth:
1 boiling fowl or free-range chicken
2 onions, roughly chopped
2–3 bay leaves
2 tablespoon huascas or 2–3 sprigs fresh basil
Salt and peppercorns

Ajioco santafereno, Colombia's favorite Sunday lunch

The vegetables:

*1 cassava root, sliced lengthwise, hard core
  removed, peeled, and cut into chunks*
*2 pounds patuso potatoes, peeled and
  cut into chunks—about 5^1/$_2$ to 6 cups
  (if unavailable, use any firm-fleshed reds)*
*1^1/$_2$ pounds sabanero potatoes (if
  unavailable, use any floury whites)*
*1 pound criollo potatoes (if unavailable,
  use any small, yellow, waxy potatoes)*
4 fresh ears of corn, broken into chunks
Salt and pepper

For serving:

*Aji (salsa) of finely chopped yellow chiles,
  cilantro, scallion, and lemon juice*
Sliced avocado
Sour cream
Capers

Simmer the bird until perfectly tender in a
large pot along with the onions, herbs,
salt, and peppercorns, in enough water to
cover generously. The surface of the broth
should tremble, no more. An old bird will
need 2–3 hours, a young one will be ready
in half the time.

Let it cool, strain the broth, lifting off the fat,
and return the broth to the heat. As soon
as the first bubbles rise, add the cassava
chunks and the first potatoes, peeled and
cut into chunks. After 10 minutes, add the
second batch of potatoes, also peeled and
cut into chunks, and return to a boil. After
another 10 minutes, add the little potatoes,
scrubbed but not peeled, and the chunks of
fresh corn. Return to a boil and allow another
20 minutes, until the small potatoes are
perfectly tender. Finish with an extra sprinkling
of huascas or basil. Serve in deep bowls.

turkey

or guajalote (Mexico), peru (Brazil)

The only barnyard bird indigenous to the region, the turkey was domesticated by the Aztecs. Spanish colonizers first encountered it in Venezuela (four live birds were brought to Seville in 1500) and for two centuries after its arrival, the Jesuits held a profitable monopoly on what was soon to become the Christmas roasting bird.

shredded turkey

Appearance and taste

In the wild, the tom—male—is a handsome, bronze-feathered bird with magnificent blue and scarlet wattles used in courtship rituals; the hen—female—is smaller and usually lacks the beardlike tassel on the breast. In its semidomesticated state, the turkey is relatively small-breasted with robust flesh. It is chewy rather than flabby, and has a markedly gamey flavor.

Buying and storing

The turkey is not a bird whose gastronomic qualities are improved by intensive husbandry. For texture and flavor, choose free-range every time. Allow a pound per person dressed weight—the bones are heavy.

Medicinal and other uses

Lean—virtually fat-free—turkey is an excellent choice for dieters.

Culinary uses

Interchangeable with chicken in all recipes for barnyard birds, the turkey is at its most interesting in the traditional dishes of the region: tacos, tamales, and the kind of slow gentle closed-pot cooking that mimics the traditional earth oven.

Peru a la brasiliera

(Turkey roasted in banana leaves)
Serves 8–10

Closed-pot cooking, a refinement of the earth oven method, produces tender, succulent meat bathed in plenty of fragrant juice.

10–12 pound turkey
2 pounds salt (don't worry)
3 banana leaves or husks from 12 ears of corn

Chili baste:
3 malagueta chiles, seeded and chopped
3 tablespoons wine vinegar
2 onions, finely chopped
6 garlic cloves, finely chopped
6 tablespoons oil
3 mild red bell peppers, seeded and chopped
1 teaspoon powdered cinnamon
1/2 teaspoon powdered cloves
1/2 teaspoon grated nutmeg
1 wineglass cachaca or white rum

A fine turkey specimen, Mexico

Rinse the bird inside and out and singe off any little whiskery feathers. Check the wings for feather stumps and remove, if necessary, with tweezers. Douse the bird inside and out with the salt. Place in a large bowl or bucket, cover with cold water, and set in the refrigerator overnight.

Next day, rinse the bird under running water, making sure all the salt is washed away, and pat it dry. Make the chili baste. Put the chiles to soak in the vinegar. Fry the onion and garlic gently in 3 tablespoons of the oil until soft and golden. Push aside, add the remaining oil, and fry the chopped pepper until it caramelizes a little. Sprinkle in the spices and add the cachaca or rum. Let it boil to evaporate the alcohol. Tip the contents of the pan into the food processor and blend, along with the chiles and their soaking vinegar.

Place the bird on the table with the neck cavity facing you. Using your fingers, work the breast skin free of the flesh. Start gently and be careful not to tear the skin—it's easier once you get started. Loosen the skin all the way down the bird almost as far as the tail, going through the membrane that covers the drumsticks. Reserving a couple of tablespoons of the chili baste, carefully work the rest of the chili down both sides, until the entire breast and the drumsticks are covered. Secure the neckflap underneath with a skewer. Preheat the oven to 475°F.

Line the bottom of a deep, earthenware casserole dish (large enough to accommodate the bird) with half the corn husks or banana leaves, first cut into 18-inch squares and softened by being held over a flame. Place the turkey on the leaves, breast-side up, and brush with the reserved chili baste. Roast at the high heat for 10 minutes. Cover with the remaining leaves, reduce the oven to 325°F, and roast for 2–2½ hours (depending on the size of the turkey), until the juices of the thigh run clear when it is pierced with a knife. Leave the bird to reabsorb its juices and let it settle for 10 minutes before carving into bite-size pieces. Serve on fresh banana leaves, if available, moistened with its own juices (pass more around separately), accompanied by soft cornmeal (polenta), white rice, black beans, and okra sautéed with garlic and lemon juice.

Tacos de guajalote

(Turkey tacos)
Serves 4, allowing 3 tacos per person as a light lunch

This is the original Mexican taco, made with the meat of the muscular semiwild woodland-bred turkeys, which provided both the Mayas and the Aztecs as well as the Pilgrim Fathers with good reason for giving thanks.

The filling:
1 poached turkey breast, cooled in its own broth
A ladleful of cooking broth
3 tablespoons oil
1 small, mild onion, chopped
2–3 green jalapeño chiles, seeded and cut into matchsticks
4 tomatoes, skinned, seeded, and diced

The wraps:
12 tortillas
Oil for shallow frying

For serving, choose from:
Roughly mashed or sliced avocado
Sour cream
Shredded lettuce or other greens
Mashed beans
Grated cheese
Pickled or fresh green chiles
Chile-tomato salsa

Prepare the filling first. Shred the turkey meat by pulling the fibers apart with two forks. In a small frying pan, heat the oil and fry the onion and chile—a minute, no more. Add the tomato and let it bubble for five minutes or so to make a smooth sauce, mashing to break down the lumps. Stir in the shredded turkey and its broth, and simmer until shiny and almost dry—about 10 minutes. Divide the mixture between the tortillas, roll up, secure with toothpicks, and fry in shallow oil until golden. Drain on paper towels and serve immediately with sliced avocados.

Tacos de guajalote, shredded and sauced turkey breast on a crisply fried tortilla

feathered game

Duck, pigeon, quail, and curassow (an indigenous species of pheasant), along with birds of the seed-eating kind—including several members of the parrot family—are traditionally hunted for the pot. Raptors, as elsewhere, are eaten only in times of famine.

Appearance and taste

It is by no means easy to tell the difference between one game bird and another once it has been subjected to long cooking. When young enough to roast, the flesh of wild creatures reflects their diet: grain-eaters taste like chicken, water birds can taste noticeably fishy. The flavor of wild meat is stronger than that of a domestic table bird.

Choosing and storing

Game birds are tender if plucked and eaten on the day of gathering; otherwise they should be left to mature for four to seven days, depending on size, the stage at which they once again become tender. Water birds should be gutted and eaten as soon as possible.

Medicinal and other uses

Wild meat is very lean—good for those watching their diet—and dense, delivering all that is necessary to sustain life. Combined with grains and legumes in the Latin American manner, a little goes a long way.

Culinary uses

The larger game birds are tough and chewy, needing gentle stewing or fine chopping if they are to be palatable. The traditional method of tenderizing wild game was by what was effectively a form of pressure cooking: the food is wrapped in leaves, packed into an earth oven—the *curanto*—and left to develop tenderness and succulence over several hours underground.

Pozole casero

(Hominy with wild meat)
Serves 6–8

The hunter's version of Mexico's famous stew—nobody knows what's in there once it's in the pot. In its land of origin, vinagretta—the sharply acidic leaves of the Bermuda buttercup—is used instead of sorrel, and anise-flavored epazote rather than dill is the flavoring herb.

1 pound hominy: lye-treated corn kernels
4 pounds game birds, whole, halved,
  or quartered (size dictates)
2–3 bay leaves
1–2 sprigs oregano
6 allspice berries
Salt

The finishing sauce:
6 tomates verdes (or 1 pound green
  gooseberries), chopped
A handful shredded sorrel or spinach, with a
  squeeze of lemon
2–3 green serrano chiles, seeded and
  chopped
1–2 stalks epasote or dill fronds, chopped
1 small onion, finely chopped
2 tablespoons lard or oil
1/4 cup toasted pumpkin or sunflower
  seeds, powdered

For serving, choose from:
Sour cream, avocado slices, shredded
  lettuce, chopped onion, lime quarters,
  chicharrones (pork cracklings), grated or
  curd cheese

Put the hominy in a roomy pan with plenty of fresh water, put the lid on loosely, and cook until tender: from 1½ to 2 hours, depending on age and toughness. If you need to add water, make sure it's boiling. You'll know the hominy's ready when the kernels "flower": the grains burst open like little blossoms. There should still be at least two cups of broth.

At the same time, cook the birds until tender in a separate pan along with the aromatics, a little salt, and enough water just to submerge. Strain the broth and strip the meat from the bones. Return the meat to the broth and set aside.

Meanwhile, make the sauce. Cook the chopped tomato with a little water until mushy, letting it boil for a minute or two to concentrate the juices; transfer to a food processor along with the sorrel or spinach, the chiles, the garlic, and the epasote or dill, and blend to a purée.

Heat the oil, fry the onion until soft but not browned, add the chopped green tomatoes or gooseberries, and simmer until thick—five minutes or so. Stir in the ground pumpkin seeds, season with salt, and cook for another 10 minutes, until the sauce is really thick. Add the flowered hominy and two cups of its cooking water, and cook for 10 minutes more to blend the flavors. The finished dish should be moist rather than soupy.

Serve ladled into deep bowls, topped with a heap of meat, well moistened with its own broth, and a dollop of sour cream. Hand the rest of the accompaniments around separately.

Pato en pepitoria

(Duck with pumpkin seeds)

Serves 4–6

The cut-up bird—include all the bits—is simmered gently in a nut-thickened sauce. Succulent and delicious.

2 wild ducks, cut up (1 barnyard bird)
1/4 cup lard or olive oil
2 garlic cloves, peeled and chopped
1 tortilla or slice day-old bread, crumbled
1/3 cup pumpkin seeds

Few sprigs oregano, chopped or crumbled
1/2 teaspoon powdered cloves
1 teaspoon powdered cinnamon
1 tablespoon pimentón dulce *(mild paprika)*
1 teaspoon chili powder
2 onions, finely sliced in half-moons

For serving:
2 sweet red peppers, roasted and cut into strips
Soft cornmeal tortillas

Rinse the pieces, which should be small enough to pick up and eat with the fingers. Fry the garlic, bread crumbs, and pumpkin seeds in half the oil or lard until they golden—don't let them brown. Sprinkle in the oregano and the spices, and set aside.

Gently fry the duck pieces with the onion in the remaining oil. When the duck is well browned and the onions are soft, stir in the pumpkin seed mixture, and add enough water to just submerge the duck pieces. Let it boil, put the lid on loosely, and turn down the heat. Simmer gently until the duck is tender—about 30 minutes. Add a little more water if necessary.

Serve with the pepper strips and soft tortillas.

pork

Of all the Old World's meat animals, none received so enthusiastic a welcome as the pig—perhaps because of its similarity to the indigenous peccary, the hunter's most valuable prize. It was imported by the Hispanic homesteaders who, unaware of the processes necessary to render the native foodstuffs palatable, imported those things they understood. The pig quickly became, and remains, the most important of the region's domestic meat animals. This was not least because its consumption was actively encouraged by Roman Catholic missionaries, since it proved that the pork-eater was neither a Muslim nor a Jew—a matter of considerable concern to the Hispanic colonizers, who had just reclaimed their southern lands from the Moorish caliphs.

Appearance and taste

Pigs reared in the Hispanic—southern Mediterranean—tradition are not expected to be as fat and soft-fleshed as northern pigs. Their meat, relatively lean, goes to make dried sausages (chorizos) while the blood is transformed into blood sausage (morcilla), variously spiced, and sometimes blended with meat and fat or bulked out with grains.

Buying and storing

Pork deteriorates quickly in a hot climate. Buy only fresh meat, salt it lightly, and store it briefly in the refrigerator. Wash it thoroughly before cooking.

Medicinal and other uses

Pork meat tastes good because it's threaded through with delicious little globules of fat. Although pork lard is considered a "bad" fat in these health-conscious times, the reputation is not entirely deserved. According to the U.S. Department of Agriculture, unhydrogenated (pure) pork fat is low in saturated fat and contains less than half the cholesterol found in butter.

Fattening pigs for the market, Paraguay

Culinary uses

Meat and fat are equally valued in the Hispanic kitchen. While pork, although eaten fresh for a celebration, is the great pantry-stored meat, the lard, melted and refined and stored as a pure-white fat, is used for frying and preserving as well as baking (see page 107).

Carne de cerdo en manteca

(Preserved pork)
Serves 4–6

One of those delicious little preparations that never seem to appear in recipe books: lean, diced pork (fillet or leg or shoulder, it doesn't really matter) is cooked very slowly in pure lard, and browned and flavored with garlic, herbs, and paprika. You will need to start a day ahead.

2 pounds lean pork, cut into bite-size cubes
2 pounds pork kidney fat (or very fatty belly pork)
1 tablespoon crushed dried oregano
6 garlic cloves, crushed with 1 tablespoon salt
2 tablespoons vinegar
2 tablespoons mild pimentón
1 teaspoon chili powder

Mix the meat cubes with the oregano, crushed garlic, and vinegar. Work thoroughly and leave overnight in a cool place to absorb the flavors. Meanwhile, prepare the lard: cook the kidney fat very slowly with a cup of water in a low oven or in a heavy pan on a very gentle flame. When the oil has separated from the fiber and is floating on the water, pour it off, strain, and reheat to evaporate all remaining moisture—gently, it shouldn't turn golden.

Drain the pork cubes and brush off excess marinade. Heat the lard in a roomy pan and add the meat. Cook very gently for 30–40 minutes: the lard should bubble gently, a sign that the meat is losing its juices. When the meat is cooked through and the lard no longer bubbles, remove from the heat and stir in the pimentón and chili powder. Pour everything into an earthenware jar, making sure all the meat is submerged, and set it in the refrigerator to firm up. Meat preserved in this way keeps for a long time in a cool pantry, provided each time you take some out, you melt the potful down to ensure the remaining meat remains submerged. The trick is to ensure that no air can get at anything perishable.

The lard can be eaten like butter or stirred into bean dishes to add flavor, richness, and color; the meat—very rich and fragrant—is delicious with black beans and soft tortillas, as part of a Mexican *plato combinado* (see page 92). To prepare, remove the required number of cubes—four per person is ample—and heat gently in a pan until the fat runs. As a quick snack, wrap in a tortilla or slip into a split arepa, with a squeeze of lime, a lettuce leaf, and a fiery pickled chile. Very delicious.

Tatemado
(Mexican pork pot roast)
Serves 8–10

A succulent pork pot roast jacketed with spices and chiles, this dish is served at weddings and christenings in northern Mexico and takes its name from the Nauatl word for pit-barbecue.

Tatemado, pot roast pork with a fragrant chili crust

1 pork shoulder on the bone—about 5 pounds
2 pig's feet, scrubbed and split
2¹/2 cups white wine vinegar
6 garlic cloves, crushed with a little salt
1 teaspoon peppercorns
4 ounces dried chili ancho (mild and fruity)
4 ounces dried chili guajillo (sharp and hot)
1 teaspoon powdered ginger
2–3 sprigs thyme
¹/2 teaspoon coriander seeds

For serving:
2–3 red onions, finely sliced, dressed with lime juice and salt
Shredded lettuce
Sliced radishes
Tortillas

Put the meat and pig's feet in a roomy bowl. Pierce the skin in several places with a knife. In a blender, blend the vinegar with the garlic, a little more salt, and the peppercorns. Pour this aromatic bath over the meat and set aside in a cool place for a couple of hours. Slit the chiles open and scrape out the seeds and pale veins. Keep 1 teaspoon of the seeds. Tear up the chiles and soak in a bowl of boiling water for 20 minutes or so.

Preheat the oven to 300°F. Drain the meat, reserving the vinegar juices, and transfer to a casserole dish. Put the vinegar in the blender, add the chiles a little at a time, and blend between each addition until smooth. Strain and discard the bits. Return the liquid to the blender along with the ginger, thyme, chile seeds, and coriander; blend to a smooth paste. Spread the paste over the meat and add enough water to come halfway up the roast. Cover tightly, transfer to the oven, and cook for 2–3 hours, until the meat is tender but not yet falling apart. Remove the lid, raise the heat, and cook for another 20 minutes or so, to brown the skin and reduce the sauce. Serve with sliced onion, shredded lettuce, and radishes—all ready to wrap in a tortilla fresh from the comal.

beef

Beef cattle, a post-Columbian introduction to the grasslands of the New World, provided a new crop—beef, preserved first by salting and barreling, and later by freezing—for shipping back across the Atlantic to the cities of Europe to feed the newly affluent workers of the Industrial Revolution. Vast cattle ranches were established throughout the temperate zones of the territory—the borderlands of northern Mexico, the pampas of Argentina, Uruguay, Paraguay, Chile, and Peru, and the southern grass plains of Brazil. Recipes reflect this profitable trade. The *asado*, the Argentinian gaucho's barbecue, is a whole carcass of young beef, killed on the spot, skinned, split, and roasted on a spit set over a couple of forked branches, or on a pole hammered into the hard red earth at an angle to the fire. In the great cities of Brazil—Rio de Janeiro and São Paolo—*churrascarías*, restaurants that mimic the gaucho's daily dinner, serve nothing but roast meat, big slabs of it turning on the spit to be carved to the customer's order.

Medicinal and other uses

The cowboys and herdsmen who roamed the range lived exclusively on meat for months at a time, for practical reasons as well as preference, without suffering ill effects. Whether meat-eating brings toughness, resilience, and resourcefulness is arguable—Hollywood says it does, and the rest of us believe.

Culinary uses

Traditional recipes in the meat-packing lands make good use of variety meats—the butcher's cast-offs and the food of the urban poor— readily available only where there's a market for the rest. In Peru, *anticuchos*, grilled beef hearts, are the most popular street food. In the cities and ports where the meat is processed, tongue, tripe, and cow heel are combined with beans to produce nourishing stews, while the bones are prized for broth.

Tostadas de carne apache
(Tostadas topped with marinated steak)
Serves 4–6

Carne apache—Indian steak—is a popular street snack in the cattle herding borderlands of Mexico's northern states. The principle is the same as steak tartare, though nowadays the tenderizing agent is lime juice rather than the cowpoke's saddle. Start a day ahead.

12 corn tortillas

The topping:
1 pound twice-chopped or fine-ground steak (about 2 cups)
Juice of 4–5 limes
1 onion, finely chopped
1 red bell pepper, seeded and diced
2–3 fresh serrano chiles, seeded and finely chopped
2–3 tablespoons chopped cilantro
(Optional) 1–2 tablespoons chopped green olives
Salt

Spread the tortillas on the table to dry. In a large, clean bowl, mix the chopped steak with the lime juice, cover, and set in the refrigerator overnight. Turn it from time to time so it takes the lime juice evenly. Drain, bring back to room temperature, and blend with the remaining ingredients.

Toast the tortillas in the broiler or fry them until crisp and brown, and pile with the prepared steak. Tomatoes, shredded lettuce or cabbage, radishes, olives, pickled chiles, and Tabasco sauce are all appropriate accompaniments.

Herding cattle in the dry season on the slopes of Mount Concepción, Nicaragua

Estofado argentino, lean beef braised with aromatics, red wine, and root vegetables

Estofado argentino

(Argentinian pot roast)

Serves 6–8

More sophisticated than the cowboy's barbecued carcass, this is a homestead dish cooked in a closed pot, earth oven style, with vegetables and aromatics and the rough red wine of the countryside. If convenient, leave it overnight in the lowest possible oven—in the morning you will be rewarded with the most succulent beef you've ever tasted.

About 4 pounds round roast
About 2 pounds large carrots
2 cups finely chopped parsley
4 garlic cloves, finely chopped
1/4 cup oil
About 1 pound small onions, peeled
  (about 4–5 cups)

A few sprigs thyme and oregano, a bay leaf
1 bottle rough red wine
Pinch sugar
Salt and pepper

To finish:
3–4 red and yellow bell peppers, seeded and
  cut into chunks
About 2 pounds scrubbed new potatoes
  (or floury potatoes, peeled and cut into chunks)

For serving:
Chimichurri salsa (see page 199)

Shove a sharp knife right through the heart of the roast to make a deep incision from end to end—starting at the blunt end, the knife-point should appear at the tip. Grate a quarter of the carrots, mix with parsley and garlic, and stuff this fragrant paste into the incision. If necessary, tie the roast with string.

Heat the oil in a roomy, flameproof casserole dish or other flameproof and ovenproof pot, and brown the meat on all sides. Remove the meat and set aside. Cut the carrots into chunks the same size as the onions, and fry them with the onions in the pot. Return the meat to the pot, tuck in the aromatics, add the wine and the sugar, and season with salt and pepper.

Bring to a boil, cover tightly—use foil as well as a lid—and transfer to a very low oven. Let it steam gently in its own juices—overnight is not too long. When perfectly tender, remove and let it rest. Add the finishing vegetables to the pot juices and cook until tender. Slice the meat and arrange it on its bed of fragrant vegetables.

Serve with a chimichurri salsa: finely chopped thyme, parsley, garlic, and onion, marinated with olive oil and a little wine vinegar.

exotic & wild meats

air-dried charqui meat

In the absence of reliable refrigeration, it is in the form of *charqui* or jerky— meat preserved by natural dehydration— that most wild meat comes to market. This, the most ancient method of conserving the hunter's bounty, is simply fresh meat, trimmed of sinew and fat, cut into thin strips, and hung to dry in the ice cold mountain breezes from the Andes, without salt or preservatives or flavorings. Once perfectly dehydrated, it can be stored almost indefinitely and rehydrated at will.

The process, well known to all primitive peoples, was (and is) chiefly used for conserving and transporting valuable protein gathered by hunting animals like the Andean herd animals— grazers that include the llama and vicuna—and who forage their own foods rather than depend upon foodstuffs supplied by herdsmen.

Exotics—meat animals reared for the table as well as wild-gathered—include rodents such as the guinea pig or *cuy* (pronounced "kwee"), a prolific breeder first domesticated by the Incas and still valued. The traveler new to Peru will be startled to see the little creatures running around under the table in rural households, much as chickens or rabbits—whose meat is very similar. Argentina and Chile have the agouti, a small rodent bred for the table, as are the rather larger paca, viscacha, and the world's biggest water rat, the capybara, which earned the distinction of being classified as a fish by the early missionaries in order that it could be eaten on Catholic fast days. Elsewhere, particularly among the Amazonian peoples, turtle and tortoise are both considered good eating when roasted in the shell or baked in an earth oven.

Both meat and eggs of iguanas and snakes are still eaten in country districts, offered for sale by children at the roadside—though these days the hope is that the tourists will ransom the unfortunate creature, which can then be recaptured and recycled.

Appearance and taste

Rodent meat is much like wild rabbit: tender and mild-flavored when young, tough and chewy in its maturity. Reptile meat has a stringy consistency, close to the texture and flavor of chicken's neck—actually, it's indistinguishable from chicken as a filling for tacos or empanadas, the form in which it usually appears.

Medicinal and other uses

Wild meat is lean, low in cholesterol, and full of all necessary nutrients. It is not usually fed to small children or the elderly, since it's considered overfortifying and indigestible.

Guinea pig is part of the feast in this portrayal of the Last Supper in Cuzco Cathedral, Peru

Culinary uses

Dried meat is best used sparingly: quality wins over quantity. If you get the chance to cook rodent, think rabbit; South American rodents are herbivores, delicately flavored and as tender as chicken.

Conejitos ajímaní

(Little rabbits with garlic and peanuts)
Serves 4

The Peruvian way with any edible rodent— but particularly good with guinea pig, the rabbit of the New World. You will need to start up to a day ahead to allow time for the meat to marinate.

2 pounds cut-up rabbit or any midsize rodent such as cuy, cut into bite-size pieces

For the marinade:
1 teaspoon crumbled chile
2 tablespoons oil
2 tablespoons white wine vinegar
1 teaspoon achiote, crushed
2 garlic cloves, skinned and finely chopped
2/3 cup cream
2 tablespoons crushed toasted peanuts
Salt and pepper

Turn the meat pieces in the marinade ingredients, cover, and leave overnight. Drain and pat dry. Strain and reserve the marinade.

Broil or barbecue the meat over medium heat for five minutes per side if you like it rare—more if you like your meat well done. Or roast in the oven: allow 15–20 minutes at 400°F. Leave by the side of the fire or in the lowest possible oven for 20 minutes.

In a small saucepan over medium heat, let the reserved marinade boil, along with the cream, to make a little sauce. Taste and season, and pour over the meat. Finish with a sprinkling of toasted peanuts.

Charquicán

(Jerky stew)
Serves 4

A sophisticated version of a classic Chilean vegetable stew finished with a fried *charqui*, strips of wind-dried hunter's meat prepared in the old way. If you can't find jerky, steak roasted on the barbecue will have to do.

1 thick slice squash, cut into bite-size pieces
1–2 carrots, cut into chunks
4–5 small potatoes
1¹/4 cups fresh corn kernels
1¹/4 cups fresh peas
2¹/2 cups broth or plain water
Salt

To finish:
8 ounces charqui (jerky, biltong, or any
  wind-dried meat)
2–3 tablespoons oil
2–3 onions, finely slivered
1 teaspoon crumbled oregano
1 teaspoon paprika or dried mild red chili,
  finely chopped
1 teaspoon cumin
Salt and pepper

For serving:
Pickled pearl onions
Pebre chileno (see below)

Put all the vegetables in a roomy pot along with the broth or water, season, bring to a boil, turn down the heat to simmer, put the lid on tightly, and cook for 15 minutes, until nearly tender.

Meanwhile, remove any sinew from the jerky and chop. Heat the oil in a small frying pan and gently fry the onions until they soften and color. Add the jerky and flavorings, season, and cook for five minutes or so, until well blended. Stir the contents of the frying pan into the vegetables, remove the lid, and let it boil to evaporate the juices. The stew should be deliciously moist but not soupy.

Serve in bowls, with pickled pearl onions and *pebre chileno*—Chilean pepper salsa. To prepare: pound 3 fresh hot chiles to a paste along with 2 tablespoons cilantro, 1 tablespoon oil, 1 tablespoon chopped onion, and 1 chopped garlic clove.

variety & salted meats

offal, morcilla, chorizo

The salt drawer, the draining hook, and the brine pot are where the pig ends up when the weather is too warm and damp to permit the conservation of meat in any other way. There was a time when all households with access to a backyard kept a household pig to eat up the scraps and provide the family with its annual supply of cured meats: sausages, morcilla (blood sausage), bacon, and ham. In the outlying districts, many still do. The brine pot, too, is where the bits and pieces of the butcher's shop end up—and these have become the food of the urban poor. In lands like Brazil and the Caribbean where the indigenous peoples were either forced off their land or, worse, slaughtered by the incoming slave traders, and who were eventually replaced with African slaves, dishes were made with offal, the bits of the pig considered unfit for the master. The stupendous Brazilian *feijoada* and the fiery Caribbean pepperpot— creations that not only delight the palate but have come to define an entire culinary habit—emerged from these sorry beginnings.

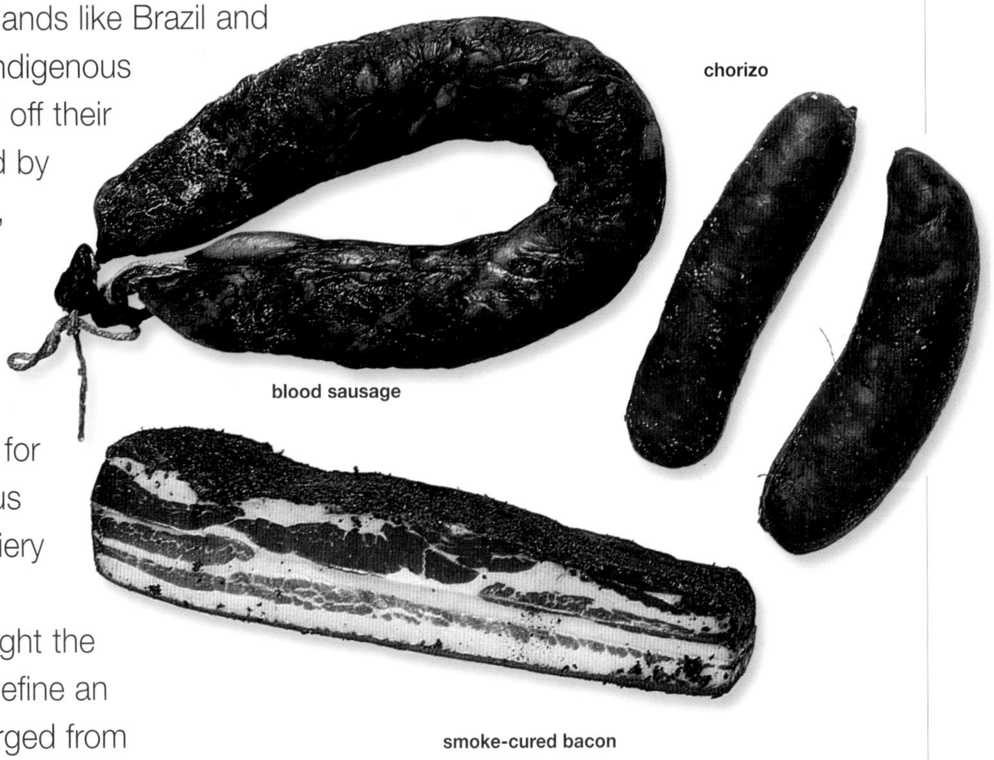

chorizo

blood sausage

smoke-cured bacon

Buying and storing

When choosing chorizo, pick the right one for the job. Fresh chorizo—soft, brightly colored, juicy—is good for frying or broiling. Mature chorizo—firm, with a soft white bloom on the skin—is good for slicing to eat raw, or for including in a slow-simmered stew. When choosing meat from the brine pot, ask the butcher for instructions: he'll know how long it's curing and how long you need to soak it. Store chorizo out of its plastic or any other wrapping on a hook in a dry corner, never in the refrigerator. Once the meat is out of the brine pot, use it as soon as possible.

Medicinal and other uses

Salt-cured meats are as high in sodium as they are in protein—use sparingly. You have been warned.

Culinary uses

Cured meats and sausages are the mainstay of the rural kitchen, added in small quantities to improve the flavor and boost the nutritional value of roots, gourds, beans, and grains. As for variety meats, variety is what makes it festive. It's the thrill of discovery: a bit of this and a bit of that allows everyone to choose exactly what they like.

Anticuchos peruvianos

(Peruvian beef heart kabob)
Serves 6–8

Spicy, chile-spiked, and deliciously succulent scraps of meat threaded on skewers and grilled to order on every street corner in Peru. The name comes from the Quechua meaning "Andean food cooked on a stick." The correct chile for marinade is the fiery *ají mirasol* (the sunseeker), the dried version of the fruity yellow *ají amarillo*, a long pointed torpedo-shaped chile, thin fleshed and hot as Hades—but jalapeños or serranos will do.

1 beef heart, about 4 pounds, trimmed
   of fat and fiber

The marinade:
1/4 cup wine vinegar
1/4 cup oil
2–3 fresh chiles, seeded and finely chopped
2 tablespoons chopped cilantro
2 garlic cloves, finely chopped
1 small onion, finely chopped
1 tablespoon powdered cumin
1 tablespoon dried oregano
Salt and pepper

For cooking:
6–8 long skewers, or bamboo or fine metal
   knitting needles

Rinse the beef heart and pat dry. Cut into bite-size cubes and mix in a bowl with all the marinade ingredients, then cover with plastic wrap and let it absorb the flavors—overnight in the refrigerator is best.

Light the barbecue or heat the broiler. If using bamboo skewers, they should be soaked for an hour or two first.

Remove the meat from the marinade and drain thoroughly. Strain the marinade and reserve the liquid. Thread the meat on the skewers and broil fiercely until the outside caramelizes—about two minutes a side—basting with the marinade as they cook. Serve with hot arepas or freshly baked bolillos: crisp-crusted, dense-crumbed rolls just right for holding in the hand.

Lots to choose from in a Montevideo market

Feijoada

(Brazilian cured meats with black beans)
Serves 12

A stupendous dish for a party, Brazil's national treasure. The meats are variable— don't worry if you can't get them all. Fresh oxtail can be substituted for *carne seca*, the Brazilian beef jerky, available in Portuguese or Latin American delis. Start on Friday to serve for lunch on Saturday.

5 cups black beans
2 bay leaves, a quartered onion, 2–3 garlic
  cloves

The meats:
1 salted, smoked beef tongue
1 pound carne seca (strips of air-dried beef)
2 pounds salt pork (sparerib for choice)
1 pound slab (fatty) bacon
2 pig's ears (singed and scrubbed)
2 pig's feet (scrubbed and split)
2–3 pig's tails
1 smoked ham hock
4–6 links linguica or chorizo (paprika sausage)
4–6 links morcilla (blood sausage)

To finish:
2 tablespoons olive oil
2 onions, finely chopped
2 cloves garlic, finely chopped
2-3 large tomatoes, grated
1–2 malagueta chile peppers, chopped

To accompany:
Finely shredded greens (kale or Swiss chard),
  wilted in a little olive oil
Plain cooked white rice
Toasted manoic meal (farofa, page 60) for
  sprinkling
Pickled malageta peppers
Quartered oranges

Put the beans to soak overnight in a large pot with enough water to cover generously. Soak the tongue at the same time, if not already soaked by the butcher.

Next day, bring the dried beef and the tongue to a boil in a roomy pot with the pork bits, turn down the heat, cover loosely, and simmer until all is tender, 2–3 hours. Add the pickled pork

Feijoada, Brazil's ultimate bean feast, strictly for Saturday lunchtime

for the last hour of the cooking. Remove the meats to a large platter. As soon as it's cool enough to handle, skin the tongue and remove the little bones and gristle.

Meanwhile, drain the beans and bring them to a boil in plenty of fresh water with their aromatics, turn down the heat, and simmer for 30 minutes. Add the ham hock to the beans and simmer for another 1½ hours.

Slice and fry the sausages and blood sausage in the oil until well browned (you can boil them in a separate pot, but they taste even more delicious when crisped). Remove and reserve while you prepare the flavoring sauce.

Gently fry the onion and garlic in the oily sausage drippings until soft and golden, then stir in the tomatoes and chile and squash down to break up the fibers. Let it boil to make a rich little sauce, then stir in a couple of ladlesful of the cooked beans, mashing to

blend. Stir this mixture into the beanpot, along with the fried sausage and the reserved meats. Simmer for another hour, adding boiling water when necessary, to make sure the water level never drops below several inches. Remove the meats from the beans and leave in separate dishes in the refrigerator overnight.

Next day, reheat with more boiling water for an hour. Arrange the cooked meats, suitably sliced—de-rind, if necessary, and cube the bacon slab, slip the meat off the ear-gristle, slice the tails, and bone out the pig's feet—on a single large platter or several smaller ones, and moisten the meat with a little bean liquid. Serve the beans in their sauce in a large, warm bowl. Arrange the accompaniments around the bean bowl for everyone to make their own combinations. A pitcher of Caipirinhas—fresh lime juice, white rum or cachaça, sweetened with sugar cane juice (see page 183)—makes the party even livelier.

lamb & kid

Sheep are mainly confined to the southern tip of the landmass—Patagonia and the Andean highlands—while goats, the universal forager, are pastured on marginal land throughout the territory. Recipes are inherited from the repertoire appropriate to their predecessors on the high plateaus, the Andean llamas, alpacas, vicuñas, guanacos—all of which have been domesticated since the earliest times.

Appearance and taste

The meat from animals pastured on the Andean uplands is lean and sweet. If it smells a little strong, wash it thoroughly before cooking.

Buying and storing

Meat does not have a long shelf life down on the plain—particularly that from young animals—any more than it does on the butcher's shelf. It is best to buy it as fresh as possible and consume without delay. In the Andean mountains in winter, storage is not a problem since the meat will remain frozen and safe so long as it's hung out of the reach of predators.

Culinary uses

Mountain lamb is sinewy and tough compared to the soft-living, valley-reared lamb. Chop the meat thoroughly unless you intend to subject it to long cooking. Kid, the meat of young goats, has a gluey texture particularly good in a slow-simmered stew; when roasting, a gentle heat is better than high heat.

Ropa vieja
(Old clothes)
Serves 4–6

A hash by another name—one of those leftover dishes into which anything goes—just as they like it in Venezuela. The principal is the transformation of something soft and bland into something crisp and tasty. Patience, expressed as long gentle frying, is key.

1 pound cooked meat—lamb or kid
4–5 tablespoons olive oil
1–2 onions, finely sliced into half-moons
2 garlic cloves, skinned and cut into slivers
1 tablespoon chopped fresh marjoram or oregano
2–3 fresh chiles, seeded and chopped
Salt and pepper

Shred the meat, fat and all. Fry in the oil along with the onion, garlic, and other flavorings. Season and continue frying, turning over the mixture as it browns. Eventually it will acquire the most exquisite crust and a wonderful fragrance. Eat with plain boiled potatoes, arepas, or whatever strikes your fancy.

La señalanda—marking sheep for purposes of identification—in Argentina

Pastel de choclo

(Chilean shepherd's pie)
Serves 4–6

A savory base of *pino*—a variable mixture of meats topped with puréed corn—is given a crisp crust under the broiler. The traditional cooking pot is a dish of unbaked red clay from the village of Pomaire, in the mountains to the east of Santiago.

Pino:
1 1/2 pounds finely chopped lamb or kid
2 pounds onions, finely sliced (about 7 cups)
3 garlic cloves, finely chopped
1/4 cup oil or butter
2 rounded tablespoons mild paprika (pimentón)
1 teaspoon powdered cumin
1 teaspoon dried oregano
2 1/2 cups diced squash
3 tablespoons raisins
A dozen pitted green olives, roughly chopped
Salt and pepper

The topping:
10 cups fresh corn
2 1/2 cups milk
1 egg, broken up with a fork

To finish:
3 hard-boiled eggs, quartered lengthwise
Powdered sugar and chili flakes

First prepare the pino. Put the lamb or kid, onions, garlic, and oil in a heavy pan, add a ladleful of water and cook gently, the lid on loosely, for about an hour, until the meat is tender. Add the remaining pino ingredients and cook for another 30 minutes (add water if it looks like it's drying out). Let it boil to reduce the juices to a rich gravy. Stir in the raisins and olives and season with salt and pepper.

Meanwhile, purée the corn with the milk, transfer to a pot, and cook until the mixture has thickened a little—5 minutes. Remove from the heat and let it cool a little. Stir in the egg, and salt lightly.

Preheat the oven to 350°F. Spread the pino in an earthenware gratin dish, top with the hard-boiled eggs, and finish with the corn purée and a powdering of the sugar and chili flakes. Bake for half an hour, until brown and bubbling. For an even more caramelized topping, slip it under the broiler.

fish & shellfish

The fishermen of the region—as a glance at the map will confirm—have access to one or another of three great waters: Pacific, Atlantic, and Caribbean. A fortunate few, mainly those who inhabit the lands of the Maya and Aztecs, have access to all three. But the richest of these fishing grounds is where the chilly waters of the Antarctic meet the warmth of the Pacific, when the cold Humbolt current curves around the shores of Chile. Here, great drifting clouds of plankton feed the rainbow shoals that spawn on Chile's narrow continental shelf and provide molluscs and other rock-dependent sea creatures with a reliable food source. The shelf, a shallow pasture out of reach of ocean predators, serves as a nursery for vulnerable offspring. Names are confusing: a gilt-head bream, for instance, is known as dorado among Spanish-speakers, whereas in Caribbean markets, dorado is the local name for dolphin-fish, known on the west coast as mahi-mahi, which is not a warm-blooded sea mammal but a blunt-nosed seafish with brilliant golden flanks—hence its name. For this reason, I have not given exact species, but have chosen ingredient groups for culinary purposes—round-bodied whole fish, steak fish, and so on—remembering there are many more fish in the sea than I have room to list.

bivalves

Clams and related shellfish

Clams and all manner of assorted bivalves are to be found all along the coastlines. Since none of the bivalves are mobile—with the exception of the scallop—they are concentrated wherever there is a ready food source. All are edible and most are appreciated locally, while a few have commercial value and are exported.

Habitat

They are found all along the shoreline from the chilly Straits of Magellan to the Sea of Cortez by way of the tropical sands of Brazil.

Appearance and taste

Size, color, and flavor are very variable: there are literally thousands of hinged-shell molluscs, some more delicious than others. Since the bivalves get their nourishment by pulling water through their shells, any danger normally comes from what the creatures have ingested. As for culinary virtues, price in the market is the best indication of quality. The taste is usually a little salty, although the more delicately flavored are as close to an oyster as anyone might wish.

Buying and storing

When buying fresh, check that fish are still alive in their shells: a quick shake will encourage them to close. Too many open shells—or worse, dried-out and gaping ones—indicates they're not perfectly fresh. Discard any that are cracked or dirty. Local names are usually derived from the local language.

Medicinal and other uses

Shellfish, though of general value as a supplementary food source since prehistoric times, supplied all the dietary needs of the coastal dwellers of Chile who subsisted comfortably on a harvest of razor clams, a seemingly inexhaustible shore crop, judiciously supplemented by sea vegetables.

Culinary uses

Bivalves can be eaten raw or cooked. If the former, bear in mind that raw clams are even harder to pry open than oysters: use a short, strong, double-bladed knife, either inserted between the shells or in the hinge, whatever works. If the latter, they are best cooked until they open in a closed pot in a minimum amount of liquid for the shortest possible time: longer cooking or reheating makes them rubbery. If gathering your own bivalves, to clean them, put them in a bucket with plenty of cold water and enough salt to produce the same salinity as seawater—½ cup salt to 4 quarts water—and leave them for a couple of days to spit out their sand. For inclusion in stews, large clams should be chopped; small ones can be left whole.

Cazuela del pescador

Cazuela del pescador
(Fisherman's clams)
Serves 4

A fisherman's dish, nothing fancy. Simple but good. Let the clams soak overnight in cold water and discard any with cracked or gaping shells and those that feel too heavy—a sign they're full of something other than live fish. Shellfish can stay fresh for as long as they can hold water in their shells.

4 pounds clams or any fresh shellfish
2 tablespoons olive oil
2 garlic cloves, finely chopped
1 green frying chile, seeded and chopped
1 fresh red chile, seeded and finely chopped
1 tablespoon chopped parsley

Pick over the clams and rinse thoroughly. Heat the oil in a roomy pot and fry the garlic and chiles for 2–3 minutes, just enough to perfume the oil. Tip in the shellfish, turn up the heat, and let it simmer for 3–4 minutes, until all the shells gape open in the steam—turn them with a spoon so that the ones on top can get to the heat. When all are open, they're done—discard any that do not open. Remove the pot from the heat immediately—shellfish toughens if it's overcooked. Finish with freshly chopped parsley.

Empanadas de mariscos al horno
(Oven-baked seafood turnovers)
Serves 6–8

Little turnovers stuffed with seafood, a reminder of pre-Columbian feasts, these are baked in the wood-fired baking oven that, in modern Chile, takes the place of the old earth oven, the *curanto*.

The filling:
2 pounds shellfish—clams or mussels
1 glass white wine
1 pound shrimp
2 tablespoons olive oil
2 onions, finely chopped
2 garlic cloves, finely chopped
1 red bell pepper, seeded and diced small
1 teaspoon crumbled thyme
1 chile, seeded and chopped
Salt and pepper

The pastry dough:
2^1/$_2$ cups self-rising flour
^{1}/$_2$ teaspoon salt
^{1}/$_4$ cup olive oil
2 tablespoons white wine
^{2}/$_3$ cup warm water

Cook the shellfish in a pot with a tablespoon of the wine: let it boil, put the lid on tightly, and shake over the heat until they open. Remove and let cool. Cook the shrimp in the remaining juices along with the rest of the wine, removing them as soon as they blush scarlet. Shuck the shellfish and chop the meat if necessary (small clams can be left whole). Peel the shrimp and chop roughly. In another pan, fry the onion, garlic, and pepper in the oil until soft. Sprinkle with the thyme and chile, season with salt and pepper, add the wine juices, and let it boil to reduce to a fragrant sauce. Stir in the prepared shellfish and shrimp and let it cool while you make the pastry dough.

Preheat the oven to 400°F.

To make the pastry dough, sift the flour with the salt. In a small pan, heat the oil, wine, and water until just bearable to touch. Pour the warm liquid into the flour, and knead to a soft, elastic dough ball. Form the dough into a thin roll and divide into 20 pieces. Roll out each piece on a well-floured board into a thin circle the size of a coffee saucer. Dot with a teaspoon of the filling, wet the edges, and fold one half over the other to enclose the filling, pressing down with a fork to seal. Continue until you have 20 little turnovers. Transfer to an greased cookie sheet.

Bake for 15–20 minutes, until crisp and brown.

oysters

Oysters are shore-dependent bivalves with rough shells and delicately flavored, soft, succulent flesh: the cream of the shellfish crop.

Fishing boats in Valparaiso, Chile

Habitat

The oyster is a tidal creature, at home in the alternately salt and sweet waters of estuaries and river mouths.

Appearance and taste

The oyster family divides into two main species: the long narrow-shelled *Crassostrea* (varieties of which include the Portuguese *angulata* and the giant Pacific *gigas*) and *Ostrea* spp., the smaller, smoother, rounder natives—also known as *belón* or plate-oyster—which are considered the more delicate in flavor. A fresh oyster tastes of sea spray, without a hint of fishiness.

Buying and storing

A reliable supplier is the best guarantee of freshness and wholesomeness. Kept cool and damp, oysters can remain alive for as long as they can keep water in their shells: ten days is not unreasonable. Oysters for cooking are perfectly good from the freezer—a process, which, if you freeze your own, has the advantage of opening the shells.

Medicinal and other uses

Oysters are a reputed aphrodisiac. It's something to do with appearance and scent—but I'm sure you can work it out for yourself.

Culinary uses

To open, hold the oyster firmly in a clean cloth, and slip the point of a short, strong knife in around the side of the hinge. It will open with a gentle pop. (It's easier with a specially designed knife with a fist-guard.) Slide the blade across, parallel with the top shell and sever the connector muscle, taking care not to lose any of the delicious juices. Then slip the knife underneath and sever the bottom muscle. To serve raw, leave the oyster on the deeper of the two shells and on no account rinse away all the delicious sea juices. When cooking, save the juices and use them to flavor the sauce.

Chupe de ostras con elote

(Chilean oyster and corn chowder)
Serves 4

A delicate soup in which the sweetness of the corn complements the fresh flavor of the oysters. To make a stock, get about 2 pounds of white-fish bones and heads from your fish market and simmer in a quart of water with a quartered onion, a stick or two of celery, a bay leaf, peppercorns, and salt. After 20 minutes, strain and boil rapidly to reduce to 4 cups of well-flavored stock.

4 cups fish stock
24 oysters
1 1/4 cups fresh corn kernels

To finish:
2 egg yolks
2 tablespoons heavy cream
Salt and pepper
A few basil leaves, torn

If using fresh oysters (frozen are perfectly acceptable), open them carefully and save all the liquid. Bring the fish stock to a boil with the wine, and let it boil for 5 minutes or so, until the steam no longer smells like alcohol. Add the oyster liquid and the corn and simmer for 5 minutes, until the corn is tender.

Slip the oysters with all their juices into the hot soup. Simmer for 3 to 4 minutes, then remove from the heat.

To finish, whisk the egg yolks with the cream, and then whisk in a ladleful of the hot broth. Stir into the soup and reheat gently. Taste, and season with salt and pepper, and serve sprinkled with a few torn leaves of basil. Do not re-boil, or the egg will scramble and the oysters harden.

Seviche de ostras

(Guatemalan oyster seviche)

Serves 4

Guatemala's favorite seviche. In neighboring Mexico, shrimp are often included, while expense dictates an increase in the vegetable quota—avocado, mild green peppers, and tomato often come in a halved avocado. In Ecuador, a conch seviche dressed with bitter orange juice is the morning-after pick-me-up.

2 dozen oysters, shucked and roughly chopped
2 yellow or green chiles, seeded and finely chopped
2–3 scallions, trimmed and roughly chopped
¹/₄ cup lime or lemon juice or white wine vinegar
Salt

For serving:
Chopped cilantro
Pickled chiles
Quartered limes or lemons

Combine all the ingredients, let them marinate for 3 to 4 hours, drain, spoon back into the shells or glass bowls, dress with freshly chopped cilantro, and serve well chilled, with pickled chiles and quartered limes.

Seviche de ostras, a cool salad of marinated oysters

mussels

You can tell the difference between shore- and rope-grown mussels by the clusters of tiny barnacles on the shore-grown ones, the color of the shell, which is blue-black in shore-grown mussels rather than browny-gold, and the shape, which in the shore-grown is shorter and broader than the relatively easy-living rope mussel.

Browny-gold rope-grown mussels

Habitat

The mussel is a prolific breeder that clings to any available sea-washed surface, reaching full maturity in three to four years, colonizing estuaries, rocky promontories, and anywhere a mollusc can find something to cling to while it feeds on passing debris. For this reason, when gathering, make sure you pick a clean shoreline well away from any sewage.

Appearance and taste

Shells are blue-black to honey-gold and the meat is ivory to a deep orange, depending on diet and time of year. Small mussels are more tender than large ones: anything over 3 inches long is inclined to be tough. The taste is sweet, sea-breezy, and only mildly fishy.

Buying and storing

Bivalves can remain alive for as long as they can hold water in their shells. Store them under seaweed in a cool damp place—no longer than a week in a tropical climate, two weeks if the weather is cool and damp.

Medicinal and other uses

There is an official quarantine in North America on all wild bivalves from May 1st to October 1st—the summer months, the breeding season—which, if applied in the Americas of the southern hemisphere, would run roughly from December to March. The quarantine is imposed because mussels, clams, and oysters are filter-feeders that can concentrate quantities of a toxic one-celled organism that "blooms" in warm waters in summer. The toxin, which is not destroyed by freezing or cooking, can be fatal. Aqua-cultured shellfish such as rope-grown mussels are regularly monitored and tested for toxic build up, so can be considered safe throughout the year.

Culinary uses

Mussels are visually dramatic in their blue-black shells with pearly white linings, which cradle plump little orange cushions—particularly when served with a snowy pile of rice. Don't scrub or scrape the mussels until you're ready to cook them: once de-bearded, they die.

Mejillones gratinados

(Broiled mussels)
Serves 4

Big fat bay mussels given a fragrant little hat of parsley and cheese.

2 pounds live mussels in the shell
2 cloves garlic, finely chopped
2 tablespoons finely chopped parsley
1/4 cup fresh white bread crumbs
1/4 cup olive oil
Tabasco or any hot chili sauce
2 tablespoons slivered parmesan or any hard
  cheese

Scrub and de-beard the mussels. Rinse and transfer to a roomy pot with a splash of water. Put the lid on tightly and shake over the heat until the shells open.

Open the mussels completely, leaving the meat on one half of the shells and discarding the other. Arrange neatly on a broiler pan. Sprinkle each mussel with a little garlic, parsley, and bread crumbs, trickle with oil and a shake of chili sauce, and finish with a sliver of cheese. Broil under high heat until the bread crumbs are brown and crisp and the cheese melted.

Mariscada do Baiana

(Mussels with rice and coconut milk)
Serves 6–8

Big fat mussels that thrive on the rocky headlands of the Bay of Bahia are served in a deliciously soupy rice enriched with coconut cream.

2 glasses white wine
1 bay leaf
2¹/₂ quarts mussels, de-bearded and
* scrubbed*
3 tablespoons extra-virgin olive oil
1 large onion, skinned and chopped
2 garlic cloves, finely chopped
2 cups long grain white rice
1 pound skinned, chopped, fresh tomatoes or
* canned plum tomatoes (about 2¹/₂ cups)*
Finely grated peel of an orange
1 tablespoon chopped parsley
1 tablespoon chopped basil
1 teaspoon chopped cilantro
²/₃ cup unsweetened coconut milk
Salt and pepper

For serving:
Malagueta pepper sauce (see page 51)

In a large, heavy pot, bring the wine to a boil with the bay leaf. Add the cleaned shellfish, cover, and steam over high heat until the shells have opened, about 5 minutes. Remove the mussels, discarding any that haven't opened.

Strain and reserve the liquid. Heat the oil in a heavy pan over medium heat and sauté the onion and garlic until translucent. Add the rice and turn it in the hot oil. Add the tomatoes and let it all boil for a couple of minutes. Finally, add the orange peel, mussel liquid, and a mugful of boiling water. Let it return to a boil, cover, and simmer for 10 minutes, stirring from time to time.

Stir in the herbs and season with salt and pepper. Simmer for another 5 minutes and stir in the coconut milk. Return to a boil, add the mussels, and continue cooking until the rice is tender but still soupy—a few more minutes. Hand around the pepper sauce separately.

shrimp, prawn, crayfish, and lobster

All the usual crustaceans, including shrimp, prawns, crayfish, and lobster—both common and spiny—are prolific on the eastern and western shores of the region. Brazil is particularly blessed, as are those parts of the Caribbean where stocks have not been fished to extinction. Lobster, though in short supply on the Atlantic coast, provides a livelihood for the creel-fishermen of Juan Fernández, a volcanic archipelago 500 miles off the coast of Chile, the islands that gave shelter to the shipwrecked Alexander Selkirk, Robinson Crusoe's alter ego.

Appearance and taste

When raw, shrimp and prawns are generally gray-green to almost transparent, though some deep sea species can be a beautiful carmine. All turn browny-pink to a deep red when cooked. The flesh is sweet, fragrant, and, when perfectly fresh, a little chewy. Deep sea lobsters, when uncooked, are a darker blue than those that live in shallower waters. Crawfish—variously called langouste, langoustine, and crayfish—are mottled orange-red when caught and don't noticeably change color in the pot.

Buying and storing

Buy fresh whenever you can. If in the market, buy your lobster live (the tail should snap back when flattened). With shrimp and prawns, check for firmness and bright, black, button-eyes, and use your nose. If already cooked, lobster should have a curl to the tail—a sign it was still lively when popped in the boiling pot; prawns and shrimp should look plump and bright rather than dull and shrunken.

Culinary uses

To cook shrimp or prawns, bring to a boil in plenty of salted water, re-boil, wait for a minute or two until the carapaces turn red, and drain under cold water. To prepare live lobster, shove a sharp instrument into the space between the back of the head and the shell, then plunge it into boiling water, holding it under until the shell reddens and the water re-boils. Allow 15 minutes for a one-pound lobster, 20 minutes for a two-pounder, and so on, adding 10 minutes per pound. Allow it to cool in the cooking water and then split it straight down the middle with a sharp knife. Carefully lift out the dark intestinal sack that runs around down the back, and remove the feathery little "dead men's fingers' (gills) from the head.

Croquetas de gambas

(Shrimp croquettes)
Serves 6–8

Time-consuming, to be sure—but patience is well rewarded by the pleasure of these crisply jacketed little morsels with their melting, creamy hearts. It is best if you make your own stock—simmer the shrimp debris with plenty of onion, carrot, and green celery—though store-bought will do.

*1 pound shelled, cooked shrimp or
  prawns, chopped*
*1/2 mild onion, grated, or 4–5 scallions,
  finely chopped*
1 heaped tablespoon parsley

The sauce:
1/4 cup butter
*1/4 cup flour (more, if you're not
  confident of your skill)*
2 1/2 cups hot fish stock
Salt and cayenne pepper

To finish:
A plateful of seasoned flour
*1–2 eggs, lightly whisked with an equal volume
  of milk*
A plateful of fresh bread crumbs
  Oil for frying

Mix the chopped shrimp or prawns with the onion and parsley.

Melt the butter in a heavy pan. As soon as it froths, stir in the flour. Lower the heat and stir for a moment or two, until it looks sandy (don't let it brown). Whisk in the hot stock in a steady stream, until you have a smooth, thick sauce. Season with salt and cayenne pepper. Continue simmering for 5 minutes to cook the flour. Stir in the prawn mixture, scoop it out and spread it in a dish, let cool, cover with plastic wrap, and set in the refrigerator to firm for an hour or two or overnight. Form the mixture into neat little bite-size pockets—work as quickly and lightly as you can and have a bowl of warm water ready for dipping your hands. Dust the pockets through the flour, dip in the egg and milk mixture, and then roll delicately in the bread crumbs. If there are any bald patches, repeat the egg-and-bread crumbing. Leave in a cool place for 30 minutes to set the coating.

Heat enough oil to submerge the croquetas. Wait until the oil is very hot, then slip one in. If the coating splits open, the oil's too hot. If it stays soft, the oil's too cool. The first croqueta is simply experimental.

Once you have adjusted the heat, fry in batches, a few at a time. Remove and drain as soon as they get crisp and lightly brown. Serve with chili sauce for dipping, or a dish of pickled chiles.

Moqueca de camarão, a spicy shrimp stew enriched with coconut cream

Moqueca de camarão
(Bahian shrimp stew)
Serves 6

The sauce in which the fish is cooked— *moqueca*—**takes its name and approach, steam-cooking, from the** *pokekas,* **the Guarani earth oven. Following the earth-oven principle, the ingredients are simply what's on hand, in any combination. The shrimp can be replaced with chicken and a grander version can be made with lobster; it can even be made with vegetables alone. The two constants are the rice and the finishing with dende oil or oil colored with paprika or anatto.**

1 1/2 pounds fresh raw shrimp or prawns
2 tablespoons vegetable oil
8 ounces chorizo, sliced
1 large onion, finely chopped
2 garlic cloves, skinned and finely chopped
1 red bell pepper, seeded and chopped
1–2 red chiles
1 pound tomatoes, skinned and chopped (about 2 1/2 cups)
2/3 cup coconut milk
Salt

To finish:
Cooked white rice
1 tablespoon dende oil, or vegetable oil colored with anatto or a pinch of paprika

Pick over the shrimp and rinse. Peel them or not, as you please. Heat the oil in a heavy frying pan. Fry the chorizo slices until the fat runs and it browns a little, then remove and set aside.

Add the remaining oil to the hot juices in the pan and fry the onion, garlic, red pepper, and chiles gently until soft—don't let them burn. Add the tomatoes and let it boil, mashing with a wooden spoon to soften the fibers. Add the coconut milk and simmer for 10 minutes until rich and thick. Taste and add salt. Lay the shrimp on top to cook in the steam—a minute or two. Pile on white rice and finish with a trickle of dende or paprika oil.

crab

centolla (spider crab), cangrejo (common crab), caranguejo (Brazilian mangrove crab), siri (common crab)

A round-bodied crustacean with or without claws, the crab varies when alive from pale, almost translucent green to brick red, but it is always red when cooked. Like all crustaceans, the crab is a scavenger.

Habitat

Opportunist and voracious feeders, crabs are found wherever there's a ready source of edible debris—human or piscine—on beaches, rocks, and in shallow waters, with some species—Brazil's mangrove crabs—living their lives on shore. Lobstermen hate them because they devour everything in the creel. Shore fishermen use them for bait and take home the claws that get caught in their nets. Deep-water crabs take refuge in wrecks during storms.

Appearance and taste

Of all the many species of crab, the most interesting gastronomically are the common crab, Cancer sp., including the small-clawed Dungeness native to the Pacific coast as far as Alaska; the blue crab, an Atlantic species found in the Caribbean—also known as the soft-shell for its annual shedding of its carapace; and the spider-crab, more troublesome to pick over but with the sweetest flavor, which is popular in Chile. In Brazil, mangrove crabs, *caranguejo*, are held in high esteem—they are more often found on restaurant menus than sea crabs. All crabs, when cooked, have delicate, slightly sweet, snowy-to-cream flesh that flakes easily.

Crabs for sale by the roadside, São Francisco do Sul, Brazil

Buying and storing

Crabs are available alive (and they must be truly lively—don't pay money for dead meat); cooked and in the shell; as dressed crab—the meat picked and packed back into the shell; or picked, meat only, sold by weight (best for freezing).

Culinary uses

To cook live crabs, allow 12 minutes for a 2-pound crab, brought gently to a boil in unsalted water (add salt as soon as it boils), timed after the water returns to a boil; in a steamer, allow 15 minutes. Once it is cooked, pull the body from the shell and let it drain, cool, and set. Separate the body from the shell, crack off the mouthpiece, and remove the feathery gray gills that fringe the carapace. Now you're ready to pick your crab with whatever you can; use one of the legs as a prodder to get into the corners. As well as the white meat that has to be carefully picked from the body, all crabs have darker, smoother meat just inside the shell: the crab-butter or dark meat. Don't discard this, but incorporate it in your dish. Picked crabmeat is perfect for soups and sauce-based dishes such as croquettes. Soft-shells—molted crab—are best fried whole: there is no need to pick. Mangrove crabs have the most delicate meat and need no sauce: boil and eat with a squeeze of lemon and a shake of malagueta pepper.

Pil-pil de cangrejo

(Chile crab)

Serves 4

Chileans like their seafood—including baby eels and frog's legs—cooked in a little sauce of oil, chile, and garlic, and served so hot you need a little wooden fork to eat it with.

2¹/₂-pound crab, yielding 1 pound meat
4 cloves garlic, slivered
1 teaspoon small dried chiles or 2 fresh chiles, seeded and chopped
²/₃ cup olive oil
1 small glass brandy
Salt

If your crab is alive, bring it gently to a boil in plenty of salted water. Allow 15 minutes for the first pound and 10 minutes for each subsequent pound. Pick all the meat out of the shell and claws: the only nonedible bits are the mouth-piece and the feathery gray gills. Heat the oil in a shallow pan until very hot. Add the garlic and chiles and fry for a moment. Stir in the crabmeat and the brandy. Let it all cook fiercely to evaporate the alcohol.

Jamaican crab patties

Serves 6

Delicious little handheld appetizers—these should be served with a rum punch.

The meat from 1 large crab or 2 smaller ones
2–3 tablespoons oil
4 scallions, rinsed and chopped
1 teaspoon peppercorns, roughly crushed
1 teaspoon turmeric
¹/₂ teaspoon salt
1 tomato, roughly chopped
1 pound puff-pastry
1 egg, beaten

Pick over the crab, discarding any bits of shell. Warm the oil in a frying pan and add the onion and the spices and salt. Stir for a moment. Add the tomato and let it boil, crushing down to make a sauce. Add the crabmeat. Fry gently for a few minutes and set aside to cool.

Preheat the oven to 375°F.

Roll out the puff pastry and cut into hand-size circles with a 3-inch pastry cutter or a wineglass. Put a dab of the crab mixture on each circle, wet the edge, and fold it over to make a semicircular patty. Paint the tops with beaten egg. Bake for 15–20 minutes, until well risen and golden.

Pil-pil de cangrejo, sizzling crabmeat with chile

dried shrimp

or camarão or camarón seco

These sun-dried shrimp are spread out to dry in the warm sea breezes of the coast and sent inland to be enjoyed by those who don't have ready access to the shore. Dried shrimp are important in Brazil and Mexico, both of which have large Catholic populations for whom it is a useful resource for fast days when meat cannot be eaten: the forty days of Lent and the eves of all the saints' days.

Manufacture

In Brazil, dried shrimp are prepared by the shrimp fishermen themselves who rub the catch with a little dende oil and spread it in the sun to dry. To prepare your own, toss fresh shrimp in dende oil (or any oil infused with anatto) and dry in the highest possible oven temperature for 12–20 minutes. Finish under the broiler to crisp the shell (don't let it blacken), then toss with salt. They keep for a week in the refrigerator.

Appearance and taste

Bright red, crunchy, salty but sweet, with a flavor of parmesan and honey, sun-dried shrimp are the ingredient that defines the cooking of Bahia, Brazil's most populous province. In all the fishing villages along the coast, you'll see the fishermen tossing glistening hills of tiny crustaceans dyed bright red with dende oil, raking them over and over again in the scorching sun. At night the heaps are covered with a tarp to protect them from the ocean breeze. The process is repeated for two days until the shells are crisp and crunchy and the flesh tender but still a little chewy. Sometimes they're smoked as well, to add a little extra shelf life.

Buying and storing

Dried shrimp are to be found in West African grocery stores and are readily available in packaged form in Asian grocery stores. The Asian shrimp may be a little chewier than the Bahian version, and will lack the remarkable color of the dende oil, but are perfectly acceptable. Stored in a jar in a cool, dry place, they keep almost indefinitely.

Medicinal and other uses

A long shelf life is dried shrimp's great virtue, delivering protein, minerals, and vitamins that may be in short supply.

Culinary uses

Particularly good as a finishing sprinkle for a bean salad or a soupy dish of rice, dried shrimp add texture as well as flavor. To prepare for any recipe that calls for fresh shrimp, soak in warm water for half an hour to rehydrate.

Casting a fishing net over Lake Vittoria Espíritu Santo, Brazil

Camarón seco con frijole blanco

(Mexican dried shrimp and white beans)
Serves 4

Dried and semidried shrimp—moist and orangey in color—form an important part of fast-day food throughout Latin America. This is a Lenten dish from the beautiful valley of Oaxaca in Central Mexico, where fresh fish is hard to come by.

1¹/2 cups dried shrimp
2 large tomatoes, skinned (or 1 can plum
  tomatoes)
1 small onion, roughly chopped
4–5 garlic cloves, chopped
3 tablespoons sunflower oil, sesame seed oil,
  or pumpkin seed oil
2¹/2–2³/4 cups cooked, drained white navy beans
2–3 epasote leaves or dill fronds

Put the dried shrimp to soak in a little warm water for 10 minutes, then drain. Blend the tomatoes to a thick pulp along with the onion, garlic, and a little water until smooth. Heat the oil in a frying pan, add the puréed tomato, and simmer until thick—about 15 minutes.

Stir the tomato mixture into the soft beans along with the epazote or dill. Stir in the shrimp, add a cupful of boiling water, and simmer until the shrimp are tender—10 minutes, no more.

Serve with soft tortillas for scooping, Mexican style. A ripe avocado, roughly mashed with a little salt and lime juice, would be an appropriate accompaniment.

Camarón seco con frijole blanco, a white bean salad topped with crunchy shrimp

Vatapá

(Bahian dried shrimp relish)
Serves 4–6

A relish or dipping sauce, vatapá is made with crushed nuts, coconut milk, and sun-dried shrimp, thickened with bread and served with seafood in much the same way as mayonnaise. It is eaten as street food with acarajé, black-eyed pea fritters (see page 77), or—for more formal dining—a skewerful of barbecued shrimp, a fish stew, or a grilled lobster. Vatapá is also used to thicken the juices of Bahia's surf-n-turf dishes—pork and shrimp, poultry and prawns—and is indispensable with a shrimp moqueca (see page 139) or to thicken the juices of a chicken-and-shrimp xin-xim (see page 173).

1/2 pound day-old, dried-out white bread (about 6–8 slices)
1¹/4 cups coconut milk
1 cup dried shrimp
1 cup roasted cashews and roasted peanuts
1 walnut-size piece fresh ginger, grated
Salt and malagueta pepper sauce (see
  page 51)

To finish:
Juice of half a lime
1 tablespoon dende oil or any oil with achiote

Crumble the bread, soak with the coconut milk, and let it swell for at least an hour.

Put the shrimp and the nuts in a mortar or a food processor and pound, or blend, to a powder. Mix with the soaked bread in a heavy pot, and transfer to the stovetop. Add the ginger, season with salt and malagueta pepper, dilute with a glass of water, and, over medium heat, let it boil, turn down the heat, and cook gently for about 10 minutes, until thick and smooth. Beat in the juice of half a lime and a trickle of oil. The consistency should be light and soft rather than dense and porridge-like—a little more coconut cream will lighten it if necessary. Serve with quartered limes, plain boiled rice, and farofa (see page 60), for sprinkling.

large steak fish

Swordfish, tuna, shark, dolphin-fish: these are the predators, the lords of the ocean, using all the world's waters as both thoroughfare and food source.

tuna steak

Habitat

These migratory fish are to be found wherever a food source can be assured, particularly near the large coastal cities, where smaller fish find nourishment among the effluent.

Appearance and taste

The firm, steaklike flesh ranges from the pure-white flesh of the swordfish to the deep ruby red of the tuna.

Buying and storing

The larger the fish, the longer its shelf life—a fact that is both a blessing and a curse. On the one hand, steak fish comes fresher to market than its smaller cousins. On the other hand, it's more difficult to tell the good from the almost-bad. Use your nose and finger. Steak fish should smell sweet—never like ammonia—and be firm to the touch.

Medicinal and other uses

Tuna and dolphin-fish—mahi-mahi—contain measurable quantities of histidine, an amino acid that turns to histamine when the fish is caught in tropical waters and not properly cooled and stored. Histamine poisoning—the main symptoms are flushing, dizziness, and a headache—can be treated with antihistamines, which make the effects quickly disappear.

Culinary uses

Throughout the territory, but particularly on the Pacific coast, fresh fish—filleted and diced, or beaten to tenderize—is eaten raw in the form of seviche: small pieces of fish marinated in an acid bath, a remarkably rapid process. In pre-Columbian times, before the Europeans planted citrus groves, the marinade was the juice of the indigenous passion fruit.

Reed fishing boats drying on a Peruvian beach

Seviche de atún peruviana

(Lime-marinated tuna)

Serves 6

In Peru, a seviche is served as a full meal with a variety of accompaniments.

1 pound fresh tuna, skinned and diced
1 level teaspoon sea salt or kosher salt

For the dressing:
6 tablespoons lime or bitter orange juice
1 mild onion, chopped
3 tablespoons peanut oil
2 tablespoons roughly crushed toasted
  peanuts
1 fresh red chile, seeded and finely chopped

Dice the fish and turn it with the salt in a bowl. Mix the dressing ingredients together and toss them with the fish. Cover and leave in a cool place for at least an hour to absorb the flavors. Taste, adjust the seasoning, and finish with a little more oil. Serve with slices of cooked sweet potatoes and corn, shredded lettuce, fresh or pickled chiles, and onion rings soaked to soften in a little salted water.

Budín de cazón

(Baked fish pudding)

Serves 6–8

Shark meat—*cazón***, dogfish—straight from the blue waters of the bay of Mexico, is a favorite of the housewives of Campeche who prepare it as a** *sopa seca* **or dry soup. Here it's given a quick oven-gilding, much like a lasagne. Any other firm white fish can be substituted.**

1 pound shark meat (dogfish) or any
  firm-fleshed white fish
1 onion, thickly sliced
1 bay leaf
1 stalk epazote or dill (optional)
1 tablespoon white wine vinegar
Salt

To finish:
6–8 wheat tortillas, cut into squares
6 tablespoons unsalted butter

Seviche de atún peruviana

6 chiles poblanos, charred, seeded, and cut
  into ribbons
2¹/₂ cups fresh tomato sauce
1¹/₄ cups sour cream
¹/₄ cup grated white cheese (cheddar is fine)

Preheat the oven to 400°F.

Poach the fish in the aromatics, vinegar, salt, and enough water to cover in a lidded pan. When the fish is firm and opaque— 8 to 10 minutes—remove and let the poaching liquid boil until it is reduced to a couple of tablespoons. Skin, bone, and flake the fish, and moisten it with the poaching liquid.

Meanwhile, fry batches of the tortilla pieces in a little of the butter, until golden and crisp, and set aside. Heat the tomato sauce in the remaining butter and let it boil, mashing down to thicken, and set aside.

Assemble the budín. Cover the bottom of a gratin dish with half the tortilla pieces and top with a layer of shredded fish, chile ribbons, and half the tomato sauce. Follow with a layer of the remaining tortilla pieces, then the rest of the sauce, and finish with the sour cream and the cheese. Bake in the oven for 20–25 minutes, until deliciously brown and bubbling.

medium-size, round-bodied whole fish

Sea bass, congrio, scrod, mullet, and grouper are all white-fleshed fish that can be cooked whole.

Appearance and taste

Sea bass and related fish of the drummer family—*Sciaenidae*—whose means of communication is a loud drumming sound produced by snapping their air bladders, are slender, round-bodied, silver-scaled fish with easily visible bones and flesh, which cooks to large creamy flakes. Congrio is not, as it would be in Spain, an eel but a big-headed, narrow-bodied member of the grouper family that looks and cooks like monkfish: firm, white, and dense.

Buying and storing

An open mouth and gaping gills are a sign a fish is very fresh. The most sought after members of this group are close to being

fished beyond recovery. Among these, the corvina or Chilean sea bass, *Dissostichus eleginoides*, also known as the Patagonian toothfish and Australian sea bass, has been fished to the edge of its sustainable level—in other words, we shouldn't be eating it at all. A great many very fine fish are sold under the general name of sea bass—go for the farmed varieties.

Medicinal and other uses

Fish is the ideal food. Without going into detail, this is practically fat-free, unadulterated protein in easily digestible form: in other words, all a person needs to sustain life in one easy package. The only part of a fish that can be toxic is the liver, although it is a delicacy in some, such as skate and members of the cod family; it is best avoided unless you're sure of your species.

Culinary uses

All fish share the same anatomy, a basic knowledge of which will help you deal with unfamiliar species. The spine—a jointed, highly flexible central bone from which grow finer lateral bones that support the flesh and provide an anchor for the dorsal fins—runs from head to tail. When the fish is raw, pressing along the spine loosens the flesh ready for filleting. When cooked whole, the flesh can be lifted off the bone without disturbing the central spine or the lateral bones (which also form the rib cavity). Easy does it.The cheeks are a delicacy, as is the sweet, just behind the head—one reason for cooking the fish with its head on.

Fishing boats, Ciudad de Carmen, Mexico

Causa a la chiclayana
(Fisherman's seafood platter)
Serves 6

A Peruvian assembly of fish, potatoes, cheese, eggs, and vegetables—a fisherman's dish, made with whatever swam into the net too late or too early to sell at the market. All are welcome, none indispensable.

1¹/2 pounds congrio or monkfish fillets
1 tablespoon seasoned flour
¹/4 cup olive oil
2 pounds yellow-fleshed potatoes,
  peeled and cut into chunks (about 6–7 cups)
2 tablespoons finely chopped parsley
1 garlic clove, finely chopped
Salt

Vegetable accompaniments:
2 fresh ears of corn, each broken into 3 pieces
1 pound sweet potato, peeled and thickly sliced
1 pound cassava root, peeled and thickly sliced
3 ripe plantains, peeled and sliced lengthwise,
  then crosswise
oil for frying plantains

Dressing:
3 onions, finely sliced
2 hot red chiles, seeded and cut into strips
¹/2 cup white wine vinegar
¹/2 cup olive oil

For serving:
Crisp lettuce leaves
3 hard-boiled eggs, quartered
6 slices fresh white cheese
A handful black olives

Lightly salt the fish fillets, dredge through the seasoned flour, and fry quickly in half the oil for a minute or two, turning once, until firm and a little golden. Remove and place on paper towels and set aside. Boil the potatoes in plenty of salted water until tender—about 20 minutes. Drain, mash with the parsley, garlic, and remaining oil, and heap in the middle of a serving dish.

Meanwhile, attend to the vegetables: boil the corn without salt for 5 minutes; boil the sweet potato and cassava until tender—about 30 minutes; and fry the plantains in a little oil until they brown. Arrange all the accompaniments on a serving dish around the mashed potato.

Now make the dressing. In a small pan, bring the onions and chile strips to a boil in enough salted water to cover. Drain, return to the pan, and add the vinegar and oil. Bring to a boil and pour the hot dressing over the mashed potato. Arrange the lettuce leaves around the edge of the platter and top with the fish fillets, hard-boiled eggs, cheese slices, and olives.

Corvina colombiana

Corvina colombiana

(Sea bass baked in coconut milk)
Serves 4–6

Simple but delicious: the coconut milk keeps the fish moist and makes its own creamy sauce. Any medium-size, round-bodied, white-fleshed fish will do—bream and congrio are also excellent candidates—so long as your choice is beautifully fresh and bright-eyed.

1 whole fish, 3–4 pounds
Salt
1 yellow or red chile, seeded and finely chopped
1 sprig thyme
2–3 whole heads fresh fennel (or 6 baby fennel), sliced lengthwise
1 large onion, finely sliced
2 1/2 cups coconut milk

sea bass

Rinse the fish inside and out, season the cavity with salt and a few scraps of chopped chile, and tuck in the sprig of thyme.

Preheat the oven to 350°F. Lay the fish on a bed of fennel in an oval heat-proof casserole dish with a lid (or use a roasting pan and cover with foil). Cover with sliced onion, season with salt and the remaining chile, and pour the coconut milk around it. Bake for 45–55 minutes, until the flesh is firm when pressed. The time it takes is dictated by thickness rather than weight.

medium-size, flat-bodied whole fish

bream

Species in this category include bream, porgy, snapper (sometimes known as redfish), and dorado (a name applied to bream on the West Coast but to dolphin-fish, otherwise known as mahi-mahi, in the Caribbean).

Habitat

These fish are found in harbors, estuaries, and tidal waters as well as deep sea. As a child in Uruguay, I used to fish half-pound dorado—young gilt-head bream—off the harbor wall at Punta del Este, now a fashionable seaside resort but at the time, in the 1950s, a small fishing village at the mouth of the River Plate.

Appearance and taste

These flat-bodied fish of medium size share one important culinary characteristic: their bodies are compressed—flattened—allowing them to be quickly cooked without needing to be filleted or cut into steaks. Although they don't fetch high prices in the market, they're excellent everyday eating, succulent and sweet-fleshed.

Buying and storing

Look for a bright eye, flesh that is firm to the finger, and a clean, sweet sea-scent.

Red snapper for sale on the pier in La Libertad, El Salvador

Medicinal and other uses

While all sea creatures are edible, a few store up toxins in their livers or ovaries—a protective measure against predators. Two of the Pacific's coastal fish have poisonous roes, the cabezón and the alligator garfish.

Culinary uses

The most valuable characteristic of these flat-bodied fish is their shape—even the largest can be poached, steamed, baked, or fried in no more than 10 minutes.

Patacones del pescador

(Fisherman's fishcakes)
Serves 4–6

Easy, convenient, delicious, and cheap: make these spicy fishcakes with leftovers or frozen fish if you can't find fresh.

The fritters:
8 ounces flaked, cooked fish
1¹/₂ pounds potatoes, cut into chunks
1 mild onion, grated
2 tablespoons grated cheese
3 eggs
1 tablespoon pimentón (mild paprika)
1 teaspoon chili flakes
Olive oil for frying

The salsa:
1 green chile, seeded and finely chopped
1 mild onion, finely chopped
2 garlic cloves, finely chopped
6 tablespoons finely chopped parsley
2 lemons, juice and peel
1 teaspoon sugar

Boil the potatoes in enough salted water to cover. Drain and mash thoroughly with the grated onion and cheese. Beat in the eggs and mix in the flaked fish, and season with pimentón, chili, and a little salt. Refrigerate for half an hour.

Meanwhile, combine the salsa ingredients and set aside in a cool place to marinate—the flavors need a little time to blend.

Heat a panful of olive oil for shallow frying. When very hot, drop in teaspoonfuls of the fish mixture—not too many at a time. Wait until they puff and turn golden, turn them over once, then remove with a slotted spoon and drain on paper towels. Serve straight from the pan, with the salsa handed around separately.

Brotola al horno

(Oven-baked bream with root vegetables)
Serves 4

This is the way Esperanza, my mother's cook in Uruguay, liked to prepare the morning's catch. Because my father was a diplomat, we were the proud owners of the first electric oven in Montevideo, and Esperanza made the most of it. Any of the medium-size estuary fish can be given the same treatment, accompanied by any root vegetables, though an element of sweetness is essential.

1 sea bream or porgy, weighing about
2 pounds cleaned weight, head left on
1 pound sweet potatoes, peeled and
cut into chunks (3–3^1/$_2$ cups)
1 pound potatoes, peeled and cut into chunks
(3–3^1/$_2$ cups)
1 pound smallish yellow onions, skinned
and quartered (about 3–4 cups)
1 pound ripe firm tomatoes, cut into chunks
(about 2^1/$_2$ cups)
^{1}/$_2$ cup dry white wine
^{1}/$_4$ cup olive oil
coarse salt and chili flakes

Rinse the fish, salt the cavity, and set aside until it reaches room temperature.

Preheat the oven to 350°F.

Arrange the vegetables in a roasting pan, pour in the wine, trickle with the oil, and finish with a liberal dusting of salt and chili flakes. Cover with foil, shiny-side down. Bake for 20 minutes, until the vegetables are nearly tender. Carefully remove the foil. Place the fish on the bed of vegetables, sprinkle the fish with salt and chili flakes, replace the foil, and bake for another 10 minutes, until the fish is cooked right through. It's ready when it feels firm to your finger. Remove and set it to one side for another 10 minutes, so that the heat can penetrate right through to the bone.

small fish and fry

fresh anchovies

Sardines, anchovies, herring, pejerreyes (the Chilean smelt), and the small fry of larger fish are the bread-and-butter of the inshore fishing fleets. A short shelf life—the result of natural oiliness and relatively small size—means that the catch, unless salted or preserved in some other way, stays close to home.

Habitat

Small fish—shoal fish whose survival strategy depends on numbers—provide larger fish with a food source. Find one, and you'll find the other. Perhaps because of this, the movements of small fish shoals are notoriously unpredictable, but when you catch one, you catch plenty. While fritter-fish are usually a sea harvest, the small, silver Chilean smelt, very delicate and delicious, is found in rivers and lakes as well as the ocean.

Appearance and taste

Sardines are silver all over, with large, visible scales that loosen and flake off as the fish deteriorates; they have short, blunt heads and shiny, dark eyes, and the heads take on a bloody look the longer they've been out of the water. In size, they vary from small as your thumb to twice as long as your hand. Anchovies and smelts are noticeably more slender, with small, pointed heads and no visible scales. The anchovy has a dark stripe down the flanks and a distinctly emerald sheen.

Buying and storing

Small oily fish are vulnerable to spoilage: it is best to buy as close to the fishing grounds as possible—or pay a good price to a reliable fish seller. When buying on the harbor front, test for freshness by dipping a finger in the brine and touching it to your tongue; if the run-off is noticeably salty, the fishermen have waited too long on the tide.

Casting nets over Lake Janit-Zio, Mexico

Medicinal and other uses

The virtues of oily fish are well-known: they are rich in protein, vitamins, minerals, and those all-important omega fatty acids that help in the prevention of heart disease.

Culinary uses

Small fish with a high fat content deteriorate quickly—a matter of hours rather than days. Until refrigeration was available, ingenuity was needed to make the catch last long enough to get it to market. One solution was salting and barreling, which led in turn to the sardine-canning industry. The canning factories of Baja California—made famous in John Steinbeck's stories of Cannery Row—were established to take advantage of the huge hauls of sardines and anchovies landed by the fishermen of the Sea of Cortez. One day, the silvery hoards simply vanished—no one knows where or why—and the industry with it.

Choose the preparation method appropriate to the size. Flour and deep-fry the tiny ones—head, guts, scales, and all (sardine and smelt scales slip off easily with a little encouragement under the tap); medium-size fish can be butterflied: slit the fish down the belly with your thumb and remove the backbone and innards along with the head; anchovies never grow too large to fritter, while large sardines are best kept for the grill.

Pescaítos fritos
(Little fried fish)
Serves 4

A blend of wheat flour and cornmeal produces a deliciously crisp crust, especially if you twice-fry them. The real secret is the absolute freshness of the raw materials: the smaller the fish, the shorter its shelf life. This treatment is suitable for all fish of any breed so long as they're no longer than your hand: sardines, smelts, squid, snapper, as well as fillets of larger fish.

1 pound fresh anchovies
1/4 cup flour
1 heaped tablespoon cornmeal
1 heaped teaspoon coarse salt
a sprinkling of crushed, dried oregano (optional)
Olive or vegetable oil for frying

For serving:
Quartered lemons

Gut the fish (unnecessary if they're tiny) and leave the heads on if the fish are no longer than your thumb. If they're larger, run your finger down the backbone to loosen, and pull it out, leaving the two halves joined. Nip the heads off. Rinse and drain but don't pat dry.

Mix the flour with the cornmeal, salt, and optional oregano on a flat plate.

Heat the frying oil in a pan—Hispanic cooks only use as much as will submerge the food to be cooked. When the oil is hot enough to fry (a faint blue haze will rise from the surface), flip the wet fish through the flour one by one and drop them in the hot oil. Fry in small batches to avoid the temperature dropping, and remove while still quite pale. Transfer to paper towels to drain. Continue until all are done. Repeat the process, frying all the fish once more, to crisp and color them.

Serve piping hot with quartered lemons, a plate of fries, and a salad of diced tomatoes, onion, and cucumber, just as they do in the harbor-front cafés of Valparaiso.

Pescaítos fritos, crisply jacketed little fried fish

Pejerreyes en vinagre
(Vinegar-pickled smelts)
Serves 4 as an appetizer

This is a good recipe for the larger small fish, caught by the inshore fishing fleets who sell them fast and cheap in the morning market. This—a light pickle—adds at least a week to the shelf life in a cool pantry, even without refrigeration. Start 48 hours ahead.

1 pound fresh smelts (or anchovies or sardines)
2/3 cup white wine vinegar
2 tablespoons water
1 tablespoon salt
2–3 garlic cloves, cut into fine slivers
1 green chile, seeded and finely chopped

To finish:
1 tablespoon olive oil
2 tablespoons flat-leaf parsley

Rinse the smelts and drain thoroughly. Press lightly down the body of the fish to loosen the flesh from the bones. Holding the head firmly between finger and thumb, pull down through the belly toward the tail. The spine and ribs should slip easily through the soft flesh, gutting and splitting all in one movement. Nick the spine at the base of the tail, leaving the tail still attached. Continue until all the fish are gutted and butterflied.

Open each fish flat and lay it, flesh upward, in a single layer in a shallow dish. Mix the vinegar with the water and salt, and pour over the fish—they should be well-soaked. Sprinkle with the garlic and chile, cover with foil, and leave in the refrigerator to marinate for 48 hours. (They will keep for a week in the refrigerator.) To serve, drain and finish with a trickle of olive oil and a sprinkle of parsley.

flatfish

Flounder, sole, brill, turbot, halibut, plaice, dab: a family of many faces—all of which are worn on one side of the head, a convenient arrangement for a fish that feeds on the sea-bed, allowing it to keep both eyes out for predators.

Habitat

Flatfish are bottom-feeders, subsisting on a delicate diet of sand-burrowers.

Appearance and taste

Some flatfish, such as the sole and the flounder, which are dextral flatfish, have their faces on the right side of the body, while others, sinistral flatfish, a group that includes turbot and brill, have theirs on the left. The flesh is pure white and lean in all species, the texture threadlike rather than flaky, though firmness and delicacy of flavor varies.

Buying and storing

Buy on the bone and make sure the flesh is firm and the skin veiled rather than slimy, with the tiny scales still firmly attached. As for quality, let price be your guide: the firmer and sweeter and thicker the flesh, the higher the price.

Culinary uses

Flatfish have, as their name suggests, a long, flat skeleton that makes it easy to lift the flesh from the bone once it's cooked. Some flatfish can be filleted easily when raw, while others, the cheaper varieties, are harder. For reasons of camouflage, the top skin is dark and beautifully patterned and the underside is pale; the upper skin is relatively easy to pull off, the underside is harder. This matters little if grilling or poaching the fish whole, but is less convenient when filleting.

Buñuelos de pescado

(Seafood fritters)

Serves 4–6 as an appetizer

An easy solution to the problem of what to do with the lesser members of the flatfish family—all that skin and bone and very little else. You'll need more than 2 pounds of fish to get 4 tablespoons of meat. Don't bother to gut or trim, simply poach or bake in foil, then separate the flesh from the rest.

About 4 tablespoons cooked, flaked fish
2 pounds floury potatoes, scrubbed
1 small onion, very finely chopped
2 tablespoons finely chopped parsley
1 chile, seeded and finely chopped
3 eggs
Salt
A little milk (optional)
Oil for frying

Pick over the fish, discarding any stray bones.

Cook the potatoes until tender in plenty of salted water. Drain, skin, and mash well. Beat the fish into the mashed potato with the onion, parsley, and chile. Add the eggs one by one, beating between each addition. The mixture should be so stiff a spoon can stand up in it. Add a little milk if it's too dry and let it cool completely.

Preheat a panful of oil to the point where a cube of bread crisps and browns immediately.

Using two wet spoons, shape the fish mixture into egg-size patties and drop them directly into the hot oil in batches, no more than will comfortably float on the surface. Flip them over several times to puff and brown. Reheat the oil between batches. Drain on paper towels and serve piping hot with a dipping sauce—peanut, chile, tomato, or whatever strikes your fancy.

sole, the king of the flatfish tribe

El biche

(Ecuadorian bouillabaisse)

Serves 4–6

A delicate fish soup finished with chopped peanuts, fortified with banana dumplings and new potatoes.

1 pound flatfish fillets
Salt
5 cups fish stock (made with a fishhead)
1/4 cup oil
2–3 white onions, finely chopped
1 teaspoon cumin seeds
1 teaspoon crushed hot chili
1 pound new potatoes

Banana dumplings:
2 green bananas or plantains, grated
3 tablespoons toasted, crushed peanuts
2–3 tablespoons fish stock
1 tablespoon chopped cilantro

To finish:
3–4 green bell peppers, roughly chopped
1 cup peas
1/4 cup toasted, crushed peanuts
1 lemon, grated peel and juice
2 tablespoons chopped cilantro

Salt the fish fillets and set them aside. Strain the fish stock, heat the oil in a big pan, and add the onions. Cook gently until the onion softens. Sprinkle with cumin seeds and chili. Add the fish stock and potatoes and simmer for 20 minutes.

Meanwhile, work the grated banana with the peanuts, cilantro, and enough fish stock to make a dozen little balls. Slip the balls into the simmering broth and add peppers and peas.

When all is tender, add the peanuts and stir. Slip the fish fillets into the broth and let them become firm and opaque—three to four minutes. Taste and season. Finish with lemon juice and peel and a sprinkling of cilantro.

oil-rich fish

mackerel, bonito, salmon, kingfish, herring

Pacific mackerel—*sierra*—is plentiful on the West Coast, while the Eastern Seaboard has bonito, shad, and Atlantic mackerel. The native salmons are the Pacific Chinook and the smaller silver salmon. As stocks in the wild vanish through overfishing, farmed salmon has become an important export crop and a major source of Chilean fishermen's income. Those who live in the Andean uplands stock their lakes with trout—*trucha*—an alternative method of ensuring a good fish dinner.

mackerel

Appearance and taste

Mackerel is one of the most handsome fish in the ocean: long, slender, and silver, with no visible scales and dramatically black-patterned, blue-green flanks. Salmon is silver from top to "toe" with rose-pink flesh, a rich flavor, and a fragrance reminiscent of its main food source, shrimp. Really fresh salmon has a creamy curd between flakes; the flesh is pink and falls into large flakes when cooked. Color is simply a matter of diet: overly red flesh in a farmed salmon is a sign of too many additives in its feed; the paler the flesh, the more likely it's wild-caught. Farmed salmon can be flabby if not given sufficient space to swim against the current. Mackerel is strong meat, with a distinctively cod-liver-oil flavor, and flesh that separates into strings.

Buying and storing

To choose fresh, whole fish, check the brightness of the eyes and the color and scent of the gills—you're looking for a deep crimson with a fresh seaweed scent.

Medicinal and other uses

Oil-rich fish are a prime source of omega-3 fatty acids, which are good for our hearts, brains, and eyesight. A word of warning: salmon—both wild and farmed—is occasionally infested with tapeworm, and is therefore not recommended for seviches unless preliminary precautions are taken. If you want to use salmon in a seviche, first freeze it for 24 hours.

Culinary uses

Oily fish can be baked, steamed, poached, or included in a soup—but grilling and frying suits its character. Fish from the freezer is excellent hot-smoked, treatment for which mackerel and bonito as well as salmon and any large river fish are suitable.

Salmon ahumado

(Hot-smoked salmon)
Serves 6

Hot-smoking—the application of heat and smoke to food in a closed pot or earth oven—is a technique familiar to the river peoples of the Amazonian basin. In the absence of any form of refrigeration, hot-smoking was used for practical rather than epicurean reasons, to add a little shelf life to the river catch. Since river dwellers had no salt, the addition of salt in this recipe is a modern refinement.

A whole small salmon, about 3–4 pounds. cleaned, scaled, with the head left on
4–5 tablespoons salt
Sawdust for smoking or dry rice and green tea

You'll need a fish poacher or a large turkey-roasting pan with a grill rack on the bottom.

Rinse the fish and pat dry. Remove the dark red vein that runs down the bone inside the cavity. Sprinkle with the salt, inside and out. Leave in a cool place for a couple of hours. Let it come back to room temperature and dust off any excess salt. Line the fish poacher or roasting pan with foil, shiny side down. Sprinkle in a layer of the smoking material—sawdust or rice and tea—about ¼-inch thick. Place the rack on top of the smoking material and settle the fish on the rack. Put the lid on tightly or cover securely with a double layer of foil.

Place the container over a high heat—you'll probably need two burners—and wait until you can smell the smoke. Turn the burners down to medium, open the window, and leave the kitchen. Allow 15 minutes for steam to build up and penetrate the fish. Remove from the heat (without opening) and set aside—outside would be even better. The fish will continue to cook as it cools. Your reward for a smoke-wreathed kitchen will be moist, succulent flesh with an exquisitely delicate flavor. Serve at room temperature, with a chile-peanut salsa, baked plantains, and roasted sweet potatoes.

Sierra en escabeche

(Hot-pickled mackerel)
Serves 4

As a method of conservation in prerefrigeration days, a spiced pickle-bath was not only useful but added variety to the diet. A Mexican recipe in the Hispanic tradition.

2 large or 4 small mackerel, gutted and
* beheaded*
Salt
1 heaped tablespoon of flour
2 tablespoons of olive oil
¹/₂ onion, skinned and finely sliced
1 garlic clove, skinned and crushed
1 mild green chile, sliced
1 tablespoon chopped parsley
1 bay leaf, torn
6 peppercorns, roughly crushed
3–4 sprigs thyme
¹/₄ cup sherry vinegar (or any other
* good vinegar)*
2 tablespoons water

Chop each mackerel straight through the bone to give four to six thick steaks (your fish seller will do this for you). Sprinkle with salt and dust with flour. Heat the oil in a shallow frying pan, put in the fish, and fry gently until golden and firm (4 to 8 minutes depending on thickness).

Transfer to a wide shallow dish. Add the onion, garlic, and sliced chile to the oil remaining in the pan (or a little new oil, if using leftovers) and fry gently for a few moments so that the flavors blend. Add the remaining ingredients and let

the mixture boil. Pour this warm scented liquid, unstrained, over the fish. Cover loosely with a clean cloth, and leave overnight, at least, in the refrigerator. Ready to eat in a day, but better in two.

Sierra en escabeche, mackerel steaks marinated in a fragrant vinegar bath

cephalopods

Cephalopod means head-footed, of which two members, squid and octopus, are found throughout the region. A squid has ten legs; an octopus has eight. Both are highly intelligent predators. While squid are shoal fish, hunting in packs, the octopus is solitary, hugging the rocks and inlets.

Appearance and taste

Squid is eaten at all stages of maturity, from pin-head to more than three feet in length; occasionally giant specimens, kraken, are washed up from the deep. Immature squid can be floured, fried, and eaten whole, including their tiny ink sacs, which dye everything jet black and have a faint flavor of violets. When more mature, the flesh is chewy, sweet, and white—but only if you take care to remove the ink sacs (save them to cook with rice). Octopus, whose interior bone has been reduced to a small sharp beak, is a more daunting task since it needs to be thoroughly pounded, although a spell in the freezer has the same effect.

Cleaned squid, Panama

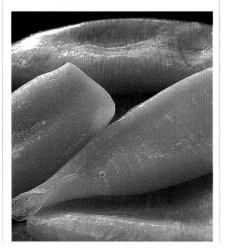

Buying and storing

Squid is a commercial crop landed by the inshore fishing fleets: meet the boats when they dock. The octopus, too smart for the net, is line-caught, a rowing boat crop, brought home on the tide and thrashed to tenderness against the harbor wall. Buy fresh and cook immediately, or gut, slice, and freeze.

Medicinal and other uses

For all practical purposes, octopus and squid are fat-free.

Culinary uses

Anatomy is important when preparing the cephalopods. Squid has no bone but a clear plastic-like quill. The tentacles have little circular "toenails" embedded in their suckers that need to be scraped loose. To gut, pull the tentacles from the caplike outer body, bringing the soft innards with them. Trim off the innards just below the eyes, and discard. Scrape and rinse off the violet membrane that veils the cap. Slice the cap into rings and chop the tentacles—or not, depending on size. Rinse your hands in cold water afterward so they don't smell fishy.

squid

Pulpo en escabeche

(Pickled octopus)

Serves 6–8

Fishermen don't easily give away their secrets, but here it is: "First catch your octopus. When you have caught it, throw it forty times against a rock. Fewer times are needed if it's small, more if it's large. First the flesh is hard, but slowly it softens. Now you must rinse it in seawater so that it foams. Unless you do this, it will never soften. You'll know when it's ready because the tentacles will curl. You must not take off the skin as so many ignorant people do. The skin turns red when you cook it, and this is what tells you it is fresh and good. To prepare for an escabeche, put it in a pan and cook it gently with a ladleful of sea water until it's perfectly tender. The alternative is a few days in the freezer."

2 pounds tenderized octopus
1¹/₄ cups water
1 tablespoon salt

For the dressing:
6 tablespoons extra virgin olive oil
Juice 2 lemons
A handful of oregano, leaves only
1 crumbled dried red chile
Salt and pepper

Cook the octopus in the water with the salt until soft—30 to 40 minutes. Keep the water just trembling; don't let it boil. Let cool in its broth, then drain and chop into bite-size pieces. Toss with the dressing ingredients.

Cazuela de calamar

(Squid casserole)

Serves 4–6

A Chilean way with the cephalopod. One of those dishes for which there is a perfect moment: when you dip into a squid shoal, you catch plenty. The recipe can be made with octopus, though the eight-armed sea monster needs a good preliminary pounding to tenderize it.

1¹/₂ pounds squid (calamari)
3–4 tablespoons olive oil
4–5 cloves garlic, skinned and chopped
2–3 celery stalks, diced
1 red and 1 green bell pepper, seeded and diced
1–2 fresh yellow chiles, seeded and finely chopped
¹/₄ cup fresh peas
1 pound small yellow potatoes, scrubbed and diced (about 3–3¹/₂ cups)
1 teaspoon oregano
2–3 bay leaves
¹/₂ bottle dry white wine
¹/₄ cup heavy cream
Salt

Cazuela de calamar

Pick over and rinse the squid. If preparing your own, see Culinary uses.

Warm the oil in a roomy saucepan and add the chopped garlic. When the garlic begins to sizzle, add the fish. Stir over the heat for a few minutes until the flesh stiffens and turns opaque.

Add the vegetables, herbs, and wine, bring to a boil, turn down the heat, cover loosely, and let it simmer gently for about 40 minutes, until all is tender and the juices well-reduced. Taste, season, and stir in the cream.

gastropods

Gastropods, that weird company of one-footed sea creatures that includes abalone, conch, sea urchins, barnacles, snails, and slugs, grow fat and sweet on the transparent pin-head shrimp, shoals that drift through the Straits of Magellan on the icy tides of the Humboldt Current.

Habitat

The rocky cliffs of coastal Chile, which plunge steeply to the depths mirroring the steepness of the mountains above, provide a precarious perch for all manner of sea creatures, including the prized abalone—most of which goes to the sushi bars of Japan.

Appearance and taste

Chilean notables are *locos*—giant abalone; *choritos*—small black-shelled mussels; *machas*—razor-shells; *picorocos* ("stick-to-the-rocks"), giant rough-shelled barnacles that taste like lobster; and *ostras*—delicious little cold-water oysters. But the star of the show is the *erizo* or sea-hedgehog, a sea urchin that achieves an astonishing size: some are as large as a football—one per person is certainly enough; only the females are of gastronomic interest since it's just the five little ovaries that are eaten. Conch, also known as *lambi*, is appreciated in the Caribbean: a large reddish-colored sea snail with bright yellow eyes, it lives in a beautiful rose-tinted shell: its meat, when thoroughly beaten to tenderize, is said to be sweeter than clam.

Buying and storing

Freshness is everything. Buy live and store in a cool place for the minimum amount of time. Never eat a shellfish that is already dead.

Medicinal and other uses

Shipwrecked sailors can survive for years on a diet of mollusc—as did thousands of coastal dwellers for centuries. Some people suffer from shellfish allergies triggered by toxins either inherent in the fish or produced by parasites. Once acquired, the allergy is unlikely to go away.

Culinary uses

Abalone, which must first be tenderized by pounding, can be eaten raw or lightly cooked (long cooking toughens it). It is delicious sliced, dipped in egg and bread crumbs, and fried in very hot oil. The same rules apply to all other shellfish: at its simplest, eat raw with a squeeze of lemon; if applying heat, make it brief and don't reheat.

Mariscal

(Chilean seafood platter with green sauce)
Serves a party

A seafood selection as served straight from boat to plate and opened to order in the picadas—the little harborside restaurants of Valparaiso, and every other coastal town that shelters an inshore fishing fleet. The selection depends upon whatever is local—the only constant is that is must be exquisitely fresh.

The shellfish—choose from:
Abalone, beaten to tenderize
Razor-shells or cherrystone clams (steamed or raw)
Mussels, opened
Oysters, opened
Scallops, opened, sand sac removed
Shrimp and prawns, cooked and peeled

Machas, razor-shells, look strange but taste delicious

Giant barnacles (picorocos), cooked briefly in salted water
Crab claws, cracked
Sea urchins, snipped around the waist to expose the five little roes

The sauce (for 4)
1/4 cup finely chopped onion or scallion
1/4 cup chopped cilantro
1/4 cup chopped parsley
1–2 green chiles, seeded and finely chopped
6 tablespoons lemon juice
1/4 cup oil
1/2 teaspoon salt

For serving (optional)
Ulte or any edible seaweed, cooked to tenderize, chopped

Raw shellfish can be opened by inserting a short, strong, double-bladed knife into the hinge, or slipping it around the side; py the shells apart and serve the meat and the juices on the deeper of the two shells. Crustaceans must be cooked in plenty of boiling salted water for just long enough for them to change color all over. Sea urchins have to be slit in half to expose the five little roes in a starfish shape—careful, the prickles are sharp. Abalone needs first to be thoroughly tenderized by battering it against the rocks until it froths, then sliced.

Combine the sauce ingredients, taste, and adjust the seasoning. More salt? More lemon juice? A pinch of sugar?

Arrange the seafood on a large platter and serve the sauce separately, or, if you prefer, spoon a very little into each shell.

Curanto en olla
(Seafood, pork, and chicken stew)
Serves 8–10

The *curanto*—the pit-barbecue or earth oven—was used in pre-Columbian times, mainly as a method of preserving perishable food in times of glut, particularly when more seafood had been gathered than could conveniently be

Mariscal, a medley of seafood served with a piquant sauce

consumed fresh. Modern *chilenos* maintain the tradition in the form of the beach pit-barbecue, a family outing undertaken in much the same spirit as Long Island's surfers set up a clambake—although the Chilean *curanto* is likely to include more substantial food such as suckling pig, potatoes, and corn. Here, the food—a surf-n-turf blend of shellfish, chicken, and pork with potatoes, is cooked in an *olla*: an all-purpose earthenware cooking pot, heatproof so it won't crack on an open flame.

about 4 pounds fresh shellfish: razor-shells, prepared abalone, barnacles, etc.
6 tablespoons oil
1 pound pork shoulder, cut into cubes
1 small chicken, cut up
2–3 links chorizo sausage, sliced
1 onion, roughly chopped
1 sweet red pepper, seeded and cut into chunks
2 fennel bulbs with their fronds, roughly chopped
24 small new potatoes
1 bottle dry white wine
2 tablespoons finely chopped chile or chili
paste or red pepper flakes
2 garlic cloves, finely chopped
2 tablespoons chopped cilantro
Salt and pepper

Scrub the shellfish and leave them in a bowl of cold water to spit out their sand.

Heat the oil in a roomy earthenware *olla* that won't crack on a direct flame, or in a large stewpot, and fry the assorted meats until they brown a little. Add the onion and chopped red pepper and fry for a moment more.

Add a layer of chopped fennel and potatoes, pour in the wine and enough water to submerge the meats completely, and sprinkle with the chile, garlic, and cilantro. Season, bring to a boil, top with a plate so that everything stays submerged, and simmer gently for about 20 minutes, until the potatoes are nearly tender. Arrange the seafood on top, put the lid on again, and let it cook for another five minutes, until the shells open.

Serve in deep plates, bathed in its own aromatic broth, with bread for mopping.

bacalão

or bacalhão, salt cod

Salt cod provisioned the wooden ships that made the perilous early Atlantic crossings. Later, it was established as the fast-day food of the Roman Catholic Church. Once cheap and plentiful, it's now a luxury item sold in small quantities, often soaked and vacuum packed.

Appearance and taste

A large kite-shaped sheet of rock-hard fish—though scarcely recognizable as such—salt cod is pungent and mouth-puckeringly salty. When soaked in several changes of water for at least 24 hours, it rehydrates to about three times its volume and loses much of its saltiness. It's a mistake to oversoak: it's nicest when still a little chewy.

Buying and storing

Choose with care. The white of the flesh should be ivory rather than snowy—a sign of chemical bleaching—and check the backbone for traces of pink: an indicator that too little time was spent in the salt. The middle cut is the best; the tail used to be hung up in the dovecote at Christmas for the birds to peck.

Medicinal and other uses

This is not for anyone cutting down their salt intake, for obvious reasons. Otherwise, it is an excellent source of protein.

Culinary uses

Salt cod can be used in any fresh fish recipe, but is most delicious in combination with sweet-sour flavors, such as tomatoes and peppers. Ackee saltfish, the national dish of Jamaica, combines the saltiness of the fish with the blandness of ackee, the fruit of a West African native tree established on the island by Captain Bligh of the *Bounty*, the texture and flavor of which are much like scrambled eggs. The Dominican Republic's *morue en chemise*—saltfish scrambled with eggs—confirms the popularity of the combination. In Brazil, where culinary habit derives from Portugal—the original salt-cod experts—you'll be told it's used in as many ways as there are days in the year.

Salted fish on sale in El Salvador

Fanesca

(Ecuadorian beans and corn with salt fish)
Serves 10–12

A combination of fresh fava beans, corn kernels, and vegetables with salt cod go into this family dish eaten during Easter week—which, in the southern hemisphere, falls in the autumn, at harvest time. It's traditional to send a bowlful of it to the neighbors.

*1¹/2 pounds fresh fava beans, shelled
(about 4¹/2–5 cups)*
*1¹/2 pounds fresh corn kernels (about
3¹/2 cups)*
*1¹/2 pounds fresh navy or cranberry beans
(about 4 cups)*
*1 pound fresh, mature peas, shelled
(about 4 cups)*
2²/3 cups short grain or risotto rice
5 cups milk and 5 cups water, mixed
1 pound diced squash
1 pound diced large zucchini (about 3¹/2–4 cups)
1/2 small cabbage, finely sliced
8 ounces salt cod, soaked, boned, and skinned

Refried beans:
2 tablespoons butter or oil
3 onions, finely chopped
2 garlic cloves, finely chopped
*1 tablespoon color chileno (see achiote,
page 186), or oil colored red with paprika*

1 teaspoon powdered cumin
Pepper, no salt

To finish:
1–2 chayotes (choko) or zucchini, diced
2/3 cup heavy cream
1 cup roasted peanuts, crushed

For serving (optional):
A handful ready-to-eat lupini (edible lupin seeds)
Roasted salted corn kernels (masitas fritas)
Hard-boiled eggs, peeled and quartered
Chopped parsley
Chopped fresh chile
White cheese in slivers or matchsticks

Cook the fava beans in boiling water without salt for 20 minutes. Drain and slip off the skins when they are cool enough to handle: the beans crumble if skinned when cold. In another pot cook the corn, the navy beans, and the peas until tender—also about 20 minutes. Drain, reserving the cooking water. Cook the rice in half the milk and water mixture until tender. These preparations can be made the day before.

The next day, cook the diced squash, large zucchini, and cabbage in a tightly lidded pan in a very little water until tender—10 to 15 minutes. Cook the soaked cod in the remaining milk and water. Drain, reserving the cooking liquid, and flake the fish.

Meanwhile, prepare the refried beans. Heat the oil in a large saucepan or a well-tempered, flameproof, earthenware casserole dish and gently fry the onion and garlic until soft and a little caramelized. Add the color chileno (or one tablespoon paprika mixed with a little oil), sprinkle with the cumin and pepper, and fry for another five minutes to blend the flavors. Add the reserved bean-cooking water and let it boil. Stir in the reserved beans, corn, and rice, along with the reserved vegetables, and simmer gently for 10 minutes, stirring constantly to blend the flavors. Stir in the reserved cooking liquid from the salt cod and cook for another 10 minutes. Finish with the diced chayote, cream, salt cod, and crushed peanuts.

Serve hot in bowls, with the optional accompaniments.

Bacalão colorão. Salty flakes of bacalão contrast with the sweetness of the peppers and onion

Bacalão colorão
(Salt cod with red peppers)
Serves 4

A Mexican fasting dish for Lent—very good. Choose middle-cut salt cod and give it no more than 18 hours' soaking, or you'll lose all the flavor.

8 ounces salt cod, soaked in several
  changes of water
2/3 cup olive oil
6 red bell peppers, seeded and cut in ribbons
2–3 fresh red chiles, seeded and finely
  chopped
1 large onion, finely sliced
4 garlic cloves, chopped
1/4 cup chopped parsley or cilantro

Skin, bone, and flake the soaked salt cod. If it's still too tough to flake, simmer in water for 5 minutes first.

Heat 4 tablespoons of the oil in a heavy pan and fry the peppers and the chile. When they're soft and caramelized at the edges, remove and set aside. Fry the onion and garlic (let it turn golden but not brown), remove, and set aside.

Fry the soaked cod in the pan drippings until the edges curl and it crisps a little. Combine the salt cod with the pepper and onion mixtures, and the parsley or cilantro, and serve. It is nicest at room temperature.

For a more substantial dish, serve with quartered hard-boiled eggs and soft tortillas for scooping.

nuts

The cooks of the region use nuts as thickenings for sauces, to add a little protein to roots and grains, in desserts, and to enrich soups and stews. Of the nuts used, two are native, two are shared with other continents, and one is an import—what the botanists call an alien.

Brazil nuts and cashews are both exclusive to the Americas—unknown elsewhere until the arrival of the Old World's colonizers. The peanut, in the New World native to Peru, is also an Old World staple, grown in Africa since the earliest times, and the pine nut—a forest harvest that fed the Mapuche Indians of southern Chile—also appears as a staple food of the Aboriginal peoples of northern Australia. The coconut, on the other hand, is an imported crop. Although it probably self-seeded on the Pacific coast, drifting from the South Sea islands on the ocean current, the circumstances under which it established itself on the Atlantic coast were grim. The coconut palms that shade the beautiful beaches of Rio and Bahia, and the shores of Cuba and the Caribbean, are a by-product of the slave trade: coconut was the main provision loaded aboard the ships that supplied the sugar plantations with their workforce. The captives packed into the stinking holds of the trading ships were provided with their own weight in coconuts, a supply intended to serve as both food and water, and at the end of the voyage, the amount of coconuts remaining gave an indication of the mortality rate of the cargo—evidence, maybe, of carelessness. The leftover coconuts (along, no doubt, with the bodies) were simply tipped overboard to self-seed on the shore.

brazil nut

or nuez de brasil, castanhas do Pará (Brazil)
(*Bertholettia excelsa*)

Brazil nuts are the seeds of one of the most impressive
of the Amazonian forest trees, which can reach a height
of about 165 feet, topped by a canopy up to 100 feet
in diameter.

How it grows

So far the trees remain wild, having resisted
all attempts at cultivation. The fruit, which
contains the nuts, is round and smooth-
skinned, about the size and weight of a
coconut, and falls to the ground when
ripe, occasionally causing casualties among
the unwary.

Appearance and taste

Each fruit contains as many as twenty nuts,
arranged like the segments of an orange. Once
you manage to crack it, the meat—which has
to be pried off the shell—is crisp but tender,
and very rich and buttery, thanks to a
remarkably high oil content. The nuts of the
sapucaya or paradise-nut tree, its close
relation, though not commercially marketed,
are considered even more exquisite.

Buying and storing

Although about a quarter of the crop exported
from the Amazonian city of Pará is shelled
before shipping, Brazil nuts are best bought
in the shell. They should be satiny and a little
oily: avoid any that look dried out or dusty.
Keep them in the refrigerator, whether shelled
or unshelled.

Medicinal and other uses

Brazil nuts are high in protein, with an oil
content of nearly 70 percent. As a prime
source of amino acids, Brazil nuts are
particularly good for bringing balance to a
vegetarian diet; nourishing and fortifying, they
are perfect for athletes and anyone involved in
hard physical labor. Brazil nuts are not part of
the native diet of Amazonia, being too rich and
oily for the climate.

Culinary uses

Only crack as many as you need: once
extracted from their stone-hard covering, the
oily nutmeat rapidly turns rancid.

Crema de castanhas do Pará

(Brazil nut soup)
Serves 6–8

**A sophisticated cream soup enriched with
Brazil nuts and finished with shrimp and
avocado—sophisticated enough for the
salons of Rio.**

2 cups shelled Brazil nuts
2 quarts chicken stock
1/4 cup unsalted butter or oil
1/2 cup all-purpose flour
A pinch freshly grated mace
1 1/4 cups heavy cream
Salt and pepper

To finish (optional):
1 ripe avocado, diced
*1 cup cooked, peeled shrimp or a
   handful dried shrimp*

Preheat the oven to 400°F.

Spread the nuts on a baking tray and roast for
10 minutes—halfway through, shake the tray to
turn and toast them evenly. Let them cool, then
rub off the husks. Tip into a food processor
and grind to a powder. Remove and reserve
two tablespoons of the powdered nuts, leaving
the rest in the food processor. Heat the stock,
add a ladleful to the powdered nuts in the food
processor, and blend again.

Meanwhile, melt the butter in a large soup-pot,
sprinkle in the flour, let it sizzle but not take
color, and slowly add the rest of the stock,
whisking to avoid lumps. Bring back to a boil,
turn down the heat, and simmer for 10 minutes
to cook the flour.

Stir in the nut-broth, mace, and cream, and
reheat. Taste and add salt and pepper if
needed—or maybe a shake of malagueta
pepper. Ladle into bowls and finish each
serving, if you like, with a little diced avocado, a
few shrimp, and a sprinkling of the reserved
powdered nuts.

**Pedacinos de chocolate
con nueces de brasil**

Pedacinos de chocolate con nueces de brasil

(Brazil nut cookies)

Makes about 18 cookies

Crisp, nutty, chocolatey, and delicious with a glass of iced coffee. The basic ingredients make the difference: choose a high-quality cocoa powder and crack the nuts yourself.

²/₃ cup Brazil nuts
1 cup all-purpose flour
1 heaped tablespoon cocoa powder
¹/₂ teaspoon baking powder
¹/₂ teaspoon salt
¹/₂ cup softened unsalted butter
¹/₂ cup brown sugar
1 egg, lightly beaten with a fork

Reserve 18 of the best Brazil nuts. Crush the rest to a coarse powder and toss with the flour, sifted with the cocoa, baking powder, and salt.

Beat the butter with the sugar until light and pale. Beat in the egg, then the flour and nuts. The mixture should be soft enough to drop from the spoon, so you may need a little milk.

Preheat the oven to 375°F. Butter a cookie sheet and sprinkle lightly with flour. Drop spoonfuls of the cookie mixture onto the cookie sheet. Using a damp finger, press one of the reserved whole Brazil nuts into the middle of each cookie. Bake for 10 to 12 minutes. Let cool a little before transferring to a cooling rack—they crisp as they cool.

peanut

or maní (Peru), cacahuete (elsewhere), groundnut, monkey nut (*Arachis hypogaea*)

A Peruvian native cultivated by the Incas, and possibly also a native of Equatorial Africa, the peanut is one of the world's major foods. It is not a true nut but a legume, a member of the pea family—hence its English name.

How it grows

The peanut's growing habit is equally interesting: the blossoms appear in the usual way, but the flower stalks thrust themselves into the ground as soon as the pod begins to develop, ensuring that the seeds—peanuts—are already planted in the earth by the time they mature.

Appearance and taste

The skin that covers the nut can be any color from pale cream to a reddish brown or even piebald. An oil nut as well as an eating nut, the flavor is starchy and beany when raw, developing its delicious nuttiness only when roasted.

Buying and storing

When buying peanuts in the shell, check for dusty patches that indicate the presence of bugs; when buying roasted, if possible, taste for freshness before buying.

Medicinal and other uses

With 30 percent protein and 50 percent fat, the peanut is the perfect food—fortifying and digestible. Unfortunately, increasing numbers of people are developing a peanut-allergy, which can, in the worst affected, be fatal.

Culinary uses

To roast peanuts, shell them, spread them on a baking sheet in a single layer, and roast them at 325°F for 15 to 20 minutes; to skin them, shake them vigorously in a sieve while blowing off the papery residue, or rub them with a clean cloth.

Galletas de maní con canela

(Peanut and cinnamon cookies)
Makes about 2 dozen cookies

A basic beaten cookie—very easy and delicious. Serve with an exotic sorbet—chirimoya or lucuma.

3 cups all-purpose flour
1/2 cup crushed peanuts or peanut butter
3/4 cup butter
1/2 cup sugar
1 tablespoon powdered cinnamon
1 egg
Salt

To finish:
2 tablespoons whole, split peanuts

Sift the flour and cinnamon with a pinch of salt into a bowl and mix in the crushed peanuts. Beat the butter with the sugar until light and fluffy, then beat in the egg. Work in the flour and nut mixture until you have a ball of soft dough—you may need a little more flour. Cover with plastic wrap and let it rest in the refrigerator for an hour to firm up.

Heat the oven to 425°F. On a lightly floured board, roll out the dough. Cut out circles with a cookie cutter or glass, and arrange on a buttered cookie sheet. Brush the tops with water and sprinkle with the whole peanuts: push them lightly into the dough. Bake for 15 to 20 minutes until golden, and transfer to a cooling rack to crispen.

Chupe de maní

(Peanut soup)

Serves 4

A simple soup popular in Ecuador and Bolivia. You can use smooth peanut butter if you don't want to grind your own peanuts.

2 tablespoons peanut oil
1 onion, finely chopped

1 floury potato, peeled and diced
1 red bell pepper, seeded and finely chopped
2 dried red chiles, seeded and crumbled
5 cups strong chicken or beef broth
¼ cup finely ground toasted peanuts
Salt and pepper

To finish:
2 tablespoons chopped cilantro
Diced tomato
Extra peanuts for sprinkling

Heat the oil gently in a heavy saucepan. Fry the onion, potato, and pepper until soft—don't let them brown. Stir in the chile and add the stock. Bring to a boil, turn down the heat, and simmer gently for 20 minutes, until fragrant and well-blended. Blend half the soup to a purée with the peanuts and stir it back into the rest. Taste, season, reheat gently and ladle into bowls.

Finish with a sprinkle of cilantro, diced tomato, and extra peanuts.

cashew nut

or castanha-de-cajú (Brazil), marañón (Mexico)
(*Anacardium occidentale*)

A relative of the mango and the pistachio, the cashew is the edible fruit and nut of a Brazilian tropical shrub. It was known as *acajú* to the Tupi, the indigenous people for whom it was (and remains) an important food—hence the name given to it by the Portuguese colonizers.

How it grows

The fruit that contains the seed (the cashew) is suspended beneath a large fleshy apple, which is eaten fresh or pulped for its juice and is delicious in puddings—unfortunately, the apple rots within two days, so can only be appreciated in situ.

Appearance and taste

The nut is poisonous when raw and has to be first heated and then shelled—labor-intensive, but a process perfectly understood by the indigenous inhabitants of Amazonia, who are accustomed to the necessity of detoxifying tropical fruits and roots. The nutshell contains an oil that irritates the skin, but is useful in waterproofing and is of value to the chemical industry. The nut, which is the shape and size of a large kidney bean, white, and buttery in flavor, is 45 percent fat and 20 percent protein, both of which say the right things to the tastebuds—hence its popularity, particularly when roasted, as a cocktail snack.

Buying and storing

Because they're toxic when untreated, the nuts are never sold in the shell. To check for freshness, look for a clean, clear color with no sign of powdering.

Medicinal and other uses

Fresh cashew-apple juice is a local remedy for sore throats and upset tummies, including dysentery. The nuts have a high oleic acid content and are recommended for tooth and gum problems and gastrointestinal disorders (although are not recommended in combination with starches, particularly bread).

Culinary uses

Bahian cooks pound the nuts for thickening sauces or for infusing in water to make a nutmilk (refreshing on a hot day), as well as powdering them for inclusion in cakes and pastries. The apple can be conserved in syrup—the only way it ever appears on the export market—and is delicious with vanilla ice cream.

Sango de quinua y marañón

(Cashew nut and quinoa risotto)
Serves 6

A combination of grains and nuts from Ecuador's Amazonian highlands—perfect as a vegetarian party dish.

12 ounces quinoa, picked over and
  rinsed (about 2 cups)
5 cups water
2–3 tablespoons peanut oil
2 cups cashews
1 onion, finely chopped
2 garlic cloves, finely chopped
1 yellow chile, seeded and chopped
Salt and pepper
2–3 tablespoons cream

To finish:
Quinoa or spinach leaves, wilted in a covered
  pan with a little peanut oil
Salt and chili flakes

Rinse the quinoa in a strainer under the faucet until the water runs clear, transfer to a heavy pan along with the water, bring to a boil, turn down to simmer, and cook for about 20–30 minutes, until the water has completely evaporated and the grains are soft and fluffy.

Meanwhile, heat a tablespoon of the oil in a frying pan and fry the cashews for a few

Sacks of nuts in a Mexico City market

minutes, stirring until lightly browned, then remove and set aside. Add the remaining oil, onion, and garlic to the pan and fry until soft—don't let them brown. Add the chopped chile, fry for a minute, then stir in the cream and let it boil. Stir in the cooked quinoa and all but a tablespoon of the browned cashews, roughly crushed, and toss it all together over a gentle heat for another 5 minutes. Season.

To serve, top each portion with some of the greens and finish with a sprinkling of the toasted cashews, tossed with salt and chili flakes.

Horchata de cajú

(Cashew nut milk)

Makes 5 cups

A refreshing nutmilk, a legacy of the Moorish occupation of Iberia that was imported as a chile-taming thirst-quencher.

2^1/2 cups powdered cashews
5 cups water

2 tablespoons sugar (more if you like)
Short stick of cinnamon

Stir the ground nuts into the water and let them infuse overnight. Next day, strain the milky liquid into a saucepan, stir in the sugar, and add the cinnamon stick. Bring to a boil, and let it cool. Refrigerate, removing the cinnamon stick just before serving.

Serve well-iced, in tall glasses.

Horchata de cajú

pine nut

or piñones (*Araucaria araucaria, A. angustifolia, Pinus cembroides*)

Chief of the native pine nuts are seeds extracted from the cones of the araucaria or monkey-puzzle, a close relative of the Australian bunya-bunya tree. This pedigree makes it, along with the peanut, one of the few botanical candidates that support the theory that all the continents once formed part of the same landmass.

Buying and storing

Use your nose: the scent should be sweet and resinous, with no powdery residue to indicate the presence of small uninvited guests. The flavor deteriorates once the nuts are shelled, so keep them in a sealed jar in the refrigerator and use within a month.

Medicinal and other uses

In my opinion, a miraculous food. Forget fillet steak: a handful of pine nuts a day supplies protein, fat, and other nutrients. The Latin American varieties are particularly rich in vitamins and minerals.

Culinary uses

All pine nuts—including the pine nuts of commerce, the seeds of the Mediterranean stone-pine (*Pinus pinea*)—are interchangeable for culinary purposes. They are traditionally used throughout the territory in nut-thickened sauces of Mediterranean origin as well as in indigenous pre-Columbian dishes.

Araucaria trees in Cani National Park, Chile

How it grows

A pine tree that grows to a remarkable size, the araucaria is a native to southern Chile and has a prodigious lifespan—around fifteen hundred years—which makes it one of the oldest living things on earth. The nuts remain an important food source for the south Chilean Mapuche Indians—the "people of the land"—for whom the trees are sacred. Unfortunately, only vestiges of the once vast forests remain, and even these are vanishing with alarming rapidity. In Brazil, a similar gastronomic niche is filled by the Parana pine (*A. angustifolia*); in Mexico, the seed-cones of *P. cembroides* provided the Mayas and the Incas with a high-protein food source.

Appearance and taste

Commercially sold pine nuts are preshelled, and with good reason. As I well remember from childhood holidays in the Andes, you need a pair of heavy stones and a great deal of patience to crack even a small handful. The Mapuche of southern Chile harvest the cones in the autumn and store them underground through the winter as a source of protein during the cold months, cracking them to order and eating them raw, or toasting and milling them for flour, or cooking them and fermenting the pulp to make a form of chicha.

Locro con piñones

Torta de piñones

(Pine nut tart)

Serves 6–8

When crushing the nuts, don't reduce
them to a powder or they'll get oily. The
sugar sounds like a lot, but it makes the
nut filling wonderfully chewy. This is
also good made with Chilean hazelnuts,
Gevuina avellana, a relation of the
macademia, which grows wild on the
snowline and is usually sold roasted,
like peanuts.

Pastry dough:

2 cups flour

1 teaspoon powdered cinnamon

1/4 cup sugar

3/4 cup butter

*1 egg yolk, mixed with 1 tablespoon cold
  water*

Filling:

1 cup pine nuts, roughly crushed

6 tablespoons granulated sugar

1/2 teaspoon crushed allspice

1 egg white, whisked until stiff

1 1/4 cups heavy cream, lightly whipped

Make the pastry dough first: mix the flour with
the cinnamon and sugar, rub in the butter, then
work in the egg and enough water to give a
soft, firm dough—use the tips of your fingers
and don't overwork, just press it together
lightly until it forms a ball. Cover with plastic
wrap and let it rest for 30 minutes.

Preheat the oven to 400°F.

Roll out the pastry dough into a disk and use
it to line a 7-inch fluted tart pan. Prick the
bottom, and slip it into the oven for 10 minutes
(no need to fuss with beans and foil) to set
the crust.

Meanwhile, mix the filling ingredients together.
Spread the mixture in the pie shell, return it to
the oven, and bake for another 30 minutes or
so, until the filling is set and the crust crisp.

Locro con piñones

(Potato soup with pine nuts)

Serves 4–6

A winter soup from the cold uplands of
Chile's altiplano, fortified with monkey-
puzzle pine nuts, though any pine nuts will
do. On the other side of the Andes, the
cowpokes of Argentina make their stock
with the roasted bones left over from the
asado—but if water is all that's available,
water will do.

*2 pounds potatoes, peeled and thickly
  sliced*

about 2 1/2 quarts bone stock or water

1 large clove garlic, chopped

2 small onions, finely chopped

Salt and pepper

To finish:

1 cup pine nuts

1 tablespoon finely chopped garlic

Cilantro or scallions

In a roomy pan, cook the potatoes in the stock
or water with salt, garlic, and onion for about
30 minutes, until completely mushy. Mash
roughly (don't blend in food processor).

Meanwhile, lightly toast the pine nuts in a dry
pan, stir in the garlic, and crush the mixture if
using plain water, leave whole if using stock.
Stir this aromatic panful in the soup and
simmer for another 10 minutes. Taste and
adjust the seasoning.

Serve steaming hot in bowls, with sprigs of
cilantro or scallions.

coconut

or nuez de coco (*Cocos nucifera*)

The coconut is the fruit and seed of the coconut palm, a cultivar that probably originated in Malaysia and the islands of Polynesia. A primary food source— sometimes sole food source— throughout the tropics, it self-seeded in the Americas by way of Africa.

How it grows

The coconut palm, as is usual with a native of the tropics, crops constantly, blooming and seeding all year.

Appearance and taste

In spite of the dismal circumstances under which it was introduced to the New World, this is a crop of many useful parts. The fiber— coir—is used to make matting and baskets; the outer shell, when hard and dry, provides fuel for the cooking fire; young buds, known as pine-cabbages, are eaten as a vegetable; the leaves can be used as fans and for roofing material; the nut can be eaten ripe or unripe and yields a clear, highly perfumed oil; the flower buds are infused and fermented to make an alcoholic drink; the shell, when green, is full of clear, slightly nut-flavored water much appreciated as a refreshing drink, while the unripe flesh is a soft neutral-flavored jelly; and the nutmeat, when ripe, can be eaten immediately or stored. Once the coconut has been cracked and exposed to the air, keep it in the refrigerator.

Buying and storing

When buying a whole mature coconut, shake, it—you should hear a sloshing sound, which tells you it's fresh and full of liquid. Check the three little dimples—the "eyes" that give it a face like a monkey (*coco* in Spanish)—for signs of dampness or mold. To crack a coconut, shove a sharp instrument through the dimples and drain off the liquid. Then tap with a heavy hammer all around the circumference until it cracks, or drop it onto a concrete floor, or heat it in the oven at 350° for half an hour, after which a light tap will do the trick. Remove the meat from the shell, bag it up, and keep it in the refrigerator. Eat within a week, or grate and dehydrate in the lowest possible oven, and store in an airtight jar.

Medicinal and other uses

Coconuts are high in iodine, making them useful in the treatment of thyroid conditions. In the form of milk, its chemical balance is comparable to mother's milk. The oil extracted from the ripe flesh has been used for centuries for cooking; in its natural state, coconut fat is easily digested and appears not to cause weight gain. When refined—the odorless colorless state in which it usually comes to market—it's more than 90 percent saturated fat, even higher than butter or lard. In this form, it's extensively used in commercial cream preparations, such as ice creams, "dairy" whiteners, and whips, to which it delivers an instant cholesterol hike. Unrefined oil goes rancid quickly, but is lovely as a cosmetic rub, particularly good as a hair conditioner, and wonderful for treating stretch marks after pregnancy.

Related products

Coconut milk and cream are both available in a can, boxed, and as a block. To make your own coconut milk: measure a half cup of grated coconut (fresh or dried) into 2½ cups hot but not boiling water, blend in the blender and strain. Put the pulp, and another 2½ cups water, into the blender; blend and strain. Mix the two strainings to give you coconut milk; the first straining gives you cream.

Culinary uses

Puerto Rican piña colada is made with fresh coconut milk, pineapple juice, corn syrup, and rum. The milk is delicious in rice puddings and milky desserts; in Brazilian and Colombian cuisines, coconut cream is used to enrich soups and sauces, particularly those with chicken or fish.

Enyucado de coco

(Cassava coconut cake)
Serves 8–10

A deliciously moist coconut cake from the Caribbean coast of Colombia. Bake it in a ring mold for a celebration.

3 pounds peeled cassava
1 large fresh coconut
4 cups shredded white cheese (cheddar
  is fine)
A little salt
2 egg yolks
1 1/4 cups milk
1 cup sugar
1/4 cup softened butter
1 teaspoon aniseeds, lightly toasted and crushed

Enyucado de coco, a moist coconut and cassava cake

Grate the cassava, the coconut, and the cheese into a bowl. Add the remaining ingredients and mix together to make a smooth soft dough. Set it aside for an hour to swell.

Preheat the oven to 300°F. Transfer the dough to a buttered baking pan—a large loaf pan is perfect—and bake for an hour, until firm to the finger, well-risen, and browned. Surprisingly light and moist—it is delicious with fresh pineapple.

Ximxim

(Bahian chicken and shrimp with coconut milk)
Serves 6–8

Pronounced chim-chim, this is the classic one-pot stew of Bahia, Brazil's most populous province. The combination of poultry and seafood with coconut milk is particularly delicious—wonderful food for a party.

1 free-range chicken, cut into bite-size pieces
2 limes
1 pound fresh prawns or large shrimp
  (about 3–4 cups)
1/2 cup oil (olive and dende is perfect)
2 mild onions, diced small
2 garlic cloves, finely chopped
1 mild red bell pepper, seeded and diced
1 mild green bell pepper, seeded and diced
1 pound ripe tomatoes, chopped (about
  2 1/2 cups)
1 malagueta or habanero chile, seeded and
  diced
2 heaped tablespoons crushed, toasted
  cashews
2 heaped tablespoons crushed, toasted
  peanuts
2 heaped tablespoons dried shrimp (see
  page 142)
1/2 teaspoon grated fresh ginger
Salt and pepper

To finish:
1/4 cup finely chopped cilantro
2/3 cup unsweetened coconut milk
2 tablespoons dende oil, or vegetable oil
  colored with achiote (see page 186)

Pick over the chicken pieces and trim off excess flaps and any whiskery feathers. Season with salt and pepper and toss with the juice of one of the limes. Let marinate for half an hour.

Pick over the prawns—if they are large, peel, removing the heads and leaving the tails, and devein (remove the dark intestine that runs down the back). Season with salt and pepper, toss with the juice of half the remaining lime, and let marinate as above.

Heat half the oil and fry the chicken pieces until nicely browned. Push to one side and add the prawns—they'll only take a minute or two. Remove and reserve both the chicken and prawns. Fry the onion, garlic, and chopped red and green peppers in the remaining oil added to the pan drippings. Let soften but don't let them brown. Add the tomatoes and chile, and let it boil, squashing down to make a sauce. Add a glass of water, let it boil again, and return the chicken to the pan. Cover loosely and simmer for 20 to 30 minutes, until the chicken is perfectly tender. Stir in the well-pounded nuts and dried shrimp. Let it boil again, add the ginger, and simmer for another 5 minutes. Stir in the chopped cilantro, coconut milk, and dende oil, lay the prawns on top, and reheat gently.

Delicious with white rice, a sprinkling of farofa, and a drop of malagueta pepper sauce. Now pour yourself a caipirinha and shake those hips.

the pantry

When considering the Latin American pantry, it's worth remembering that before the arrival of the Europeans, salt was not available—neither mined nor produced by evaporation. For many centuries, the main method of preservation was through prolonged cooking in an earth oven (with or without the addition of smoking), plus, sometimes, an additional plant-based antibacterial substance such as allspice or cassareep. Freeze-drying was known to the Incas, who used the method to preserve potatoes; meat—in those areas where the climate was not too damp to prevent the quick dehydration essential without salting—was preserved by air drying.

Such a diet, lacking the savor of salt, needed enlivening with chiles, chocolate, vanilla, and many other flavorings of local interest. Notable plant-based additives include achiote (annatto seeds, used as a colorant), allspice (for its fragrance), and angostura, valued both for its medicinal properties and its palate-stimulating bitterness.

As for those things whose function is to soothe, stimulate, or give pleasure, a wide variety of infusions—tisanes—are enjoyed for their medicinal or stimulant properties. Maté, a tea brewed from the leaves of a member of the holly family, is the most popular, taking the place of chocolate in the southern parts of the region. In the tropical lands of the region, coffee—an Old World import that found its natural habitat in the New World—swiftly became both locally popular and economically important as a crop for export.

The people of the pre-Columbian civilizations were perfectly familiar with the pleasures of strong drink, preparing fermented beverages from a wide variety of raw materials. Among these, a Mexican beer—*pulque*—is remarkable for being made from the collected juice of a desert cactus; it is famous in its distilled form as tequila, a colorless, odorless, white brandy.

cocoa

or chocolate, cacao
(*Theobroma cacao*)

The tropical tree that produces this valuable crop is highly temperamental.
Dependent on a tiny mosquito for pollination, it refuses to flower at all unless provided with
year-round moisture and a temperature that never falls below 64°F, confining itself to no
more than 20 degrees latitude on either side of the equator. The tree is singularly wasteful of
its creamy little blooms, since only one in every hundred bears fruit.

How it grows

Theobroma cacao is a lower-canopy tree
indigenous to equatorial America, whose pods,
born on the main trunk rather than the
extremities, vary in color as they mature from
ocher to red. Inside are rows of pale beans,
much like a corncob embedded in soft white
fluff. The harvesters split the pods and heap
them under damp leaves to ferment, a natural
process that develops the flavor as well as
inhibiting sprouting. The beans are then
exported to the manufacturing country, where
the raw materials undergo their metamorphosis
into chocolate bars and cocoa powder.

Buying and storing

Among bean varieties, the *criolla*, the original
bean of the Maya, is held to be the best: fruity,
fragrant, with a touch of palate-tickling acidity.
The *forastero*, the wild bean native to the
forests of Brazil—now extensively cultivated in
equatorial Africa—is considered a little on the
bland side, needing high roasting to intensify
the flavor. The *Trinitario*, the Caribbean bean, is
a hybrid of the two: mellow, with flavors of oak,
honey, and hay. Most chocolate is a blend of all
three. When assessing the quality of dark
chocolate for cooking purposes, read the label:
the cocoa-solid content should be at least
70 percent. When unwrapped, the surface

should be glossy and smooth. A reddish
tinge is good: dark chocolate should be a
deep mahogany, never black. When
breaking, listen for the crisp snap and look
for a tree-bark texture in the break. Melt a
small piece on the tip of the tongue: the
taste should be clean (aromas as for wine:
caramel, hay, fruit, flower, spice); the
texture creamy rather than oily (a quick
melt indicates high cocoa-butter content);
the "finish" (aftertaste) should be long, as
for wine. To store, keep wrapped in a cool,
dry place.

Medicinal and other uses

Among the Aztecs and their predecessors,
cocoa was a cure-all. As an aphrodisiac,
its consumption was confined to the
emperor who was expected to bear
many children. To his priests, it was a
panacea for stomach pains, an antidote to
any form of poisoning, a disinfectant for
cuts, and a balm for burns; for the ordinary
mortal, it provided a form of currency—
exchangeable throughout the empire for
goods and services. This is the form in
which it was first encountered by the
Spanish colonizers.

Culinary uses

Cocoa is bitter tasting in its raw form and,
like coffee, must be fermented and roasted.
In the civilizations of the Maya and the Aztecs,
beans were prepared in much the same way
as they are today: dried in the sun and
fermented in their pods, then ground over a
fire to a powder, and formed into pellets for
storage. In this form, the taste is bitter and
must be balanced by the sweetness of honey,
a thickening of sweet cornmeal, and a flavoring
of vanilla or chile or both. This aromatic blend
was then stirred into boiling water and beaten
until foamy. Today, the cocoa butter is heat-
extracted and the shells are ground to produce
plain cocoa or, alternatively, extra cocoa butter,
and sweeteners are added to the ground shells
to make a solid chocolate block. Cocoa is best
used in its unsweetened form in savory dishes,
although high-quality bitter chocolate will do
well enough.

A harvest of fresh coca leaves in Peru

Mole negro de guajalote

Mole negro de guajalote

(Turkey in chocolate and chile sauce)
Serves 10–12

One of the great dishes of the Mexican kitchen, said to have been invented by the nuns of a convent in Oaxaca. Don't be intimidated by the length of the ingredient list—the cooking's easy.

1 whole turkey breast, on the bone
1 large onion, cut into chunks
3 cloves and 3 allspice berries
6 peppercorns
2–3 sprigs thyme
2–3 sprigs dried marjoram
Salt

The sauce:
8 ounces dried medium-hot chiles, seeded
  and torn (the chiles should be this year's—
  not totally dehydrated but still a little moist)
6 tablespoons rendered pork fat or oil
6 garlic cloves, roughly chopped
1 onion, finely sliced
1 corn tortilla, torn in small pieces
1/4 cup roughly chopped peanuts

2 tablespoons pumpkin seeds
2–3 tomatillos (or ordinary tomatoes), chopped
1/4 cup raisins
1/2 cup unsweetened cocoa powder or
  grated black chocolate
1 teaspoon orange peel
1 teaspoon powdered cinnamon
Salt

Simmer the turkey breast with the aromatics and a little salt in enough water to cover for 1½ to 2 hours, until perfectly tender—the poaching liquid should not boil. Strip the meat from the bones and set aside. Strain the broth and reserve.

Toast the chiles in a dry frying pan for about a minute, until they change color, then put them in a bowl with enough boiling water to cover.

Heat half the fat or oil in the pan and fry the tortilla pieces until crisp and brown, then scoop into a blender. Toss the nuts and pumpkin seeds in the hot drippings and stir over the heat until they toast a little, then add them to the blender. Fry the tomatoes (you may need a little more oil) until soft and soupy, stir in the raisins, and let

everything boil, then add to the blender, along with about 1¼ cups of the reserved broth, and blend all to a thick purée.

Fry the garlic and onion in the remaining lard or oil until soft and golden. Add the contents of the blender and let it all bubble up, then turn down the heat and let simmer gently for 15 minutes.

Meanwhile, tip the soaked chiles with their water into the blender and purée. Add to the sauce in the pan and let it boil. Stir in the chocolate, cinnamon, and orange peel. Add another 2½ cups of broth and let it boil again. Add the reserved turkey meat and simmer for 20 minutes until the oily sauce begins to pool a little. Taste and add salt. Heap the mole on a pretty dish and finish with extra pumpkin seeds and a few more curls of orange peel. Serve with black beans, white rice, a freshly made guacamole, and soft tortillas for scooping.

Chocolate con vainilla

(Hot chocolate with vanilla)
Serves 4

A cup of steaming hot chocolate, fragrant with vanilla, is the best pick-me-up after a night on the town.

2 ounces best-quality dark chocolate (look for
  70 percent cocoa solids)—about 1/3 cup
2 1/2 cups hot water (not boiling)
The seeds from a 1-inch vanilla bean
1 egg yolk or 1 teaspoon cornstarch slaked in
  a little cold water
1/4 cup unsweetened evaporated milk
  (or light cream)
Honey to sweeten
Chili flakes or powder (optional)

Break the chocolate into small pieces and soften very gently over low heat with 2/3 cup water. As soon as it liquefies, whisk in the rest of the hot water. Add the vanilla seeds and whisk until perfectly smooth. Remove from the heat. Use a fork to mix the egg yolk or cornstarch with the milk or cream, and whisk it into the hot liquid. Whisk over the heat until silky and smooth, removing it just before it boils. Add honey to taste and sprinkle with a few flecks of the optional chili.

vanilla

or vainilla, vainica (*Vanilla planifolia, V. fragrans*)

The vanilla bean is the seedpod of a tropical tree orchid native to Central America, known to both the Mayas and the Aztecs, who used it as a flavoring for hot chocolate. The first pods were brought back to the Spanish court by Hernán Cortes—the blue-eyed, blond-haired Conquistador who, somewhat misguidedly as it turned out, was hailed as a god when he entered the Aztec capital.

How it grows

A high-canopy orchid, it has cream-colored, lilylike blooms and flourishes 165 feet off the forest floor. When grown commercially, the orchid is treated as a climbing vine and trained up poles in long rows. Each flower opens only once a year and, in the absence of insect pollinators, must be hand-pollinated. The pods are harvested when still yellow and unripe, when they have neither fragrance nor flavor. They are then subjected to a lengthy curing process, a form of fermentation, which triggers the development of enzymes that allow the beans to acquire their characteristic fragrance. The traditional method of achieving this is by drying the beans under cover for several weeks, then laying them out on wool blankets to heat in the sun; at night they're wrapped in their blankets and taken under cover to sweat. When the beans have turned from brown to black, they are left to dry out for another two or three months before being bundled up for storage or export. The curing process takes a total of three to six months. The main Latin American vanilla-producing countries are Mexico, Guyana, Puerto Rico, Guadalupe, and Dominica. West Indian vanilla is extracted from a different species, *Vanilla pompona*.

Appearance and taste

Properly prepared vanilla beans are a luscious deep brown in color, shiny and dark, and exuberantly freckled with tiny crystals of vanillin, a chemical developed as a result of the curing process. The flavor is complex, as at home in the perfumery as in the kitchen. It is both flowery and fruity—tuberose and mangolike—while the scent is fragrant but never cloying. Mexican vanilla has a pleasantly sharp edge not found in other vanillas.

Buying and storing

The best vanilla comes as a whole pod in a vacuum-packed container—glass or clear plastic—through which you can see the goods. Look for the characteristic dusting of vanillin crystals on the pods. Fresh pods will always have a better flavor than even the most carefully prepared extract—made by steeping the pods in alcohol over several months. Price and packaging will tell you if you're buying the real thing, so it's wise to distrust anything sold loose or cheap. You can reuse the pod if all you have done is immerse it in a custard: just rinse it carefully, wipe it dry, and store it in the sugar jar, where it'll perfume the sugar. On the other hand, in a creamy dessert, the tiny seeds are irresistible for their crunchiness as well as the beauty of the tiny black freckles, adding another layer of pleasure. Avoid synthetic vanilla—usually based on euginol, a substance that occurs naturally in clove oil but is also to be found in soft wood pulp used for papermaking. Cloying and sickly rather than fresh and sweet, it lacks the subtlety as well as the spirit of the real thing.

Medicinal and other uses

A liver stimulant, vanilla assists in the production of digestive enzymes. It also has a considerable reputation as an aphrodisiac, a virtue not unrelated to its digestive properties.

Culinary uses

Vanilla delivers sweetness as well as fragrance, although since it's usually used in combination with sugar, this is not often apparent.

Chucula de vainilla

(Vanilla and guava cream whip)
Serves 4–6

A creamy Ecuadorian dessert perfumed with vanilla seeds—deliciously fragrant against the gentle background of guava and banana.

1 short length vanilla bean
2 ripe bananas, thickly sliced
2/3 cup water
2–3 ripe guavas, quartered, skinned, and cored
3–4 tablespoons sugar (or sugar syrup)
1 1/4 cups cream, whipped

Scrape the seeds from the vanilla bean and set aside. In a small, covered pan, cook the bananas in the water with the scraped vanilla bean. Remove from the heat as soon as the fruit softens—5 minutes or so. Add the guavas, re-cover, and cook for another 5 minutes. Remove the vanilla bean. Blend the fruit with the sugar and vanilla seeds and fold in the whipped cream. Let it cool—or lightly freeze, if you prefer—and serve piled in pretty glasses.

Chucula de vanilla, a vanilla-perfumed fruit whip

Ponche de vainilla

(Vanilla rum punch)
Serves 6

An eggnog, a pick-me-up—the classic remedy for the morning after. You'll find variations on the same theme throughout the region. Here's the Mexican version.

2^1/$_2$ cups creamy milk (or light cream)
^{1}/$_4$ cup sugar
^{1}/$_2$ vanilla bean
6 egg yolks
1^1/$_4$ cups pale rum

Put the milk, sugar, and the vanilla bean in a heavy pan, heat gently until almost boiling, stirring until the sugar dissolves, then turn the heat down and simmer gently for 15 minutes, until the vanilla has imparted its fragrance to the milk. Remove the vanilla bean.

Whisk the yolks until pale and light. Whisk in the hot milk a little at a time, return to a gentle heat and cook, stirring, until it thickens enough to coat the back of a wooden spoon. Let it cool before blending with the rum. Bottle and cork it. It is ready to drink in a day or two—unless the hangover can't wait. For an elegant apéritif, serve chilled or pour over ice.

honey

or miel

liquid honey

honeycomb

The food that sustains the bee grubs in the hive; although honey is the original sweetener, it is also used throughout the region to season meat and other savory foods.

Manufacture

South American bees have a well-deserved reputation for ferocity and irritability. Fortunately, their honey is delicious—particularly when gathered in the wild and sold in great glittering, bee-buzzed combs in the market.

Appearance and taste

The grubs as well as the honey are appreciated in the region—the flavor of a combful of bee grubs is rather like caramel and cream. The forest honeys of Mexico and Guatemala are particularly dark and high in vitamins and minerals. Especially delicious and well-endowed with minerals are the pine-flavored honeys of the Andean uplands.

Buying and storing

Local honeys reflect the diet of the bees that produce them, passing on toxins—including antibiotics and pesticides—as well as fragrances and other desirable attributes. When buying locally, take advice: some honeys are very strong, almost medicinal in flavor; some, if the bees have been pollinating certain blossoms, can even be toxic. Honey will keep virtually forever: it will crystallize over the course of a year, but can be brought back to a liquid state by popping the jar in simmering water. A honey that has been heated up to 145ºF can still be labeled uncooked, although the flavor and vitamin content begin to alter at 104ºF.

Medicinal and other uses

Raw honey is an antiseptic and a laxative; stirred into an infusion of thyme, it clears sinuses; in combination with vinegar or lemon, it sooths coughs; when applied topically, it heals wounds. As a food, honey is metabolized more slowly than sugar and the darker honeys are usually richer in minerals than light honeys. The comb-washings go to make a fermented liquor, the wax to make holy candles to mollify the saints who inhabit the churches and whose temper is uncertain, just like the old gods who ruled from the ancient temples on which the churches were built. With or without the intercession of a priest, the saints have an insatiable appetite for candles.

Beekeeping in San Martín, Mexico

Culinary uses

You need about 30 percent less honey than sugar to sweeten something. The flavor of a particular honey that has not been blended with other honeys is best appreciated in its simplest form, stirred into the preferred infusion of the region: drinking chocolate in the lands of the Maya and the Aztec, and maté, a mildly stimulant tea popular in southern Brazil, Uruguay, Paraguay, and Argentina. Honey can be boiled down to make a thick, toffeelike sauce—delicious poured over ice cream, or as a stuffing for doughnuts and churros. Since sweetness is associated with pleasure, honey desserts take place of honor at weddings and the seasonal celebrations of the church, particularly those associated with the Virgin Mary.

Turrón de miel de abejas

(Honey nut meringue)

Serves 6

A Chilean dessert derived from the Spanish *turrón*, who got the idea from the *halvas* of the Moors. Very light and exquisite, particularly if served with something sharp—a sorbet or a fresh fruit salad made with shredded pineapple and strawberries or, if you happen to be in Chile, shiny black murtilla berries, which are dark-juiced, with a sour cherry flavor.

6 tablespoons honey
6 tablespoons dry white wine
4 large egg whites
Pinch salt
2 tablespoons toasted pine nuts

Bring the honey and the wine gently to a boil in a small enamel saucepan, stirring to blend. Stop stirring as soon as the mixture boils, turn down the heat, and simmer for 5 to 10 minutes, until the syrup thickens to the small-ball stage and a candy thermometer reads 250°F.

Meanwhile, whisk the egg whites with the salt until stiff enough to hold soft peaks—don't overbeat or they'll be grainy. Pour the hot syrup in a steady stream onto the whisked whites, beating until cool and shiny. Spoon into pretty glasses and finish with a sprinkling of toasted pine nuts.

Cachapas con miel

(Venezuelan fresh corn pancakes with honey)

Makes a dozen

Deliciously light little pancakes that include both fresh corn and cornmeal, wonderful with a dark forest honey.

12 ounces fresh corn kernels
  (about 2 cups)
1/3 cup cornmeal (or fine-ground polenta)
1/2 cup bread flour
1 level teaspoon baking powder
Pinch salt
3/4 cup buttermilk

Cachapas con miel, breakfast pancakes drenched with honey

1 large egg
For serving:
A small pitcher of warm honey

Drop all the pancake ingredients in the blender and purée to a smooth batter. Heat a griddle or heavy iron pan and grease lightly. As soon as it's hot enough to toast a sprinkle of flour to a rich brown within 10 seconds, it's ready for cooking.

Wipe the surface with a buttery or oil-soaked paper towel. Drop tablespoons of the batter on the hot surface to make small round pancakes no bigger than a coffee saucer. Wait until bubbles form on the upper surface—a minute, no more—and flip the cakes over to brown the other side. Pile in a clean cloth to keep warm. Continue until the mixture is all used up, and serve with the warm honey.

sugar cane

or caña de azúcar (*Saccharum officinarum*)

Sugar cane was imported into the Caribbean and Brazil as a commercial crop worked by a labor force supplied through the slave trade. It's still, in spite of the proliferation of sugar beet, the world's most important sugar crop.

Crude brown sugar on sale in a Quechua market in the Peruvian highlands

How it grows

Sugar cane grows in tall, bamboolike clumps and is ready for cutting to extract the juice after the first year's growth. After that, it throws up successive clumps of canes known as ratoons, although these decrease in productivity each season.

Buying and storing

Sugar cane was a treat I enjoyed as a child: buy fresh cane in short lengths when it comes into the market at the beginning of the season, peel back the green skin, and suck the fibers to extract the juice.

Medicinal and other uses

Sugar is the world's favorite pick-me-up, either in processed form or simply chewed straight from the cane. It delivers the fastest energy buzz, though very little else, as I expect you know. It's this quick-fire delivery, combined with the body's reluctance to give itself more work than necessary that makes it addictive.

Related products

Rum, the main derivative of the sugar industry, was initially a back-porch industry, a distillation of the washings from the sugar cane extraction. It is a colorless, odorless liquor that needs outside assistance to acquire distinction. Jamaican rum is used to make a Planter's Punch: orange, grapefruit, and pineapple, sweetened with grenadine, well iced, and fortified with rum. The Puerto Rican piña colada is a blend of coconut milk, pineapple juice, and rum. The daiquiri, containing equal amounts of lemon juice and rum, well iced, was named for a small copper-mining town in northern Cuba where it was first popularized.

Appearance and taste

The darker the sugar, the less processed it is and the better the flavor—within reason: raw sugar as imported for processing in sugar refineries is full of a great many things you wouldn't want to eat.

raw, unrefined sugar

rum

sugar cane

Culinary uses

West Indians add sugar to meat when they fry it in oil, giving it a deliciously deep caramelized flavor, which not only tastes good but makes a small amount of a valuable ingredient go further. Another unusual technique peculiar to the region is that of boiling milk and sugar together until it becomes granular and caramelized: *dulce de leche* (see page 104).

Trinidad Pepper Pot

Serves a party (even better the next day)

This is a sweet-and-sour Sunday stew, seasoned Caribbean-style with sugar, vinegar, and chile. Traditionally, the pot can be kept simmering on the back of the stove for months, with something new in the way of meat or fowl added each day. Serve with white rice or plain boiled potatoes or yams, and maybe a relish of **sliced mango and ripe plantain dressed with lime juice. The Guyana pepperpot includes cassareep, a syrupy, spicy preparation based on bitter cassava, whose value as a meat tenderizer was particularly useful when cooking what the hunter caught, the only meat available before the Europeans introduced their domestic animals.**

2 pounds chicken pieces
1 pig's foot, scrubbed and split (optional)
3 pounds stewing pork or beef, cubed
2–3 red bell peppers, seeded and sliced
2 onions, thickly sliced
1–2 habanero chiles, seeded and chopped
1 short length cinnamon stick
3–4 cloves
A sprig of thyme
1–2 tablespoons vinegar
1 tablespoon Worcester sauce
2 tablespoons dark brown sugar
Salt

Put all the ingredients in a large stew pot with enough water to submerge everything, bring to a boil, turn down the heat, cover, and simmer for at least 2 hours—longer if you like—until the meat is perfectly tender. Add more water if necessary. If you prefer to use the oven, allow the same length of time at 300°F.

Taste, and adjust the seasoning, adding a little more sugar or a touch more vinegar, if you wish. Good today, it's even better tomorrow.

Trinidad pepperpot, spicy, sweet, and hot

Caipirinha

(Lime and rum highball)
Serves 1

Brazil's national drink. When made with white rum instead of Brazilian *cachaça*—sugar cane rum—it becomes a *caipirissimia*. On second thought, who cares? The only rule is that you make only one at a time.

1 lime, cut into small chunks
Superfine sugar (to taste)
A shot of cachaça or white rum
Ice cubes

Pack the lime, pulp-side up, into a tumbler. Add the sugar and crush into the limes with a pestle—don't bruise the skin or the lime oil will make the drink bitter. Add the rum and stir, then add the ice cubes.

allspice

or pimento de Jamaica, Jamaican pepper
(*Pimento dioica/P. officinalis*)

A small brown berry a little larger than a peppercorn, allspice is the fruit of the West Indian pimento tree, which is also found in Central and South America. It gets its name from the complex bouquet of spices it delivers.

How it grows

The pimento tree is a small forest tree native to the Caribbean but particularly prolific in Jamaica, which produces most of the world's supply of allspice. As with many aromatic substances (including black peppercorns and vanilla beans) the berries are picked green and spread in the sun to dry and brown, a process that allows them to ferment a little, intensifying the flavor.

Appearance and taste

Unlike peppercorns, allspice berries are variable in size. Intensely fragrant, with a scent of nutmeg, cinnamon, and clove, they have a peppery undertone that makes them suitable for both savory and sweet dishes.

Buying and storing

Choose clean, clear-colored berries with no powdery residue. They are at their most fragrant when freshly ground—buy whole rather than powdered allspice from a store that serves a Caribbean population. Store in an airtight container, and never for longer than a year.

Medicinal and other uses

A digestant, performing the same function as mint by preventing the formation of gases in the upper intestinal tract (hence the after-dinner mint). A decoction of pounded berries can be used as a pain-relieving muscle rub, and the oil can be applied topically to relieve a toothache.

A Belize plantation of allspice trees

Culinary uses

A warm spice, allspice adds depth and balance when used in savory dishes in combination with chiles. Its main use, however, is in cakes and desserts, to which it contributes a stimulating pepperiness as well as its complex blend of fragrances.

Jerked chicken with allspice

Serves 4–6

Jerk seasoning is available ready-mixed, or you can make a quantity of it and store it until needed. It is perfect with pork— delicious rubbed on a boned-out shoulder to be roasted on the barbecue (leave it overnight to absorb the flavor). For a marinade for fish, blend the seasoning with the same volume of coconut milk rather than lime juice, and give the fish just an hour in the marinade.

Jerk seasoning:
1 tablespoon ground allspice
1 tablespoon ground ginger
1 tablespoon dried thyme, crumbled
1 tablespoon dried onion, finely chopped
1 teaspoon sea salt or kosher salt
1 teaspoon cayenne pepper or chili powder
1 teaspoon sugar
1/2 teaspoon ground white pepper
1/2 teaspoon ground cinnamon

The chicken:
About 2 pounds chicken pieces
  (drumsticks and wings)
Juice of 2 limes
2 cloves garlic, crushed
2 tablespoons oil

Mix the seasoning thoroughly. Pick over the chicken pieces and remove any stray feathers. Mix 2 tablespoons of the seasoning with the lime juice, crushed garlic, and oil, and rub it thoroughly into the chicken. (Reserve the remaining seasoning for another use.) Marinate in a cool place for 3 to 4 hours—overnight if possible.

Preheat the broiler or light the barbecue. Broil the chicken pieces for 7–15 minutes, browning all sides—drumsticks take about twice as long as wings. Serve with baked plantains.

Jamaican allspice and banana milkshake

Serves 3–4

The natural pepperiness of allspice lifts the blandness of a vanilla and banana milkshake. The subtle warmth of the berries works well with the soft cool flesh of the banana, the fruit of the winter months in nontropical lands, but available all year in Caribbean markets.

4 ripe bananas
4 scoops good vanilla ice cream
2¹/₂ cups creamy milk
Sugar to taste
¹/₂ teaspoon freshly ground allspice

Put all the ingredients in the blender and blend until thoroughly combined. Serve in tall glasses, with an extra sprinkling of freshly ground allspice.

achiote

or annatto, roucou (West Indies), urucu (Brazil)
(*Bixa orellana*)

Achiote is the collective noun applied to the berries of a small tree, originally gathered by the native Brazilians of the Amazon rain forests, who used the red juice to decorate their bodies. When the Africans arrived in Brazil, they found a new use for the dye: missing the flavors and colors of home, they used the berries to give ordinary vegetable oil the same color as their beloved dende or palm-tree oil.

Appearance and taste

When fresh, the berries are bright brick-red with a very light rose-petal fragrance.

Buying and storing

Buy in small quantities (from Caribbean markets, if possible). As the seeds age, they turn brown, losing both their ability to color as well as their elusive scent.

Medicinal and other uses

As a natural dye, achiote is a safe and effective food coloring. It is used by commercial cheesemakers and—traditionally—by the buttermakers who supply the Caribbean market from the ship-victualing port of Cork, on the west coast of Ireland.

Culinary uses

Used as a food coloring throughout the region, it is particularly popular in Chile, the Caribbean, and Brazil, where the seeds—hard and not very palatable—are infused in oil and strained out.

Related products

To make *color chileno*, warm half a cup of achiote (annatto seeds) with two tablespoons pork lard and cook gently for 5 minutes. Strain off the fat and set aside. Reheat the achiote with another two tablespoons lard, strain, and set aside with the first batch. Repeat the process twice more, making four batches in all. The blending of the batches produces a very concentrated color: a quarter-teaspoon will tint a dish for four.

For oil colored like dende, add three tablespoons annato seeds to 1 1/4 cups vegetable oil, and let it infuse overnight; or heat over a low flame for 5 minutes, until it turns a sunny orange. Strain.

Huevos revueltos con color chileno

(Chilean scrambled eggs)
Serves 4

Chilean chorizo comes in short fat links, like pork sausage, and has plenty of luscious red fat. If you can only find it in a plastic pack from the supermarket, skin it, and crumble or chop.

2–4 tablespoons olive oil (depending on the amount of fat in the chorizo)
4 ounces chorizo or any other paprika-spiced dried sausage, sliced
1 small fresh red chile, seeded and finely chopped
1/4 teaspoon color chileno
6 eggs, mixed lightly with a fork
Salt

Heat the oil in a small frying pan and add the sliced chorizo. Fry until the sausage browns a little and the fat runs. Add the chile, stir over the heat for one minute, then add the color chileno, and finally the eggs.

Stir the mixture with a fork as it sets so the eggs scramble in little pieces. Salt lightly—the chorizo is salty anyway. As soon as the eggs begin to set, remove the pan from the heat and transfer to a warm plate. Serve with warm arepas or toasted country bread, over which you have poured the pan drippings.

The achiote plant growing in Brazil

Patatas bravas chilenas

(Chile potatoes)

Serves 4 as an appetizer

The colder the winter, the hotter the dressing.

1¹/2 pounds small potatoes

For the dressing:
2 garlic cloves, finely chopped
2–3 dried chiles, crumbled
1 teaspoon dried oregano
1 teaspoon cumin seeds
2 tablespoons fresh pork lard
¹/2 teaspoon annatto seeds, crushed
1 pound tomatoes, grated or chopped
 (about 2¹/2 cups)
1 tablespoon pitted black olives

For serving:
Romaine lettuce, pickled jalapeño chiles

Cook the potatoes until tender in plenty of salted water. Drain and toss over the heat to dry and split the skins a little.

Meanwhile, prepare the dressing. Crush the garlic, chiles, oregano, cumin, and annatto seeds to a paste, along with some salt, in a mortar. Heat the lard in a frying pan and fry the paste gently for 2 to 3 minutes until it softens. Add the tomatoes and let them boil, squashing down to make a thick sauce. Stir in the olives and fold in the potatoes.

Serve with romaine lettuce leaves for scooping, and pickled jalapeño chiles on the side.

angostura

Angostura is a flavoring ingredient that contains quinine—the earliest effective treatment for malaria—extracted from the bark of a South American native tree (*Galipea officinalis*).

Manufacture

It is sold in the form of bitters, made from a secret formula, and industrially bottled in Trinidad.

Appearance and taste

Angostura bitters are a pinkish brownish liquid with a spicy flavor and fragrance, in which can be identified cloves, mace, nutmeg, allspice, cinnamon, citrus peel, prunes, quinine, and rum.

Buying and storing

You have no choice: Angostura bitters come in a small bottle, which can last a lifetime.

Medicinal and other uses

Angostura bitters were originally formulated up the Orinoco river in the Venezuelan town of the same name (now renamed Ciudad Boliva), by a certain Dr. Siegart, whose patients found the preparation effective in the reduction of fever.

Culinary uses

In their exported bottled form, Angostura bitters are best known as an addition to gin, which they color pink—hence, pink gin. In the Caribbean and in Bolivia, Peru, and Ecuador, they're used as a flavor enhancer.

The familiar angostura bottle and its contents

Coctel de gambas angostureño

(Angostura shrimp cocktail)
Serves 4

This is a tomato sauce with a touch of bitterness, which works well with the sweetness of the shrimp. It is good with any plain-cooked fish—steamed, baked, or broiled.

1 pound cooked, peeled shrimp (tails left on)— 3 to 4 cups
3 large ripe tomatoes, scalded, skinned, and chopped
1 garlic clove, peeled and chopped
2 tablespoons toasted pine nuts
2 red bell peppers, roasted, seeded, and skinned
1 fresh green or red chile, seeded and chopped
1/2 cup olive oil
1/2 teaspoon Angostura bitters
1 teaspoon salt
A pinch sugar

To finish:
Shredded lettuce leaves

Drop all the ingredients except the shrimp into the blender and blend to a purée. Taste, and adjust the seasoning: more sugar, a little lemon juice? Dress the shrimp with the sauce, saving the best for decoration, and pile on shredded lettuce leaves.

Pisco sour
Serves 1

The bitterness of the Angostura bitters makes this a particularly grown-up cocktail. It is properly made with pisco, the Peruvian brandy that, though basically no different from any other distilled grape liquor, is matured in paraffin-lined barrels, so it is both odorless and colorless. The pisco sour is equally appreciated in Ecuador and Bolivia.

A shot (1 1/2 ounces) of pisco
1 teaspoon egg white
1 tablespoon superfine sugar
1 tablespoon lime juice
6 ice cubes

To finish:
Angostura bitters

Shake all the cocktail ingredients together until they foam. Strain into a chilled tumbler. Finish with three drops of bitters.

Pisco sour

coffee

green coffee beans

(*Coffea arabica*)

Coffee beans are the berries of a small tree native to the highlands of Ethiopia but grown widely throughout the tropical Americas. Its natural habitat is volcanic soil, and the higher it's grown, the better the flavor. The main coffee-grower of the Americas is Brazil, the world's largest producer—though, with the exception of the deliciously aromatic Santos, a lot of it is not much good; Colombia is the second largest in quantity but is unsurpassed in quality—look for Medellín, Manizales, Libanos, Bogatoas, and the deliciously named Buccaramangos; Costa Rica produces relatively small amounts of highly aromatic beans; Peru and Ecuador produce in limited quantities, mostly used in blends; Guatemala is distinguished by particularly fragrant beans with a mellow flavor—look for Cobán and Antiquas; Venezuelan beans rival Colombia's finest but are even more delicate—look for Meridas and Caracas; of the mellow and mild Caribbean coffees, the most famous (and absurdly expensive because the production is so small) is Jamaica's Blue Mountain; Cuba, Dominica, and Haiti also produce high-quality coffees.

brown coffee beans

How it grows

The leaves are glossy and lance-shaped; the flowers are white, sweet-scented, and grow in bracelets along the branches. The blossoms drop to form berries—called cherries—which consist of an outer skin, a layer of pulp, an interior membrane, and a pair of inner seeds that grow face to face (a few grow only one: a peaberry). The berries ripen from green to red, the stage at which they're cropped. The processing involves a preliminary light fermentation in damp conditions, followed by drying in the sun (these days, the sun is often replaced by more reliable mechanical driers). Although high-value beans are still harvested by hand, lesser quality beans are plucked by mechanical grabber.

Appearance and taste

Raw coffee beans vary in color from gray-green to yellowy-brown and come encased in a fine papery covering, which rubs off when they're roasted. This is the form—the raw but treated state—in which they're stored or exported. When freshly roasted, the beans are light to dark brown, and have a strongly aromatic scent and deep rich flavor, which is further released by milling to a fine powder before infusing in water.

Coffee pods ripening on the tree

Buying and storing

You can buy your coffee beans at one of three stages—green, roasted, or roasted and ground. If you buy green beans, they can be kept in an airtight container almost indefinitely (aged coffees command a premium).

To roast your own, stir carefully in a pan over an even heat until a rich brown toasty color is achieved, a process much like making popcorn. The process of roasting the beans releases and develops the aromatic oils that deliver the flavor; the degree to which they're roasted—light, medium, dark (very dark if coated with a little sugar right at the end—determines the final flavor; once roasted, store in a sealed packet in a cool place, and the sooner they're used the better. Once the beans are ground, the oils and their fragrance evaporate quickly. If you drink coffee regularly, you'll find it's well worth acquiring a small electric grinder of your own.

Medicinal and other uses

The active ingredient in coffee, caffeine, is a stimulant, a diuretic, and a laxative—highly desirable properties. In its pure state, unless consumed in the kind of levels that indicate addiction, there's no medical evidence that caffeine acts harmfully. When adulterated with other substances—flavorings, processings, and the like—the reverse may be true.

Culinary uses

To make a perfect cup of coffee of the simple sort most frequently encountered in the region, all you need is a pitcher and strainer and two tablespoons of medium-ground coffee per person. Put the coffee in the pitcher, pour in one and a quarter cups boiling water per person, let it steep for five minutes, give it a stir with a cold spoon to settle the grounds, then strain into warmed mugs.

La Belle Josephine

(Caribbean coffee and cream)
Serves 4

This is a delicious confection that commemorates the beauty of Josephine Baker, star of the Folies Bergères in Paris in the twenties. It is also known in the French Caribbean as *Negresse en Chemise*: Black Beauty in a White Petticoat. Exquisite, by whatever name.

1$^1/_2$ cups white curd cheese: ricotta or
   fromage frais
$^2/_3$ cup cream
1 scant cup very strong black coffee
1 scant cup dark Barbados rum
$^2/_3$ cup grated black chocolate

To finish (optional):
Sliced banana
Crushed walnuts
Cinnamon

Push the cheese through a strainer and then beat it with the cream. Gently heat the coffee with the rum, then stir in the chocolate, whisking until dissolved. Set aside for an hour at room temperature for the flavors to develop.

Drop a spoonful of each of the mixtures in individual bowls into which you have, if you wish, dropped a few slices of banana. Swirl together without blending completely. Finish with crushed walnuts and cinnamon—delicious!

maté tea

or yerba mate, Paraguay tea, yerbamá
(*Ilex paraguayensis*—main species)

A shrubby plant, maté comes from a species of holly native to South America, whose lance-shaped leaves are used to make a stimulant infusion popular in pre-Columbian times, later adopted by the Hispanic colonists. After coffee and tea, its popularity in the region makes it the most widely used stimulant infusion in the world.

Gathering and preparation

The shrub's branches are picked and dried over a fire. Afterward, the narrow, toothed leaves are beaten off with sticks, dried in ovens, and then powdered.

Appearance and taste

A touch of bitterness makes maté very refreshing. Some people say it tastes like wet haystacks—though I suspect this is mainly because the modern palate is used to more aggressive flavors. The flavor is mild and delicate, but once a taste for it is acquired, it's addictive. For the export trade, the leaves are baked twice to darken the color and strengthen the flavor.

Buying and storing

Select as you would dried herbs. The scent should be clean and sweet, the color greenish and fresh-looking. Store the leaves in an airtight canister away from direct sunlight.

Medicinal and other uses

A stimulant, with less tannin than tea, maté is not, as is sometimes supposed, caffeine-free. In its land of origin, it is considered suitable for all ages. When I was a schoolgirl in Montevideo, for my tenth birthday, my mother's cook presented me with a maté gourd of my own, inscribed with my name and complete with a *bombilla*, a silver straw with a perforated bobble on the end that acted as a strainer. On my return from school, she'd fill it for me from the kettle, and drop in a lump of burnt sugar, held in a flame until it caramelized and smoked. I would suck it slowly—taking care for the first few sips not to burn my lips on the hot metal—sitting on the steps outside the kitchen, my favorite vantage point, as well as a convenient spot for the receipt of cookies hot from the oven.

Culinary uses

To prepare, simply infuse a tablespoonful of dried maté leaves in a mugful of boiling water. Possible additions are a slice of lemon or a splash of milk, honey, or sugar. In summer, it's delicious iced, with or without a sprig of mint.

A gaucho enjoying his maté tea, Argentina

Yerba maté dulce con hielo

(Iced maté with honey)

Serves 4

Maté, while usually brewed black and taken without embellishment, is delicious in the summer, well iced, with cream and honey. Serve hot in winter.

¹/₄ cup yerba maté
5 cups water

To finish:
Cream
Honey
Ice cubes

Heat the teapot by swirling a little boiling water around inside it, and discard. Put the yerba maté in the teapot, bring fresh water to a boil, and pour it onto the maté. Stir, let it steep for five minutes, and strain it into a pitcher with cream and honey to taste. Let it cool completely. Pour into tall glasses over ice cubes.

blue agave

or maguey, octli (Aztec) (*Agave* spp.)

A spiky-leaved desert plant that looks like an enormous jagged-leaved blue-green tuft of grass; the juices from the tall bud that shoots from its heart are used to make tequila.

Agava tequilana growing in the Oaxaca valley, Mexico

How it is processed

The Aztecs made a beer with the juice that accumulates in the hollow when the cactus bud is cut out, just after it forms before it reaches maturity. The monks who arrived in the wake of the conquistadores distilled the beer to produce tequila—a white brandy named for the town in which it was first manufactured. Modern distilleries grow the cacti in serried ranks in the fields, and apply modern methods to the collection and fermentation of the juice.

Appearance and taste

Pulque, the beer made from the juice, has a strong vegetable flavor, as I well remember from a few years back—rather more than I care to admit—when the maguey grew wild in the desert, and it was simply a matter of waiting seven years for the plant to form a bud. The bud was then chopped out with a machete and the ladies of the village were summoned to suck the juice from the wound with a straw, passing it through the mouth and directing it into a receptacle—a gourd, as I remember—delivering an intoxicating beverage within the hour. Female saliva, chemists interested in this oddity have recently confirmed, is more effective in hastening the conversion of plant-sugars to alcohol than the saliva of the male. I can vouch for this through personal experience, insofar as I can remember anything at all—being only seventeen at the time and having drunk rather too deeply in order not to offend my generous hosts.

Buying and storing

Tequila, the white brandy distilled from the fermented cactus mash, is odorless and colorless in its natural state. Mescal is a refined tequila from Oaxaca that often includes a cactus grub in the bottle, though the good stuff dispenses with any such garnish. It is best drunk with a suck of lime and a lick of salt, or in any way that suits you. *Tequila añejo* is aged tequila that has had time to take color and flavor from the barrel. Store in a cool cellar—although it's unlikely to deteriorate over time whatever you do.

Sorbete margarita

(Margarita sorbet)
Serves 6–8

A delicate sorbet made by freezing the raw materials of a margarita. The alcohol keeps the sorbet relatively soft: serve it in a tall glass so you can drink the dregs.

1 cup white sugar
2$^{1}/_{2}$ cups water
Juice of 6 lemons
1 egg white, mixed with a fork until it froths
2 tablespoons tequila

Dissolve the sugar in the water in a small pan and bring gently to a boil, stirring to make sure all the crystals have melted. Let it cool, and stir in the lemon juice.

If you're using an ice cream maker, mix in the egg white and tequila and freeze as usual. If you use the freezer, as I do, then freeze the sugar-lemon mixture until solid, then take it out and beat it thoroughly, while incorporating the egg white and tequila, and refreeze.

In the Mexican town of Tequila, family-run distilleries have been producing tequila from the agave cactus for over a century

Filete azteca

(Aztec steak)

Serves 4

Serve with the full Mexican complement of white rice, tortillas, fried peppers, raw onion, and black beans.

1 pound cubed pork, dusted with flour
A little oil for frying
2 tablespoons tequila

1 tablespoon parsley, finely chopped
1–2 chiles, seeded and sliced
Salt and pepper

The sauce:
1 pound green tomatoes
3–4 scallions, finely chopped
1 garlic clove, finely chopped
1 tablespoon epazote, finely chopped or crushed
1 green chile, seeded and chopped
2 tablespoons heavy cream

Fry the pork in the oil until lightly browned and perfectly firm. Pour the tequila over the meat and let it boil. Finish with the parsley and chile, and keep warm. Blend all the sauce ingredients except the cream, but not too thoroughly. Tip into the oily frying pan, let it bubble, turn down the heat, cover loosely, and simmer gently for 15 to 20 minutes, until the sauce is reduced and concentrated. Stir in the cream, let it boil again, and pour it over the pork. Serve with all the trimmings.

herbs

thyme

basil

Four herbs usually identified with the cooking of the Mediterranean were used in pre-Columbian times: basil, oregano, thyme, and mint, and a fifth, coriander (cilantro), achieved instant popularity when the Europeans arrived. Although the New World's species are not botanically identical to those of the Old World, and in any event vary throughout the region, for all culinary purposes (and most of the medicinal) they're interchangeable. Basil—*basilio*—is often used in Colombia and Chile in combination with corn; thyme—*tomillo*—is the essential flavoring in Argentina's *chimichurri*, an oil-and-vinegar sauce that accompanies barbecued beef; oregano appears in the marinades of Mexico and Central America; and several varieties of mint—*menta*—were popular throughout the lands of the Maya and Aztecs for medicinal as well as culinary purposes. Coriander—*cilantro*—though unavailable in pre-Columbian times, has become an essential ingredient in many Mexican dishes, particularly guacamole and green chile sauces, as well as in the cooking of Costa Rica and Dominica, where an herb with a similar flavor, *Gerinium foetidum*, is also known as cilantro.

oregano

cilantro

mint

Buying and storing

Oregano and thyme, both dry-leaf herbs, lose none of their power when dehydrated—the very reverse, the essential oils appear to intensify—and are best bought in dried form, stored in an airtight container, and replaced at the beginning of each growing season. Basil and cilantro are both volatile soft-leaf herbs that don't survive drying and must be bought fresh. They are best kept in a cool place with their stalks in water, and used within a day or two. Mint is certainly more fragrant when used fresh, but develops more complex flavors when dried, becoming more like its close relations, oregano and basil.

Medicinal and other uses

Mint is a digestive, an antiseptic, a stimulant, and it clears the sinuses; basil is antispasmodic and assists with flatulence (something of a problem among bean-eaters); marjoram is a stomach calmative and expectorant; thyme is an all-purpose natural tranquilizer; and cilantro naturally aids digestion and can be used topically as a poultice to relieve itching.

Culinary uses

Apart from their intrinsic value as flavoring herbs, thyme, oregano, and mint are all effective bacteria suppressants, useful to cooks in the days when refrigeration was not an available option. Basil is used to discourage flies, and cilantro is simply the world's most popular herb.

A profusion of herbs in Copacabana market, Rio de Janeiro

Crema de elote con basilio

(Cream of corn with basil)
Serves 4–6

A Chilean recipe for a sunny yellow soup enriched with butter and milk, and finished with fresh basil.

2 tablespoons butter
1 small onion, finely chopped
4 cups corn kernels (fresh or frozen)
2¹/₂ cups chicken broth
1¹/₄ cups milk
Salt and pepper

To finish:
Large handful fresh basil leaves
1 tablespoon oil
¹/₂ teaspoon salt

Melt the butter in a roomy soup pot and soften the onion—don't let it brown. Add the corn and broth, bring to a boil, turn down to simmer, and cook gently for 10 minutes. Add the milk and blend to a purée. Reheat and season with salt and pepper. To finish, blend the basil leaves, oil, and salt to a purée, and spoon a dollop onto each portion of soup.

Sopa de albóndigas con oregano

(Meatballs in broth with oregano)
Serves 4

Miniature meatballs bulked with a little rice in the Hispanic style, flavored with oregano, and poached in a clear broth. One of Mexico's favorite midmorning snacks—perfect for hangovers, invalids, and toothless old granddads.

The meatballs:
1 tablespoon rice
1¹/2 cups finely ground meat (pork and/or beef)
1 egg, lightly beaten with a fork
1 garlic clove, very finely chopped
1/2 onion, very finely chopped
1 tablespoon chopped or crumbled oregano
1/2 teaspoon ground allspice
1 teaspoon finely chopped fresh chile or
  1/2 teaspoon chili flakes
Salt

The broth:
5 cups strong chicken, beef, or
  marrow-bone broth
1–2 habanero or malagueta chiles
1–2 sprigs dried oregano

To finish:
Chopped tomato

Put the rice in a small bowl with enough boiling water to cover, and let it soak and swell for about 20 minutes. Drain the rice and put it in the food processor along with the rest of the meatball ingredients. Blend all to a paste. With wet hands (keep a bowl of warm water handy for rinsing your fingers), form the mixture into about 24 bite-size balls.

Bring the broth to a boil with the chile and oregano (tied into a scrap of cheesecloth for ease of removal). Slip in the meatballs and bring back to a simmer. Put the lid on loosely and let it cook gently until the meatballs are cooked through—20 to 25 minutes. Serve in bowls, finished with a little chopped tomato.

Tortitas de papa con cilantro

(Potato cakes with cilantro)
Serves 4 as an appetizer

Cilantro-flavored potato cakes with a pleasantly rough texture, eaten with a fierce little cilantro/chile/avocado salsa.

The cakes:
*4 medium potatoes, boiled in their skins and
    then peeled*
2 tablespoons finely chopped fresh cilantro
2 tablespoons grated cheese
1 large egg, lightly beaten with a fork
1 teaspoon chili flakes
1 teaspoon salt
Oil for shallow frying

The salsa:
2 tablespoons chopped fresh cilantro
*1 avocado, pitted, peeled, and roughly
    chopped*
*2 green (jalapeño) chiles, seeded and
    finely chopped*
*3–4 scallions or 1 mature onion, finely
    chopped*
¹/₄ cup lemon juice
1 teaspoon salt

Put the potatoes in a bowl and mash roughly with a fork. Using your hands and without crushing out all the lumps, work in the cilantro, cheese, egg, chile, and salt. In a separate bowl, combine all the salsa ingredients.

Heat the oil in a wide, heavy frying pan and, when the oil is very hot, drop in tablespoons of the potato mixture, patting them roughly into little cakes. Fry, turning once, until golden and crisp on each side. Remove and drain on paper towels. Serve topped with a spoonful of the green salsa, or hand the salsa around separately in a bowl.

Chimichurri

(Argentinian thyme and garlic relish)
Makes 1 bottleful

A thyme-infused, garlicky, oil-and-vinegar dressing, this is the ketchup of the pampas, a must with barbecued beef—an *asado*, a young bullock roasted gaucho-style on a sharpened pole stuck at an angle over the evening's campfire. And if the meat's to be spared for another day, the sauce works wonders with a potato baked in the embers.

3–4 sprigs fresh thyme (the drier the better)
1 large onion
6 cloves garlic
¹/₄ cup flat-leaf parsley
²/₃ cup wine vinegar
2 cups olive oil

Pop the thyme sprigs in an empty wine bottle along with the onion, garlic, and parsley. Add the vinegar and oil, shake it up, and let it infuse for a couple of days. Ready when you are. Keep it in the refrigerator.

Mojito

Serves 1

Unlike rum and cola—*Cuba Libre*—this is the politically acceptable tipple in Castro's Havana.

Juice of half a lime
1 teaspoon sugar
2–3 sprigs fresh mint
A shot of white rum
Crushed ice
Soda water

Mix the lime juice with the sugar in a highball glass until it dissolves. Drop in the mint and add the rum and ice. Stir. Fill up with soda water. Finish with another sprig of mint.

fruit

The fruits of the region are a wild and wonderful mixture of the exotic, the weird, and some that are so hard to obtain you can only taste them once a year—and then only in the particular place where they're grown. Many of the more familiar fruits are used in unfamiliar ways—in unripe form as vegetables, or ripe but dusted not with sugar but with chile—while many of the more exotic and perishable jungle fruits and tropical berries are yet to be discovered outside the territory. Aware of this, whenever possible I have tried to give alternatives that, although they can never be quite the same, are the kind of substitutes a native of the region might use when trying to re-create the taste of home.

The traveler will have better luck. Anyone unfamiliar with the botanical riches of a particular area can easily sample them in the form of freshly squeezed *liquados, sorbetes,* and *batidos*—iced and frothed with cream, or topped with condensed milk—offered for sale by roadside vendors in cones of paper or plastic cups. This service, though taken for granted by the natives, is a constant source of pleasure for the visitor, as well as providing much-needed refreshment. The surprise is the offer of a drop of chili sauce along with the sugar shaker.

pineapple

or anana, piña, abaxi (Brazil) (*Ananas comosus*)

Several species of this oddly constructed fruit, both large and small, are native to the Brazilian lowlands. The Spanish conquistaders first came across it in the Caribbean and decided it reminded them of a pinecone—*piña*. The name did not travel throughout the region: elsewhere it's more commonly known as *anana*, a Tupi word for "delicious."

Fresh pineapples in transit

How it grows

The pineapple is not one but many little fruits clamped together around a single stem, topped by a tuft of narrow spiky leaves.

Appearance and taste

The fruit, which has a rough exterior with a prickly pinecone structure, ripens to a rich red-gold; the exterior roughness is reflected in the interior flesh, which is chewy rather than soft, striated like soft wood but tender, juicy, and very fragrant, its sweetness balanced by sourness—thrilling on the palate.

Buying and storing

The fruits don't ripen any more after picking, so it must be perfectly mature when harvested. Brazilian gourmets—and pineapple appreciation is a high art in the markets of Rio and Bahia—will tell you the flesh is sweeter at the stalk end. Look for firmness with no sign of withering, and a strong fragrance with no hint of fermentation; to check for ripeness, pull out one of the little leaves from the topknot—if it comes out easily, the fruit is mature.

Medicinal and other uses

The pineapple is recommended for arthritis and stiffness in the joints. But be careful when handling the fresh fruit: the juice is so corrosive that pineapple-canning factories have to provide their workers with protective clothing.

Culinary uses

The presence of bromalin, a powerful protein-digesting enzyme, makes pineapple useful as a meat tenderizer. For the same chemical reason, a gelatin dessert made with fresh pineapple won't gel if the setting agent is an animal-derived gelatin, as most of them are. The bromalin is neutralized when heated, so canned fruit or pasteurized juices don't have the same effect.

Galinha assado com abacaxi

(Roast chicken with pineapple)
Serves 4–6

The pineapple tenderizes the chicken as it roasts to make this deliciously juicy and delicately perfumed dish. It is even better with guinea fowl, an African bird that has claimed its perch in the barnyards of Brazil.

1 free-range chicken
1 small pineapple, skinned and diced (save the juices)
1 onion, coarsely chopped
2 tablespoons oil or butter
1 teaspoon ground allspice
Salt
1 teaspoon malagueta pepper sauce (see page 51) or 1 teaspoon chili powder

Preheat the oven to 400°F.

Rinse the bird inside and out and place it breast-side down on a roasting pan. Tuck the chunks of pineapple and onion inside the cavity. Trickle with the oil or slip the butter under the skin of the breast, and sprinkle with the allspice, salt, and pepper sauce or chili.

Roast for 30 minutes, turn the bird breast-side up, baste with the reserved pineapple juice and the drippings in the pan, and turn down the heat to 350°F. Roast for another 30 minutes, until tender and beautifully brown.

Cut it up neatly and serve with the onion and pineapple handed around separately.

Flan de piña, a fragrant pineapple caramel custard

Flan de piña
(Pineapple caramel custard)
Serves 6

Egg and sugar confections, a legacy of colonial rule, were the specialties of the convents, which make these little caramel custards with pineapple juice instead of milk.

For the caramel:
2 tablespoons sugar
2 teaspoons water
Juice of half a lemon

For the custard:
1¼ cups pineapple juice
1 cup granulated sugar
6 large egg yolks (another 2 if the eggs are
small)

You will need 6 little molds or 1 large one, and a roasting pan to use as a water bath. Preheat the oven to 350°F.

Make the caramel first. Melt the ingredients together in the pan, turning it over a high flame until the sugar caramelizes a rich golden brown. This will take only a moment or two. Tip it into the molds and roll it around to coat the bottom. Set aside to cool.

To make the custard, put the juice and sugar in a heavy pan, and heat gently until the sugar dissolves. Boil for about 20 minutes, until reduced by a third. Stir with a wooden spoon: it's ready when the syrup trails a transparent string when you lift out the spoon. Meanwhile, whisk the egg yolks thoroughly. Pour the hot syrup into the eggs, beating vigorously. This will begin the thickening process. Pour the mixture into the mold(s). Cover each with foil and place them in the roasting pan. Pour enough boiling water into the roasting pan to come halfway up the molds. Bake for 30 to 50 minutes, depending on the size of the container. They're ready when firm to the touch. Let them cool and shake well before unmolding—the caramel makes a deliciously dark sticky sauce.

banana

or platano (*Musa* spp.)

An ancient cultivar of Asian origin, the banana is naturalized throughout the tropical and subtropical zones of the Americas. Plants of the family Musaceae are not actually trees but grasses, with a rhizome rather than a root, and a trunk formed from its own overlapping leaves (see Plantain, page 206, for additional culinary uses).

Medicinal and other uses

The banana is excellent, fortifying, easily assimilable, and high in fiber and essential vitamins and minerals—particularly potassium. It's also a bowel stimulant, a remedy for ulcers, and a stomach calmant; it inducies sleep and encourages the production of hormones.

How it grows

The fruits develop from the small female flowers that ring the seed-head, a long stalk tipped by a single scarlet blossom whose petals peel back to expose a pointed ivory bud, the male. The weight of the bud draws the stalk downward, allowing the fruits, semicircular "hands" that circle the stem like elegant emerald bracelets, to point upward. Left to its own devices, the plant can grow to over 30 feet, although the insecurity of its footing and the weight of the fruit—as many as 200 per stalk—can cause it to topple before its time.

Buying and storing

Caribbean bananas grown on the steep slopes of the Windward Islands are smaller, sweeter, and juicier than the big "dollar bananas" of the Central American mainland—so called because they are grown on lowland plantations controlled by the two U.S.-based monopolies. In Brazil, popular varieties include *banana de agua*, lor ady-fingers, which are small, thin-skinned, and sweet, and preferred for frying to accompany meat or fish. Another popular variety is the red or apple banana, which is juicy and lemony when ripe; when green, it fries to an exquisite crispness. Bananas are exported green, the state in which they usually come to market. If the banana doesn't snap easily from the stalk for peeling, it's not ripe; ripening turns the fruit from a bright sunny yellow to a deep gold lightly freckled with brown, the moment of perfection. To slow down the ripening process, refrigerate: the skin will turn brown but the fruit will remain perfect.

Culinary uses

The red-skinned banana, floury and fragrant with pale orange flesh, cooks well: it is delicious roasted in the skin, then split and sprinkled with powdered cinnamon and brown sugar. When very ripe, it develops a bronzed skin and soft dark flesh—perfect for banana bread. The application of heat to the ripe fruit emphasizes its natural starchiness, making the flavor more robust, the flesh more chewy. When mashed before cooking, it quickly collapses to a soft mush, an advantage in baking, when the combination of starchiness and sweetness makes it an excellent cake ingredient.

Appearance and taste

The banana is the earliest convenience food: it not only tastes delicious—smooth and creamy with a vanilla-citrus fragrance and a delicately spicy flavor—but fits neatly in one's hand, ripens in the pocket, and can be slipped easily out of its skin. These virtues have made it the most widely consumed fruit in the world, much of which gets its supplies from the Americas.

Banana plantation, Honduras

Banana bread

Banana bread

Serves 6–8

Not only every island but every household in the Carribean has a favorite recipe for banana bread. It is good for breakfast and tea, and perfect for the midday break. My little granddaughters love it.

1 pound very ripe bananas (3 large ones), skinned
Generous 1/2 cup honey
2 medium eggs
1/2 cup butter, softened
1/2 cup light brown sugar
2 cups self-rising whole wheat flour
1 level teaspoon baking powder
1 teaspoon freshly grated nutmeg

To finish:
1 banana, skinned and quartered lengthwise

Preheat the oven to 350°F. Butter and line a 9 x 6-inch loaf pan with buttered waxed paper (banana bread tends to stick to the pan).

Purée the bananas thoroughly with the honey and the eggs in the blender or food processor. Sift the dry ingredients. Beat the butter with the sugar until light and pale, then beat in the banana mixture, alternating with the flour mixture, and blend thoroughly. Drop the mixture into the loaf pan, spreading it well into the corners. Top with the quartered bananas.

Bake for an hour, until the cake has shrunk from the sides and is well-risen and springy in the middle—it may need a little longer, in which case turn the oven down a notch and bake for another 10 to 15 minutes. Tip it out onto a cooling rack.

Doce de banana

(Sugared Brazilian banana)
Serves 4

A very sweet, sticky, spicy, jamlike banana compote. Take your time—it's the long, slow cooking that turns the fruit a beautiful mahogany. Try with sour cream.

4–6 ripe bananas (depending on size), skinned and thickly sliced
2 1/4 cups soft brown sugar
2 1/2 cups water
3–5 cloves
1 short stick cinnamon

Put all the ingredients in a heavy pan. Put the lid on loosely and cook over gentle heat until the fruit turns a rich dark red and the juices thicken to a clear syrup—30 to 40 minutes. Let it cool before serving. Keeps well in the refrigerator.

plantain

or plátano (*Musa* spp.)

The plantain is not, as might be supposed, a separate species of fruit from the sweet banana, but a description applied to a green unripe banana that is usually, but not always, of a variety specially grown for its virtues as a vegetable. Just to confuse matters, the name is sometimes applied to an unripe sweet banana. As if that were not trouble enough, *plátano* is the Spanish name for both varieties.

Appearance and taste

The purpose-bred varieties are mouth-puckeringly bitter when raw; when cooked, they're starchy and bland, more like a root than a fruit. The plantain is grown as a staple vegetable in those places—such as tropical jungles—where grain foods cannot thrive.

Buying and storing

The purpose-bred varieties are longer and more angular in shape than the sweet banana, often narrowing to form a short horn at the nonstalk end. The color starts a bright green and ripens to yellow, streaked with brown.

Medicinal and other uses

The plantain is indigestible and constipating when raw, though both problems are solved by cooking.

Related products

The leaves of both banana and plantain—which are actually gigantic blades of grass—are used throughout the region as wrappers to protect delicate foodstuffs from the direct heat of the fire or to keep food moist during prolonged steaming in an earth oven. A little preliminary preparation is needed: wilt the whole fresh leaf over a wide-based heat source—a charcoal barbecue or a gas flame—until the surface begins to look oily and the color changes from bright emerald to dark green. Cut out the central rib and snip the rest into sizes suitable for wrapping the food—chicken, fish, meatballs, whatever—and package in whatever way suits the recipe. The leaves give a particular distinction to the cooking of the Yucatan on the Caribbean coast of Mexico, where both fish and chicken are cooked in banana leaves, imparting an exquisite viscosity and delicate citrus flavor to the juices.

"Open market" in São Paulo, Brazil

Culinary uses

To serve plantains or green bananas as a vegetable, roast in their skins, boil, bake, or slice and fry. Use a sharp knife to peel them—or follow the instructions in the Patacones recipe on page 207—since the skin is virtually welded to the flesh. To make plantain chips, choose firm green fruits, slice thinly, skin, and deep-fry until crisp. To broil or barbecue plantains as the street vendors do in Jamaica, cut them in half horizontally without peeling them, brush the cut side with oil, and start with the skin side toward the heat. Grill for 5 minutes and turn, allowing another 2 minutes for them to soften and crisp.

Baked plantains
Serves 4

The perfect recipe for over-ripe plantains. Serve like baked potatoes in their skins: finger-licking good with spicy jerk chicken (see allspice, page 184).

4 ripe plantains

For serving:
Butter

Preheat the oven to 450°F. Arrange the plantains on a baking sheet and bake for 20 to 30 minutes, until cooked through. To serve, split right down the middle with a knife, mash the flesh a little, and drop in a pat of butter.

Patacones

(Plantain fritters)

Serves 4–6

These twice-cooked fritters—fried once to soften, a second time to crisp—are known in some places as *tostones*, in others as *patacones*—notably in Ecuador and Colombia, where you can buy special little wooden presses for squashing them flat.

2 unpeeled firm plantains or 3 green bananas, thickly sliced (2 fingers' width)

Salt

Oil for deep-frying

Soak the plantain slices in salted water for half an hour, until you can push the edible disks out of their skin; drop them back in the water to prevent browning until you're ready to cook.

Heat a panful of oil over medium-high heat.

Pat the plantain slices dry. Drop them in the oil, a few at a time, and fry gently until softish but not yet crisp. Remove to paper towels, cover with plastic wrap, and flatten with a spatula to reduce the slices to half their thickness—as mentioned, Latin American cooks can buy a special little wooden press for the purpose. You can do this in pairs, overlapping two slices and

flattening both together. Either way, the soft fruit spreads to make a pretty broken edge that browns deliciously.

Reheat the oil until very hot. Fry the flattened slices, a few at a time, until brown and crisp on the outside and still meltingly soft on the inside.

Treat as you would tortilla chips: as a scoop for a seviche, a soupy bean dish, guacamole, or a savory stew. Or serve as dessert with fresh curd cheese, honey, and nuts.

guava

or guayaba (Spanish), goiaba (Portuguese)
(*Psidium guajava*)

A Peruvian native, the guava was already established in Mexico at the time of the Hispanic conquest.

Guava tree, Cuba

How it grows

A smallish tree, about the size of an apple tree, the guava has large smooth-edged leaves and white flowers from which develop somewhat pear-like fruits.

Appearance and taste

The fruits are very variable in size and color, with skin that runs the gamut from pale green through yellow to (sometimes) scarlet when ripe. The flesh varies from creamy-white to bright pink and has an outer and inner section, the inner section being scattered with gritty little seeds in a circular pattern around the core, although some seedless varieties are grown.

Buying and storing

The fruit should yield a little to light pressure, and have a strong flowery fragrance; it ripens very rapidly, making export a problem. Choose firm fruits, discarding any that feel spongy or show signs of bruising. Store in the refrigerator and use within a couple of days.

Medicinal and other uses

The musky, spicy fragrance of a ripe guava indicates the presence of eugenol, an essential oil found in cloves, effective as a remedy for toothache, and also used as a stimulant for the lymphatic system.

Related or similar fruits

The pineapple-guava (*Feijoa sellowiana*) or feijoa is the fruit of a small evergreen tree native to southern Brazil but also found in northern Argentina, Uruguay, and Paraguay. Fruits are egg-shaped, about the size and appearance of a kiwi fruit but without the fuzzy skin. Light green when ripe, when cut they reveal a rim of flesh surrounding a hollow center filled with a soft pulp that holds lots of tiny seeds. The flavor and fragrance are complex: strawberry/guava/pineapple. The pineapple-guava ripens quickly—in nature, as soon as it drops from the tree—becoming more fragrant as it develops. Eaten raw when the first of the crop comes in, it is used for juice and jellies later. To prepare, peel off the soft skin, then slice and sprinkle with lemon juice to avoid discoloration. When ready to eat, the scent should be fresh and flowery—fruit picked when immature will be bitter even when ripe—and should have a slight give, like a pear. Medicinally, the pineapple-guava is particularly rich in iodine. It can replace apples in pies and compotes, and is also delicious raw in a fruit salad.

Culinary uses

The large, pale-fleshed, pear-shaped guavas are considered the best for eating, while the small, pink-fleshed varieties such as the strawberry guava, *P. cattleianum*—a Brazilian native that ripens to a deep purple—make the best jelly.

Mermelada de guayaba
(Guava jelly)
Makes about 3 pounds

A clear garnet-pink jelly with a flowery scent and delicate flavor.

2 pounds guavas
About 4 cups light brown sugar
Juice of 2 lemons or 3 limes

Rinse and roughly chop the guavas—skins, seeds, and all—and put them in a roomy saucepan with enough water to cover. Bring to a boil and cook for 20 minutes, until the fruit is soft and mushy. Dump the contents of the pan into a clean cheesecloth and hang it on a hook suspended over a bowl. Let it drip overnight. The next day, return the juice (save the pulp for the next recipe) to the pan with an equal amount of sugar and the lemon juice. Bring to a boil, skim off the foam that rises, and boil steadily, uncovered, for 35 minutes or until setting point is reached. To test, drop a little onto a cold saucer and push it with your finger: when it wrinkles like skin, it's ready. Pour into well-scalded jelly jars and seal. Keep in a cool pantry away from direct sunlight.

Membrillo de guayaba
(Guava cheese)
Makes about 2 pounds

A thick, slightly grainy fruit paste—very delicious. A Christmas treat, the New World version of the Old World's quince paste, guava cheese is traditionally made into little palm-leaf packages and given by the host to wedding guests to keep the memory of the encounter sweet.

2 pounds guava pulp (freshly stewed,
* or left over from the guava jelly recipe)*
2 cups light brown sugar

Push the pulp through a sieve or cheesecloth-lined strainer, discarding the skins and seeds. Put the strained pulp in a pan and beat in the sugar. Cook very, very gently for at least an hour, until the pulp and sugar have formed a soft, dark, dryish mass. Alternatively, spread on a baking tray and leave in the oven on the lowest possible temperature overnight. It'll set to a firm paste. Wrap in paper and keep in a warm, dry place—never in the refrigerator. Delicious with cheese.

Mermelada de guayaba, a clear guava jelly

musk cucumber

or sicana (Peru), cassabanana (Puerto Rico), calabaza melón (Mexico), cojombro (Nicaragua), melocotón de bresil (Guatemala), cura (Brazil) (*Sicana odorifera*)

The musk cucumber is a member of the watermelon family native to Brazil.

How it grows

An ornamental vine, as decorative as it is useful, the musk cucumber is cultivated in its land of origin not only as a fruit but also for the beauty of its foliage and flowers.

Appearance and taste

The fruit looks like a large, fat cucumber with a smooth shiny skin that can be red, black, or purple. The flesh is yellow to orange and very melonlike in flavor and texture, centered around a hollow cavity, packed with rows of flat seeds embedded in a cottonball-like fiber.

Buying and storing

Look for the musk cucumber in markets that serve Central American communities, particularly Puerto Rican ones. Tap gently—the hollower, the riper. The musk cucumber keeps well and is so deliciously perfumed that Puerto Rican housewives tuck a couple in the linen closet to scent the sheets.

Medicinal and other uses

In Puerto Rico, the juice, well sugared and slightly fermented, is used as a cold cure. The Brazilian name for it is *cura*: cure-all.

Culinary uses

When preparing it as a vegetable, peel with a sharp knife and chop. It's eaten as a vegetable when unripe, in soups and stews, in much the same way as summer squash. When ripe, it can be eaten raw, though it's more often converted into a sticky preserve popular at Christmas.

Sopa de sicana

(Musk cucumber soup)
Serves 4–6

The Peruvian way with this most fragrant of gourds. If you can't buy them or grow them, a similar culinary effect can be achieved by replacing the main ingredient with chayote and a splash of rose water. Not the same, of course—but good enough to fool the neighbors.

2 pounds unripe musk cucumbers, peeled, seeded, and roughly chopped
2 pounds tomatoes, scalded, peeled, and roughly chopped (about 5–5$\frac{1}{2}$ cups)
1 pound onions, skinned and chopped (about 3$\frac{1}{2}$ cups)
1 stalk celery, washed and sliced
2$\frac{1}{2}$ cups homemade broth or plain water
A handful of fresh basil leaves

To finish:
$\frac{2}{3}$ cup heavy cream

Put all the ingredients except the cream into a large saucepan, bring to a boil, put the lid on, and turn down to simmer for 30 minutes, until the vegetables are all soft and soupy.

Mash everything down hard with a potato masher, ladle into soup plates, and finish each plateful with a swirl of cream.

A portable Bethlehem scene, *belén*, displayed at Christmas in Peru

Dulce de cassabanana puertoriqueño

(Candied musk cucumber)

Serves 6

In Puerto Rico, Christmas wouldn't be the same without this very sticky, exquisitely fragrant preserve, traditionally offered on the best glass dish in tiny portions to guests, so their visit may be all the sweeter. It's delicious with sour cream and walnuts, and a little goes a long way.

3 pounds ripe musk cucumbers, peeled and seeded
1¹/₂ cups sugar
6 tablespoons water

For serving (optional):
Walnuts, coarsely chopped
Sour cream

Either scoop into balls with a melon-baller (pretty and appropriately festive) or dice into bite-size pieces. Layer the fruit and sugar in a heavy saucepan and add the water.

Set the pan on a very low flame, put the lid on tightly, and simmer gently for 50 to 60 minutes, until the fruit is tender and the syrup thick and shiny. You may need to splash in more water, or you may need to boil it down with the pan uncovered—it all depends on how watery it was when it started.

Let it cool in the pan in its syrup before you ladle it into jelly jars, making sure there's enough syrup to submerge the fruit completely. Or serve immediately, sprinkled with walnuts, and hand the sour cream around separately.

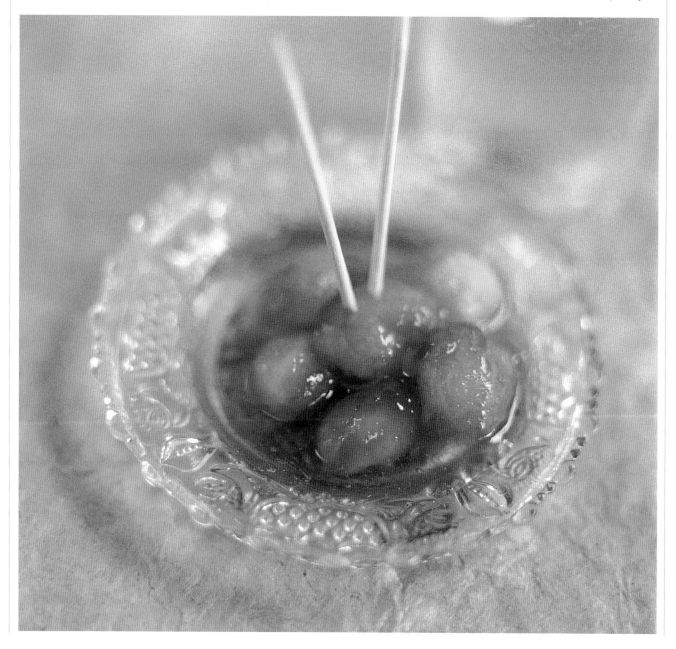

papaya

or melón zapote (Mexico), fruta bomba (Cuba), lechosa/lichisa (Puerto Rico), mando or mamão (Brazil), and pawpaw—but not to be confused with cherimoya (page 226) (*Carica papaya*)

The papaya is a pear-shaped, green-skinned fruit that grows in clusters directly out of the trunk of a small tree native to the subtropical lowlands of Central America. Cultivated since pre-Columbian times by the Mayans and their successors, the Aztecs, the common name—papaya—derives from the Mayan name, *ababai*.

How it grows

A fruit of variable size in its land of origin, the papaya can be as large as a honeydew melon. The export trade prefers smaller fruits weighing no more than a pound, which can be sold as suitable for a single portion or, at most, for sharing between two people.

Appearance and taste

When ripe, the flesh is pink, tinged with orange, and is tender and fragrant, with a flavor of strawberry and banana. Growing in popularity commercially is the *chamburo* or *babaco* (*C. pentagona*), a deeply ridged, five-sided seedless papaya of Ecuadorian origin—a hybrid of a native fruit, unknown in the wild—which has sweet, juicy, fragrant, vanilla-scented, ivory-white flesh that, lacking the hard little seeds, is edible throughout.

Buying and storing

Look for a fruit that yields to gentle pressure in the hand and feels heavy for its size, with an unwrinkled, unblemished skin blushed with yellow, ripening to red (the nonsun side remains green). Regional names are a minefield: the traveler or anyone attempting to buy the fruit in a market serving ethnic communities would be wise to exercise caution. In Cuba, *papaya* is slang for the female reproductive organs; elsewhere, eyebrows will be raised at the use of the word *lechosa*. The problem lies in the mind of the beholder, having to do with the color of the cut flesh (a beautiful orangey-pink), its softness and succulence, and the exuberant amount of small, jelly-coated seeds. I'm sure you get the picture.

Papayas and watermelons on sale in Panama

Medicinal and other uses

Papaya is digestive and stomach-settling—but be warned, don't let the corrosive juices anywhere near sensitive or broken skin, and wash your hands thoroughly before you change a baby's diaper.

Related products

The central cavity is filled with small black seeds slicked with sticky juice. These seeds, though very hard, can be cracked and eaten: crushed or milled, they taste a little like grain mustard and are good in a salad dressing. The leaves can be used as a food wrapper, imparting a delicate flavor as well as acting as a tenderizing agent.

Culinary uses

Delicious ripe and raw with just a squeeze of lime juice, papayas can be included in meat stews and marinades as a tenderizer. All parts (fruit and leaves) contain papain, a protein-digesting enzyme used in commercial meat-tenderizing powders. For this reason, it won't set as a jelly if the setting agent is a gelatin of animal origin.

Picante de papaya

(Deviled papaya)

Serves 4

A marriage of two perfectly compatible fruits—one dense and buttery, the other juicy and fragrant—given a sinful little twist with a chile-infused syrup. Roadside vendors who sell prepared fruits blended to order and ladled into plastic cups will always offer a sprinkle of chili along with the sugar shaker.

Juice of 1–2 limes
6 tablespoons sugar
1 hot red chile
1–2 papayas, peeled, seeded, and diced
1 small ripe melon, seeded and diced

Put the lime juice and sugar in a small pan with an equal amount of water. Bring gently to a boil, stirring to dissolve the sugar crystals. Add the chile, remove from the heat, and let it infuse and cool. Combine the prepared fruits in a bowl and dress with sugar syrup. Top with the infused chile as a warning to the unwary.

Guiso de chivo con papaya

(Kid or lamb stew with papaya)

Serves 4–6

A Mexican shepherd's stew, equally good made with a well-grown kid or the sinewy little lambs of the Hispanic tradition, left to cook gently overnight in the embers of the campfire, and reheated the next day.

About 2¹/₂ pounds kid or lamb on the
bone, cut into chunks
1 medium-size, unripe, green papaya, cut into
chunks
Juice and peel of 1 bitter orange, or half of a
lemon and half of a sweet orange
1 teaspoon chili powder
Short length cinnamon, broken up
1 tablespoon sugar
1 teaspoon salt
2 tablespoons oil
2 onions, finely sliced
2 garlic cloves, skinned and chopped

Mix the meat with the papaya, citrus juice and peel, chili, cinnamon, sugar, and salt in a bowl, cover, and leave for 3–4 hours to marinate.

Warm the oil in a roomy flameproof casserole dish or other heavy pot, and fry the onions and garlic gently for 8 to 10 minutes, until soft and golden. Add the meat and papaya, put the lid on tightly, and heat gently for 2 to 3 hours, until perfectly tender and deliciously gluey. Or bake: it'll take about the same amount of time in the oven at 300°F.

Picante de papaya

passion fruit

or purple granadilla, grenadilla, maracujá (Brazil), curuba (Colombia), parcha (Venezuela and Puerto Rico), ceibey (Cuba), couzou (West Indies) (*Passiflora edulis*)

Passion fruit—*granadilla*—is the fruit of a flowering vine native to the rain forests of Brazil but naturalized throughout the region, including by the Aztecs in Mexico.

How it grows

While the fruits are not particularly noticeable, the blossoms are of an astonishing beauty, as intricately chiseled as the carvings on an Aztec altar. Spanish missionaries, seeking images to assist them in their preaching, declared it a holy flower. They named it for the passion of Christ and carried it into the pulpit as a metaphor for their message: twelve petals for the Apostles, five stamens for the five wounds, three styles to symbolize the three nails, and the corolla for the crown of thorns.

Appearance and taste

On the vine, the fruit looks like a purply brown hen's egg, smooth when ripening, and crinkling a little when ready to eat, with a leathery skin whose color bleeds carmine into the soft white pith that lines the carapace and protects the

interior seeds. These seeds—small and crunchy and without any particular flavor—are encased in a soft, exquisitely fragrant, sweet-sharp, pineapple/guava-flavored jelly, which drips with juice.

Buying and storing

Choose fruits that weigh heavy for their size. When ripe, the skin crinkles up like an elderly prune: if it looks only a little bit shrunk, store at room temperature until it crumples.

Medicinal and other uses

High in vitamin C, the passion fruit is valuable in preventing colds.

Related or similar fruits

The sweet calabash, *P. maliformis*—a smallish, yellow-skinned passion fruit native to Amazonia —is particularly esteemed for its exceptionally fragrant, sweet-sour pulp: a spoonful will perfume ten times its own volume of cream.

The sweet granadilla, *P. ligularis*, is a native of Mexico whose pretty orange skin acquires, when ripe, a dusting of snowy freckles. The water-lemon, *P. laurifolia*, also called

Jamaican honeysuckle and yellow granadilla, is a Caribbean native that looks, as you might expect, like a small smooth-skinned lemon, but in all other respects serves the same culinary purpose as other passion fruits.

The banana passion fruit, *P. molissima*, is known as *curuba* in Colombia, *tacso* in Ecuador, *parcha* in Venezuela, and *tumbo* in Bolivia and Peru.

Giant or royal granadilla, *P. quadrangularis*— known as *maracujá* in Brazil—is one of the largest of the genus, up to 8 inches long. It ripens from green to gold or crimson and looks rather like a small mango. Next to the skin is a thick lining of pinkish, melonlike flesh—also edible—as well as the usual pulp-and-seed arrangement. For all its popularity (and the vine is widely planted throughout Asia as well as the tropical Americas), the flavor doesn't match the fragrance. Although acceptable raw for its juices and the odd combination of textures, the giant granadilla is disappointingly bland and is best combined with more sharply defined flavorings such as pineapple, lemon, and bitter orange.

Red granadilla, *P. coccinea*, is an Amazonian native popular in Guadaloupe, which has scarlet blossoms and speckled yellow-green fruits; *P. alatta*, the wing-stemmed passionflower, is mostly cultivated for the beauty of its blossoms, though the fruits are edible (check your gardening catalog); as is *P. caerulea*, the blue passionflower, whose fruits are bland but edible.

The Brazilian jungle-plum or *ciriguela* is a fruit of Amazonia that looks not unlike a kumquat, with thin, sharply flavored skin and soft aromatic flesh around a shiny black kernel. A Christmas fruit, it comes to market in December, after the rains.

Culinary uses

To eat passion fruit raw from the hand, use your teeth to make a small hole in the leathery skin and suck out the seeds and sweet-sour juices. As a flavoring, push it through a strainer to extract the seeds (or not, as you please): it is sensational in creams, mousses, and soufflés, and wonderful in fruit salads, delivering the same acid punch as a squeeze of lemon. Use undiluted as the acid-bath when preparing a seviche. Each fruit yields one mouthful of seed-laden jelly—the *aril*. It takes 100 fruits to produce a quart of thick juice whose viscosity comes from a high starch content. Happily, the flavor is remarkably concentrated and can be generously diluted.

Caipirinha de maracujá

(Passion fruit and rum cocktail)
Serves 1

A mouthful of sheer pleasure, tart and exquisitely fragrant—served at every fashionable Brazilian cocktail party. Make one at a time.

1 passion fruit
1 tablespoon superfine sugar
2 tablespoons cachaça or white rum
Ice cubes

Squeeze the contents of the passion fruit into a short fat tumbler. Crush the sugar into the pulp. Add the cachaça or rum and enough ice cubes to fill the glass. Stir and serve.

Baba de maracujá

(Little passion fruit mousses)
Serves 6–8

The flowery fragrance of the fruit makes each of these lightly set honeycomb mousses a mouthful of sheer pleasure. Condensed milk delivers the authentically Brazilian flavor, though some might consider fresh cream to be even better. Delicious with a crisp little cookie.

12 ripe passion fruit
2 sheets clear gelatin or 1 tablespoon powdered—enough to set 1¹/₄ cups of liquid
1¹/₄ cups unsweetened condensed milk or fresh heavy cream
4 egg whites
6 tablespoons sugar

Scoop the pulp from eight of the passion fruit and reserve the remaining four fruits. Push the pulp through a strainer to separate the juice from the seeds. Tear the gelatin into bits and put it to soak in a little cold water for 10 minutes or so, until it softens. If using powdered gelatin, follow the directions on the package. In a small pan, mix the soaked gelatin with half the passion fruit juice and dissolve it over a gentle heat, whisking to blend. Whisk in the condensed milk or the cream.

Meanwhile whisk the egg whites until they hold their shape, then whisk in the sugar, spoonful by spoonful, to make a soft meringue. Fold in the warm passion fruit cream and spoon into whatever receptacles you like— small or large. Finish with the reserved passion fruit—juice and seeds—cut in half and squeezed over the mousse.

Cape gooseberry

or physalis, uvilla (little grape, Colombia), capuli (Bolivia/Peru), topotopo (Venezuela), chuchuva (Venezuela), bolsa de amor (love-bag, Chile), cereza de Perú (Mexico), ciriguela de Peru (Brazil) (*Physalis peruviana*)

Physalis—a group that includes the tree tomato and tomatillo as well a number of cherry-like fruits of the genus Solanaceae—is a Peruvian vine fruit, a member of the potato–tomato family. It was exported north to Mexico, where it was appreciated by both the Aztecs and the Mayas, and early Portuguese colonizers established it as a crop on the Cape of Good Hope—hence its name.

How it grows

Cape gooseberries are the fruits of a perennial vine; they hang down like little lanterns where the leaves meet the stalk and are enclosed in a papery calyx. The berrylike fruits of its close relation, the decorative garden plant known as the Chinese lantern, though smaller, are interchangeable for culinary purposes.

Appearance and taste

While the flesh has a similar structure and texture to the tomato, the seeds are smaller and crunchier, and the flavor is distinctly fruity: sweet-sour, fragrant, and refreshingly sharp.

Buying and storing

The fruits start green and ripen to a brilliant yellow-orange. Buy them ripe—don't worry if the husks look a bit dingy. Stored in a sealed container in a dry place, they'll keep for months.

Mayan temple façade, Yucatán, Mexico

Consumption warning

Avoid unripe fruits: they're poisonous.

Related or similar fruits

The sweet cucumber (*Solanum muricatum*), or *pepino dulce,* is the fruit of a small bush native to the Andean regions of Peru and Chile, also cultivated elsewhere throughout the temperate zones. One form that grows on a vine looks a bit like a small cucumber—hence the name—but more usually the shape and color is that of a small, pale-skinned eggplant. The smooth golden skin is freckled with green or violet and, like the eggplant, is usually sweet but can occasionally be bitter. When ripe, the texture and appearance of the flesh—golden and juicy—is somewhere between a honeydew melon and a ripe pear, with a fragrance of vanilla and honeysuckle. The seeds and skin are both edible, though the latter is best removed since it's a little tough.

Other vine fruits of the same group, particularly *P. pruinosa*, are known as *cereza de suelo*—ground cherry—and are of local rather than commercial interest.

Naranjilla (Peru) or *naranjilla de Quito* (Ecuador), *lulún* (Mexico), *toronjo* (Colombia) (*Solanum quitoense*) is a furry little orange berry native to Peru, Ecuador, and Colombia, in all respects similar to the physalis, apart from its hairy brown skin that can easily be rubbed off. It is particularly esteemed for its juice, for which it is grown commercially.

Consumption warning

The papery calyx—inedible and mildly toxic—must be removed and discarded. When serving, just peel it back to make a feathery handle. Delicious raw (even better when dipped into a thick fondant icing), the cape gooseberry makes a fine jam, though it lacks sufficient pectin to set a jelly.

Canjica com ciriguela de Peru

(Hominy porridge with Cape gooseberries)
Serves 4

A favorite Brazilian dessert, even better at breakfast. The acidity and juiciness of the fruit contrasts beautifully with the blandness and softness of the hominy, and is balanced by the richness of the coconut milk. If using dried rather than canned hominy, cook it like a porridge in double the volume of coconut milk—allow about 30 minutes at a steady simmer. Remember that you need hominy: lye-treated, skinned, precooked and dried corn kernels; untreated corn kernels or popcorn never soften.

1 pound can white hominy
2¹/₂ cups coconut milk
2 tablespoons white sugar
8 Cape gooseberries (or physalis), hulled and quartered
1 thick slice pineapple, thickly shredded

To finish (optional):
Honey or guava jelly

Drain the hominy. Bring the coconut milk to a boil with the sugar, stir in the hominy, and cook for 10 minutes, until most of the coconut milk has been absorbed. Let it cool slightly, toss with the fruit, and finish, if you like, with a spoonful of honey or guava jelly.

**Canjica com ciriguela, a delicious
breakfast porridge**

Mermelada de lulún

(Cape gooseberry jam)
Makes about 5 pounds

A deliciously tart jam—unusual and well worth the trouble, since you won't find it sold commercially.

3 pounds Cape gooseberries (or physalis)
Juice of 2 lemons
3 pounds preserving sugar (about 6–7 cups)—if unavailable, use about 6 cups granulated sugar
Hull and rinse the berries and put them in a large pan with the lemon juice and about 1¼ cups of water. Bring to a boil, turn down the heat, and simmer gently for half an hour, stirring occasionally to prevent sticking, until the fruit is quite soft. Meanwhile, put the sugar to warm in a low-temperature oven.

Stir the sugar into the berries and keep stirring over low heat until the crystals are completely dissolved. Boil for 10 minutes, or until setting-point is reached. To test, drop a little of the jam on a cold saucer and push it with your finger: when it wrinkles, it's ready. Pour into clean sterilized jars and store in a cool dark cupboard.

tamarillo

Tree tomatoes from Colombia on sale in Panama City

or tomate de arbol, tree tomato, Peruvian tomato (*Cyphomandra betacea*)

The tamarillo—its name in the United States and when commercially grown—is the fruit of a small tree native to the Amazonian highlands, capable of surviving at high altitudes, whose self-contained habit allows it to be grown as a decorative plant in pots.

Culinary uses

The purple variety is preferred for eating raw, but the yellow has a more pronounced flavor, with a subtle, rather carroty sweetness, and a richly spicy flavor that intensifies in the cooking process—it is wonderful in sauces and pickles.

Salsa de tamarillo

(Tamarillo sauce)
Serves 4

The flavor of this close relative of the tomato deepens and becomes spicier as it cooks—a remarkable process that can be enhanced by the inclusion of warm spices, such as cinnamon and ginger. Serve in the Andean style, with arepas for scooping, or as a sauce for chicken or fish (it is particularly good with broiled shrimp).

2 pounds red tamarillos, scalded,
  skinned, and chopped
1 red onion, finely chopped
1 fresh yellow chile, seeded and chopped
1 teaspoon powdered ginger
1 teaspoon powdered cinnamon
1 teaspoon sugar
Salt and pepper

To finish:
1 tablespoon oil

Put all the ingredients in a small pan and pour in a cup of water. Bring to a boil, put the lid on loosely enough to allow a little steam to escape, turn down the heat, and simmer gently for 20 to 30 minutes, until it is richly concentrated. Taste, and adjust the seasoning. Stir in the oil and serve at room temperature as a dipping sauce.

How it grows

The fruit are oval, about the size of a small egg, and hang together in clusters.

Appearance and taste

The fruit ripens in the wild to a sunny scarlet but is captive-bred to produce yellow and dark purple varieties. When cut, it looks like a tomato, revealing small black seeds clustered around a central pillar of flesh. The flavor is wonderfully rich and spicy, with the sweetness balanced by a satisfying acidity that is underlined by a strong fragrance of sun-ripened tomato.

Buying and storing

Tamarillos are available seasonally—May through October—in the United States. Look for firm fruits that seem heavy for their size. The yellower they are, the sweeter. If they're still hard, let them ripen at room temperature.

Medicinal and other uses

The skin of the tamarillo is inedible, so always peel it whether eating it raw or cooked. Never cut it on a wooden or any other absorbent surface: the juices stain anything they touch, and you'll never be able to remove the mark.

Tamarillo growing on the eastern slopes of the Andes, Bolivia

Mermelada de tamarillo

(Tamarillo chile jam)

Makes about four 1-pound jars

A chile-spiked jam to eat with *bolillos*— dense-crumbed bread rolls baked fresh every day for breakfast—thickly spread with cream cheese. Or use as a piquant stuffing for a tamale.

A fresh-flavored tamarillo salsa

2 pounds ripe tamarillos, skinned and chopped small
1 orange, peel and juice
1 lemon, peel and juice
1 teaspoon powdered cinnamon
1 teaspoon freshly grated allspice
2 small dried chiles, seeded and torn
About 4 cups granulated sugar

Put the fruit in a roomy pan with the citrus peels, spices, and chiles. Add half a glass of water, bring to a boil, turn down the heat, put the lid on loosely, and simmer gently for 20 to 30 minutes, stirring occasionally, until completely pulped. Measure it, and return it to the pan along with the same measure of sugar, add the two juices, and bring gently to a boil, stirring until the sugar dissolves. Let it boil, stirring to prevent sticking, until it sets—put some on a cold saucer and it should wrinkle when you push it with your finger. Put in warm, sterilized jars.

prickly pear

or nopalito (leaves), higo chumbo, tuna, Barbary pear, Indian fig, cactus pear (*Opuntia* spp.)

The prickly pear is the fruit of a cactus of Central American origin now naturalized in many parts of the world—including the Mediterranean—where the prickly plant does double duty as a source of food (both fruits and young paddles are eaten) and as a protective thicket for enclosing livestock.

How it grows

The body of the plant is formed by the paddles—leaf stems on whose outer edges the flowers and fruit appear. Both paddles and fruit are protected by clusters of vicious thorns that are very hard to remove once embedded in the fingers.

Appearance and taste

Technically a berry, the fruits are oval, small enough to cradle in the palm of the hand—which would be unwise as they're covered in evenly spaced bunches of needle-sharp thorns. They ripen from green through yellow to scarlet, darkening in some species to a deep purple-black, while others remain a brilliant yellow. The flesh is studded with small tender seeds and varies in color from shocking pink to soft cream, while the flavor and texture is somewhere between a strawberry and a banana, though it lacks acidity, rather like watermelon. Juicy, but without a strongly defined character, the prickly pear is at its best when combined with a more sharply flavored fruit or juice, or with a shake of angostura bitters.

Buying and storing

When ripe, the fruits vary from dark green to a deep magenta and should be a little soft; handle with care when buying, as a few short transparent prickles will inevitably be left behind. Check for moldy spots, a sign of trouble within, and don't buy if the skin looks faded. Darker fruits are the sweetest. Mexican children deal with the problem of the prickles by picking the fruit in the early morning when the dew has softened the thorns, and rubbing them in dry sand to scrape them off. When the fruits are offered for sale in the marketplace as a ready-to-eat snack, you'll notice a bucket of water set beside the seller, who soaks the fruit and scrapes it before peeling it fresh for each purchaser. If you buy unripe fruit, let it soften at room temperature and eat it as soon as it is ripe.

Medicinal and other uses

Very rich in minerals, vitamins, and protein, the prickly pear is truly manna in the desert.

Related or similar fruits

Two other fruit borne of cacti that are locally appreciated are the Barbados gooseberry, the fruit of *Pereskia aculeata,* a West Indian native—the fruits ripen through yellow to red and the flesh is sharp—and the strawberry pear or *pitaya*, the fruit of *Hylocereus undatus*, a cactus native to Central America but widely cultivated in Florida and the West Indies. The strawberry pear is roughly the same size and shape as the prickly pear but the skin is divided into smooth cones tipped with spines, rather like small pineapples. The flesh is white, sweet, and succulent, speckled with tiny black seeds—it is excellent eaten chilled, cut in half, and scooped out with a spoon.

Prickly pear growing above a shrine to Our Lady of Guadalupe, Mexico

Culinary uses

To eat the fruits raw, serve them ready-peeled on ice, with quartered limes, lemons, or passion fruit for squeezing; warn everyone about the seeds, which are perfectly edible but a little hard. Hand sugar around for those who like it, and chili flakes for the sophisticates. In its land of origin, the fruit pulp is spread in the sun and dried as a paste for winter storage.

Nopalitos en chile rojo
(Cactus paddles with red chile)
Serves 4

Make these with the tender young cactus paddles that appear on the edges of last year's growth in the spring. At this stage, when bright green and newly sprouted, they can be eaten raw, when the flavor is somewhere between fresh asparagus and young green beans. Wear gloves when scraping off the spines. As with asparagus or hearts of palm, you can buy them canned—cut into matchsticks and blanched.

*3–4 nopalitos (young cactus paddles), scraped
  and cut into matchsticks*
Salt

The sauce:
*²/₃ cup seeded, torn, dried chiles
  (a mixture of mild and hot)*
¹/₄ cup olive oil
1 large mild onion, finely chopped
4 garlic cloves, finely chopped

Put the nopalito matchsticks in enough boiling water to cover, salt lightly, bring to a boil, and cook for about 15 minutes, until tender. Drain and set aside, saving the cooking water.

Meanwhile make the sauce. Lightly toast the chiles in a dry pan for a minute or two—only until they change color—and be careful not to inhale the fumes. Remove and set aside. Heat the oil in a heavy pan and gently fry the onion and garlic until they soften and turn golden—about 10 minutes. Add the toasted chiles and 1¼ cups of the reserved nopalito cooking water.

Dulce de tunas con mango

Let it come to a boil, turn down the heat to simmer, and cook for 10 minutes until the sauce thickens. Stir in the reserved nopalitos and cook for another 5 minutes. Taste, and adjust the seasoning. Nopalitos in red chile are traditionally served with dried shrimp fritters (see page 77).

Dulce de tunas con mango
(Prickly pears with mango)
Serves 4

A sophisticated fruit salad that combines the flavors of the desert and the jungle.

4 prickly pears with their spikes rubbed off
1 orange, juice and peel
3 tablespoons fresh lime juice
1 tablespoon tequila (optional)
3 tablespoons honey
1 large mango or 2 smaller ones, diced

Carefully remove the skin of the prickly pears—avoiding any little bumps that might conceal left-behind spines—and mash the flesh with the two juices, the tequila, and the honey, and simmer for 10 minutes in a small pan along with the orange peel. Serve spooned over the diced mango.

pine-strawberry

or fresa de piña, fresa chilena (*Fragaria chiloensis*)

This big-berried, very sweet strawberry native to Chile and the Argentine has long been naturalized throughout the territory, and was cultivated by the Aztecs of Central America, who traded with the Incas.

How it grows

The pine-strawberry thrives in the wild on the Andean uplands. Once cultivated and crossed with the smaller but more acid Virginian strain and the tiny European wood strawberry, it became the mother of the deliciously fragrant, juicy, modern hybrids that are now the universal cultivar.

Appearance and taste

In its land of origin, there are red, yellow, and white varieties of the pine-strawberry. Though named for its pineapple flavor, it lacks the depth of fragrance and distinctive floweriness of the modern hybrid.

Buying and storing

The berries should be firm, sun-ripened, and without a trace of mold, with a bright color and strong fragrance; avoid any with green or white tips as these will not have been allowed to ripen properly and can cause the skin allergy known as hives. Check the hulls for signs of withering and the skin for mold or bad patches. Store in the refrigerator, eat as soon as possible, and bring up to room temperature before serving.

Medicinal and other uses

An easily digestible berry, the pine-strawberry cleanses the blood and clears toxins; it is recommended for cardiac problems and is a source of the anticancer compound ellagic acid. When pulped and applied topically, it is a remedy for skin complaints.

Culinary uses

To enjoy its fragrance and flavor, you will do best to eat it raw with a little sharp dressing. Since the fruit is low in pectin, jams will always be runny, so take care not to overcook.

The home of the pine-strawberry, the Andean uplands of Ecuador

Tamales negros de fresa

(Black tamales stuffed with strawberries)
Makes about 24—serves a party

A steaming pile of honey-sweetened fruit-stuffed tamales (cornmeal dumplings) is the star of any *tamalada,* a tamale party held to celebrate weddings and other joyful occasions. Montezuma, last emperor of the Aztecs, was said to prefer a strawberry-stuffed tamale to all others; the Guatemalans like their festive tamales colored and flavored with chocolate—the combination is irresistible.

The filling:
1 pound ripe strawberries
Juice of 1 bitter orange or lime

The dough:
3 cups masa harina
2 heaped tablespoons cocoa powder
A scrape of seeds from a vanilla bean (optional)
$1/2$ teaspoon salt
3 tablespoons soft butter or fresh white pork lard
Warm water
3 tablespoons honey

The wrappers:
12 pieces banana leaf cut into 12-inch squares, or corn husks, dried or fresh, or squares of foil

Prepare the strawberries: hull, cut them in quarters if large, and toss with the juice. Mix the masa harina with the cocoa powder, optional vanilla, salt, and butter or lard. Add enough warm water to make a smooth, slightly sticky dough and knead thoroughly: the grain swells as you work.

Lay the wrappers on a clean cloth, shiny side up if using banana leaves (hold them in a flame for a second to make them more bendable); if using corn husks, brush lightly with oil; if using foil squares, place shiny side up. Dampen your hands and break off a plum-sized lump of dough. Work it into a ball, place it on a wrapper, and pat it flat to make a rectangle the length and width of your hand. Drop a strawberry in the middle. Continue with all.

Fresas con naranja amarga y miel

To wrap, fold one of the long sides of the wrapper over to enclose two thirds of the filling (the husk will bring the dough with it), fold over the other long side, then fold over the short sides to complete the enclosure. Use a wet finger to seal the cracks. Fold the wrappers to make little torpedo-shaped wraps, long sides first, tucking the short sides under. Secure with a strip of husk or string.

Arrange the tamales in the steamer—a strainer set over a large saucepan will do—and fill the lower part with boiling water (it shouldn't make contact with the upper container). Cover with a layer of wrapper, and steam, with the lid tightly on, for an hour, until the tamales are perfectly firm, adding more boiling water as necessary. As with any steamed pudding, the more even the cooking temperature, the lighter the dumplings.

Fresas con naranja amarga y miel

(Strawberries with bitter orange and honey)
Serves 4

Very simple and very delicious. Lemon juice or sherry vinegar can replace the bitter orange juice.

1 pound big strawberries
$1/4$ cup dark forest honey
2 bitter oranges, peel and juice

Hull the strawberries and wipe them, but don't wash. Heat the honey in a small pan with the orange juice and peel, and simmer for about 10 minutes, until the honey thickens and acquires the flavor of the orange. Dress the strawberries with the honey.

mango

The mango, though native to India and the forests of Southeast Asia, arrived in the tropical Americas during the seventeenth century and has been perfectly at home ever since.

Growing mangoes in Panama

How it grows

The tree is a handsome evergreen—at first glance, not unlike a narrow-leaved magnolia, with a smooth gray trunk and dark green foliage. The fruits, green globes, are suspended from the branches on short vegetable ropes, like Christmas baubles, and do not ripen until they drop. The shape of the fruit is simplicity itself: a smooth-skinned sphere, elongated and slightly flattened, some ending in a little point where the flower-head was. Mango groves are found throughout the tropical belt, including Cuba and the Caribbean, though Puerto Rico and Brazil are the main exporters.

Appearance and taste

When ripe, the skin color can be green or yellow or blushed with scarlet, according to its breeding; the flesh ripens from translucent green to a soft yellow, some varieties deepening to a beautiful orange. The texture of a ripe mango is juicy, buttery, and soft, a little fibrous around the hard brown pit, with an apricot/peach/pineapple flavor. When unripe and green, the pit is white and soft, the skin tender, and the flesh much like that of a sharp green apple, refreshing and fragrant.

Buying and storing

The mango gives off practically no smell at all until almost overripe—as a fruit that ripens only after it falls and that needs to spread its seed beyond the confines of the tree's canopy, it waits for the perfect moment before attracting potential sowers. To test for ripeness, cradle the fruit in the palm of your hand and give it a gentle squeeze, looking for a slight movement in the flesh. If it is very soft, or the skin is mottled with black spots, it's already over the hill. Store in the refrigerator.

Medicinal and other uses

A powerful disinfectant, the mango is valuable in treating kidney complaints and digestive problems. Applied topically, it is a skin healer and pore cleanser.

Culinary uses

The fruit is eaten at all stages of ripeness, even when green and hard, the stage when it's particularly high in pectin and can be used to set a jelly. To remove the pit, just place the fruit on its narrowest edge and slip a knife between the flesh and the pit, following the curve that mirrors the shape of the pit; repeat on the other side, then deal as neatly as you can with the margins. If the variety is particularly fibrous, roll it in your hand to soften the flesh, make a small hole in the stalk end, and squeeze out the pulp.

Downtown juice bar in Rio de Janeiro

Cebiche de mango verde y aguacate

(Green mango and avocado seviche)
Serves 4–6 as an appetizer

A refreshing Ecuadorian vegetarian seviche: the crispness of the green mango is balanced by the softness of the avocado.

1 large red onion, thinly sliced into half-moons
Salt
2 small or 1 large green mango, pitted, skinned, and diced
2 small or 1 large avocado (ripe but not mushy), pitted, skinned, and diced
1 firm tomato or 1 chayote, diced
1 fresh chile (ají—green or yellow), seeded and finely chopped
2 tablespoons chopped cilantro
1 tablespoon pitted green olives, sliced
Juice of 2 lemons
1 teaspoon sugar

Soak the sliced onion in salted water for half an hour—until it goes limp and pink—to soften the flavor. Drain and pat dry. Fold the onion with the mango, avocado, tomato, chile, cilantro, olives, and lemon juice. Taste, and adjust the seasoning, adding the sugar if necessary. Chill until needed—overnight is fine.

Serve with toasted corn kernels, popcorn, and bread rolls for scooping.

Coconut parfait with mango purée

Serves 4

A deliciously delicate ice perfectly partnered with smooth mango. A sophisticated recipe from the Dominican Republic.

The parfait:
2 14-ounce cartons coconut cream
2 egg whites, lightly whisked
6 tablespoons sugar

The purée:
1 fresh ripe mango, skinned and pitted
A little lemon juice

Pour the coconut cream into a bowl and use a fork to blend: it should be about the consistency of light cream. In another bowl set over a pan of simmering water (or in a double-boiler), whisk the egg whites with the sugar until you have a thick shiny meringue that just holds its shape. Remove from the heat and continue to whisk until cool.

Fold the meringue into the coconut cream. Divide among small metal molds, cover with plastic wrap, and freeze until firm—4 to 5 hours. About 20 minutes before serving, unmold onto pretty plates: a parfait is best if left to soften a little.

Meanwhile, blend the mango flesh to a smooth golden purée with a little lemon juice. Pour this around the parfaits and serve it before it melts.

Coconut parfait with mango purée

cherimoya

or custard apple, chirimoya, soursop, anona blanca, graveola (Brazil), guanabana blanca (El Salvador), zapote de viejas (Mexico), pox (Mexico), chirimorriñón (Venezuela), sinini (Bolivia) *(Annona cherimoli)*

The cherimoya is the fruit of a tree native to Ecuador and Peru. The Incas gave it its name—"ice-seed" in Quechua—either for the snow-white flesh (all the brighter for the contrast with the jet-black seeds) or for its remarkable ability to survive the harsh winters of the Amazonian uplands.

Custard apples in Cuba

How it grows

The fruits sprout (as do many other jungle fruits) on the trunk, branches, or twigs of the tree.

Appearance and taste

Spherical and dimpled at the stalk end like an apple, the cherimoya is about the size of a grapefruit, though some can be much smaller or considerably larger, weighing up to 2 pounds. It is marked more or less obviously with irregularly spaced facets—fingerprints—which give it the appearance of a large, jade-skinned pinecone. The flesh when ripe is soft, creamy, and deliciously fragrant, with a pineapple/banana/vanilla flavor and enough acidity to stimulate the taste buds. The texture is grainy and rather pear-like close to the skin, graduating to fibrous and pineapple-like where it cradles the seeds. "Deliciousness itself," declared Mark Twain on tasting the fruit for the first time.

Buying and storing

In all varieties, the soft leathery skin remains more or less green when ripe. Choose a fruit without brown patches or signs of mold around the stalk end. Cradle the fruit in the palm of your hand and squeeze gently: though firm, the flesh should yield a little under the pressure. Handle gently as it bruises easily. To ensure a good proportion of pulp to seed, look for fruits with large scales (fingerprints): each of these indicates the position of a seed, of which the fewer the better.

Medicinal and other uses

The cherimoya is liberally endowed with vitamins A, B, and C, as well as assorted minerals.

Related or similar fruits

Soursop or guanabana, guana agrio, or prickly custard apple *(Annona muricata)* is a dark green, avocado-like fruit, curved on one side but flattish on the other (the sunny side grows faster than the shady side), and is distinguished from the cherimoya by the smoothness of its skin that, though lacking the pinecone effect, is fuzzed with soft spines. One of the largest of the family, it can weigh up to 11 pounds. The skin is leathery in appearance but quite tender, and the flesh is white and rather cottony, tangled up with a few large black seeds—leave them alone, they're toxic. At its best—and it's very variable in quality—the fruit is fragrant, succulent, astonishingly juicy, and deliciously sharp, sometimes so acidic, it needs sugaring. It makes a refreshing drink. A native of the Caribbean and northern South America, it is extensively cultivated in Mexico.

Sweetsop or bullock's heart *(A. reticulata)*, a cherimoya native to the Caribbean, has particularly large, bland-flavored fruits that

**Manjarblanco de cherimoya,
a smooth, creamy dessert**

ripen to russet on the sunny side and yellow on the other. As its name indicates, the flesh is sweet but lacks acidity; nevertheless, it has been cultivated since pre-Columbian times throughout Central America. From Central America it was exported to Africa and thence to Asia, where its tolerance of climate and prolific fruiting habits made it suitable rootstock for many modern cherimoya hybrids.

Sugar apple, the fruit of *Annona squamosa*, a tree native throughout the American tropics (also known as the sugar apple or scaly custard apple, for the impression of scales that cover the soft, green, pale-bloomed skin) is much appreciated in Brazil, where it's known as the count's apple, after the Conde de Miranda who cultivated the trees in his garden in Bahia. The creamy yellow flesh is fragrant, sweet, and succulent, with a flavor, observed the early colonizers, of rose water; it's rarely exported since it's fragile and apt to fall to bits if roughly handled. Its counterpart, the countess's *applebiriba*, the fruit of *Rollina mucosa*, another Amazonian native, ripens to a soft yellow and has ivory flesh, fragrant and succulent.

Ilama (*Annona diversifolia*), a Mexican native tree, is of more elongated shape and has an unmarked skin—rough or smooth, bloomed with white—which ripens to any color from green to pink to purple; the flesh of the pinker varieties is satisfyingly acid, while that of the green ones is as sweet and bland as the sugar apple.

The atemoya is a delicious new sweetsop–cherimoya hybrid that combines the vanilla/banana sweetness of one with the pineapple/citrus sharpness of the other.

Culinary uses
For custard apple purée, cut the fruit in half, scoop out the pulp, and push it through a strainer to separate the seeds from the flesh. To eat raw, cut the fruit in half and eat with a spoon. If you don't want to eat it immediately, sprinkle it with lemon juice to prevent browning.

Manjarblanco de cherimoya
(Custard apple blancmange)
Serves 4

A sophisticated Chilean dessert that combines an egg-thickened *dulce de leche* with creamy cherimoya. Finish with summer fruits of which Chile has more than its share, including its own variety of blackberry, *murtilla*, described by the Spanish conquistadores as the queen of all fruits.

*1 large can (14 ounces) sweetened
  condensed milk
1 large can (12 ounces) evaporated milk
2 large eggs, separated
1 large ripe cherimoya, seeded and mashed*

To finish:
*Whipped cream
Diced cherries, plums, or berries*

Combine the two milks in a heavy saucepan and cook gently, stirring steadily, over medium heat for 20 to 30 minutes, until it is as thick as sour cream and lightly caramelized. Let cool in a bowl.

Beat in the yolks, place the bowl over a panful of simmering water, and whisk until it thickens to a custard—about 10 minutes. Remove from the heat and fold in the egg whites, well-whisked. Fold in the cherimoya pulp. Serve well-chilled in pretty glasses, topped with whipped cream and whatever berries take your fancy—strawberries, being native to Chile, would be perfect.

Sorbete de cherimoya
(Custard apple sorbet)
Makes about 5 cups

The fruit's natural viscosity makes it the perfect candidate for a sorbet—looking and tasting like an ice cream but without the cream.

*2 pounds cherimoyas (2 fruits)
1/2 cup sugar
1 1/4 cups water
Juice of l lemon*

Quarter, skin, and seed the cherimoyas. Boil the sugar and water together for 5 minutes and let cool. Blend the flesh of the cherimoyas with the sugar syrup and the lemon juice. Freeze until quite solid. Turn out, blend again, and refreeze.

Defrost for half an hour before serving: this is quite a creamy sorbet with a very subtle flavor and should not be served rock-hard. Delicious with a tall, cool glass of iced maté tea.

Barbados cherry

Cherries growing in Chile

or acerola (Puerto Rico), garden cherry, cereza de Jamaica
(Malpighia punicifolia)

The fruit of a small tree native to subtropical America, the
Barbados cherry is particularly appreciated in Puerto Rico
and the West Indies.

How it grows

This thin-skinned, three-sided berry, scarlet
when ripe, has yellow flesh surrounding three
smooth, brown, close-fitting seeds. It is a
member of the jungle berries group, which
includes myrtles as well as some of the less
familiar members of the lychee family. All bear
small, cherrylike fruit.

Appearance and taste

This particularly delicious fruit looks like a cherry,
tastes like a raspberry, and develops a sharp,
green apple flavor when cooked.

Buying and storing

Try before you buy, though you are more likely
to find Barbados cherries in the garden than the
market. Keep them in a cool dry pantry; jungle
fruits have a remarkably long shelf life.

Medicinal and other uses

Cherry fruits and jungle berries of all types are
loaded with citric acid, delivering as much
vitamin C as the rose hip. In Venezuela,
mamoncillo seeds are roasted and pounded
with honey as a cure for diarrhea.

Related or similar fruits

The Brazilian jungle berry or *Japoticaba myciaria*
(formerly *Eugenia*) *cauliflora*, a member of the
myrtle family, is particularly esteemed in the
markets of Rio de Janeiro. The fruits look like
black cherries and grow directly from the trunk
and branches of a large tree. They are mostly
eaten fresh, though they're also made into jams
and jellies.

The small round Brazilian cherry or grumichama
(Eugenia brasiliensis) is the fruit of a tree
belonging to the aromatic myrtle family that is
native to Brazil and Peru. The pulp is variable in
color—it can be crimson, yellow, or white—but
all varieties are considered equally delicious. It is
usually eaten raw.

Pitomba *(Eugenia luschnathiana)* is the small,
round, orange, cherrylike fruit of another
Brazilian native tree that is also a member of the
myrtle family. The flavor and texture are much
like that of an apricot; the fruit is usually eaten
fresh, but is also used locally in preserves.

The Surinam cherry or pitanga, pendanga
(Venezuela), cereza de cayena, or cereza
quadrada (Colombia) *(Eugenia uniflora)* is the
fruit of a berry-bearing shrub of the myrtle family
native to Amazonia. It is grown in Brazil and
Peru (and elsewhere) as an ornamental garden
plant and bears deeply ridged four-sided berries
that ripen to a brilliant scarlet. The flesh is
fragrant but a little bitter, centered on a single
resinous seed (remove the seed and chill the
flesh to neutralize the resin). It is usually eaten
raw, sprinkled with sugar.

The honeyberry or *mamón, mauco, mamoncillo,
genip,* or *grosela de miel* (honey gooseberry,
Mexico) *(Melicocca bijuga)* is a large tree of the
lychee family. A native of Colombia and
Venezuela, the honeyberry is also found in
Caribbean gardens. In Barbados, it is
considered interchangeable with ackee. The
fruits hang from the branches in clusters of what
look like miniature limes. It is sour when unripe
but juicy, crisp, and sweet when ripe—
translucent, pale green, and a little fibrous. The
single seed is edible. To eat in the hand, bite a
small hole in the skin and suck out the juices.
For a refreshing summer cordial, peel, cook, and
push through a strainer to extract the juice.

An alternative source of wintertime vitamin C is
provided by a refreshing scarlet tea prepared
from the dried or fresh flower buds of the roselle
(Hibiscus sabdariffa), a small tree native to North
Africa but naturalized throughout the Caribbean
and Central America, where it blooms exuberantly
alongside the state highways. The infusion, known
as "sorrel" in Jamaica and "Jamaica water" in
Panama, is very tart and usually drunk chilled. The
flavor is bitter-cherry, the color a festive ruby-red:
Christmas in the Caribbean wouldn't be the same
without it.

Orinoco apple or cocono and tupiro (*Solanum sessiliforum*), a jungle berry of the same family as the naranjilla, is very fragrant and sweet, with cream-colored flesh and a jelly like yellow heart.

Culinary uses

The Barbados cherry is good in pies and jams. Small fruits such as these with tough skins and large pits can be skinned, simmered in water to extract the flavor, then pulped or strained for use in syrups and sweet sauces. If the seed is edible, roast it and crush it for inclusion in a pastry or crumble.

Pastelitos de acerola

(Barbados cherry tartlets)
Makes a dozen tartlets

Deliciously sweet-sour, with a flavor and fragrance not unlike a ripe raspberry, the Barbados cherry is perfect in a tart.

The almond pastry dough:
1¹/2 cups all-purpose flour
2/3 cup ground almonds
1 tablespoon sugar
1/2 teaspoon salt
2/3 cup butter (1¹/4 sticks)
3 tablespoons cold water

The filling:
1 pound Barbados cherries (or other cherries), pitted (squeeze through the stalk end)
4–6 tablespoons sugar (depending on the cherries' acidity)
Juice of an orange and a lemon
1 teaspoon cornstarch mixed with a little water
2–3 tablespoons custard or sour cream

Toss the flour with the ground almonds, sugar, and salt in a bowl. Cut the butter into the flour with a knife and then rub it in lightly with your fingertips until the mixture looks like fine bread crumbs. Sprinkle in the water and press into a firm smooth ball of dough, still using your fingertips. Put the dough aside to rest in a plastic bag in a cool place for 30 minutes, to swell and gain elasticity.

Preheat the oven to 425°F.

Roll the pastry dough out with a floured rolling pin—use small light movements: the dough is fragile. Use a wine glass or cookie cutter to cut circles of the right size for your tartlet molds. Place the dough circles in the molds and prick the bottoms with a fork to prevent any bubbles forming. Bake for 15 to 20 minutes—the almond pastry will first whiten and then turn golden. Remove to a cooling rack to crisp and cool.

Meanwhile, put the pitted cherries in a pan with the sugar and the juices, diluted with an equal amount of water. Bring to a boil, turn down the heat, and simmer for 10 to 15 minutes, until the cherries are tender. Remove with a slotted spoon and set aside. Let the syrup cool a little, then stir in the cornstarch, reheat, and let it boil for a moment to thicken.

Put a teaspoonful of the custard or sour cream into the bottom of each tartlet, arrange a few cherries on the top, and finish with the thickened syrup.

Pastelitos de acerola, Barbados cherry tarts

Acerola and raisin relish

Makes about 2 pounds

A Barbadian sweet and sour chutney that can be eaten as a dip. It is very good with cold meats, particularly pork.

1 pound Barbados cherries (or other cherries), pitted and roughly chopped
1/4 cup raisins
2 tablespoons shredded coconut
1 teaspoon ground allspice
1 teaspoon chopped fresh ginger
1 finger-length cinnamon stick, broken
1¹/4 cups vinegar
1 cup plus 2 tablespoons dark brown sugar
1 teaspoon salt

Put all the ingredients into a large saucepan and add a half cup of water. Stir, bring to a boil, turn down the heat, and simmer, stirring to avoid sticking, until all is perfectly tender and the sharp taste of the vinegar has mellowed—40 minutes or so.

Pour into sterilized jars and seal.

mamee apple

or mamey, St. Domingo apricot, abricozeiro, abricó do Pará (Brazil) (*Mammea americana*)

How it grows

The fruit of a tropical tree, the mamee apple is a member of the same family as the mangosteen of Southeast Asia. Originally native to Brazil, it is now cultivated throughout the region but rarely exported. It is delicious eaten fresh from the hand, in a *liquado*, or sliced into a fruit salad with cream and sugar.

Appearance and taste

This round, russet-colored, tough-skinned, winter fruit is about the size and shape of a large peach, coming to a point at the base. The skin is bitter but the yellowy-orange pulp, embracing three smooth, ivory-colored inedible seeds, is sweet and fragrant, with a scent of caramel and vanilla. The texture varies from crisp and firm to soft and rather custardy.

Buying and storing

To test for ripeness, use your nose: the scent should be vanilla/caramel with no hint of fermentation. Hold the fruit in the palm of your hand and squeeze gently, rejecting any that feel soft rather than yielding. When overripe and lacking acidity, the flesh is woolly and sickly sweet.

Medicinal and other uses

Medicinally, the mamee apple has some antibiotic properties, but some people might experience digestive problems. If you're eating it for the first time, try a small slice only.

Culinary uses

To prepare the mamee apple for eating or cooking, score the skin from top to bottom and peel it off in segments. Then scrape off the whitish membrane beneath, to expose the soft orange flesh (the membrane that encloses the seeds is also bitter); it is delicious in a fruit salad with cream. Unripe fruits are best for cooking and have enough pectin to set a jelly.

Mamee apple smoothie

Mamee apple jelly
Makes 8–10 jars

Choose firm fruits and prepare carefully: score the skin from top to bottom and peel it off in segments, then scrape off the whitish membrane beneath to expose the soft orange flesh, discarding the skin, the pit, and the bitter membrane that encloses the pit. Mamee apple jelly is prepared with the pulp only. If you have trouble achieving a set, add a bottle of pectin.

6 pounds prepared mamee apple
Juice of 4 bitter oranges or lemons
3–4 cloves
About 6 pounds preserving sugar
 (about 12–13 cups)—if unavailable, use
 granulated sugar

Put the mamee apple pulp, lemon juice, and cloves into a deep preserving pan with a cup of water, and cook down to a mush. Tip everything into a jelly bag (or clean cloth pinned on the legs of an upturned stool). Set a bowl underneath to catch the juice and let it drip overnight.

The next day, measure the cloudy juice (don't press the pulp), return it to the pan, and stir in an equal amount of sugar. Stir gently over the heat until the sugar dissolves, then boil rapidly until a drop poured onto a cold saucer forms a skin when pushed with a finger—20 to 40 minutes. When cool, pour into clean jars, top with a circle of wax paper dipped in rum, and seal, or cover any way that will exclude the air.

Mamee apple smoothie
Serves 4

Fresh fruits puréed with milk—*liquado*—are prepared to order for the passers-by at roadside stands throughout the region. For the traveler,s this is one of the best ways to savor the delicate flavor of unfamiliar, rare, or exotic fruits.

2 ripe mamee apples, skinned and seeded
2¹/2 cups milk
2 tablespoons sugar

Drop the mamee pulp along with the milk and sugar into the blender and purée until smooth.

red mombin

or jocote, xocote (Mexico and Guatemala), cajá or hobó (Brazil), ciruela roja (red plum—Cuba), Brazilian plum (*Spondias purpurea*)

The fruit of a small tree native to Amazonia, the red mombin is found throughout the tropics, from southern Mexico through to Peru and northern Brazil.

Appearance and taste

The fruits are round or oval, about the size of a damson plum, thin-skinned, and rather like a small mango, ripening to a sunny yellow or even scarlet. The flesh is sharp-flavored and spicy, with a hard, nut-like core that can be cracked and eaten.

Buying and storing

Try before you buy: the flesh should be soft and juicy, sweet and not too sharp. Store in the refrigerator for no more than a couple of days.

Medicinal and other uses

The juice is drunk as a diuretic and to lower a fever.

Related or similar fruits

Yellow mombin or *ciruela amarilla* (Cuba) or hog plum (*Spondias pinnata*) is the fruit of a tree native to the American tropics, much appreciated by pigs as well as humans—though, being only mildly acidic and on the watery side, and therefore less distinctive in flavor, it is considered less good than the red mombin.

The Brazilian greengage or imbu or umbu (*Spondias tuberosa*) is the fruit of a Brazilian native tree; oval or roundish, ripening to a yellowy green, with much the same shape and size as a greengage plum, it is generally held to be the most delicious of the genus. Its skin is thickish and quite tough, the flesh soft, fragrant, and spicy; acidic when unripe, the flesh sweetens as it ripens. It makes excellent jelly.

The South Seas ambarella (*Spondias dulcis*), a larger fruit of the same family, was planted in the West Indies and is much sought-after in the markets of Trinidad, where it's used unripe in relishes, and ripe in jams.

Culinary uses

If eaten fresh, the Brazilian plum is best served chilled—it looks pretty on a bed of ice. To eat the nuts, crack the pits and extract the kernels.

Picante de jocote

(Deviled Brazilian plum)
Serves 4

A tart little relish for serving with bean dishes. Sour plums or damsons can replace the mombin.

1 pound red mombin, pitted and diced
3–4 scallions, chopped with their green
1 teaspoon honey
Juice of 1 lime
1 red or green chile, seeded and finely chopped

Toss the diced mombin with the scallions, dress with honey and lime juice, and finish with a sprinkling of chopped chile.

sapote

or zapote, lucuma (Peru), sapote de carne (flesh-sapote, Colombia), mamey (Cuba), chachas (Mexico)
(*Pouteria*—formerly *Lucuma*—*sapota*)

The sapote is native to southern Mexico and is found in the wild as far south as Nicaragua; it is widely cultivated throughout the region (and also in Southeast Asia).

How it grows

The winter-maturing fruit of a small shrubby tree, the sapote is one of several soft-fleshed, thin-skinned, winter-maturing fruits of a group that, though not necessarily of the family Sapotaceae, bear an identical or similar name—a word derived, as it happens, from the Aztec *zpotl,* which simply means "soft."

Appearance and taste

The fruits are large and oval, with reddish skins and pinkish-orange, soft, sweet flesh with a banana/pineapple/vanilla fragrance and flavor.

Buying and storing

As a winter fruit, the sapote should be tree-ripened, so avoid any that are not fully mature—they should be fragrant and yield a little when cradled gently in the palm.

Medicinal and other uses

Of the sapote and the following related fruits, some—particularly the sapote—are soporific; the star-apple is recommended for laryngitis and to clear lungs affected by pneumonia.

Related or similar fruits

The canistel or yellow sapote, *huicón, kanis, costiczapotl* (Mexico) and egg-fruit (West Indies) (*Pouteria campechiana*—formerly *Lucuma rivicoa*) looks rather like a small mango: round, but tapers to a point. The skin is smooth and thin, ripening to a smooth shiny orange, and the flesh—sometimes likened to a hard-boiled egg yolk, with the flavor and texture of sweet potato—softens toward the center, which contains the large, black, shiny seeds. The skin and flesh both ripen to a sunny yellow.

The naseberry (West Indies), or *sapodilla* or *sapote chico* (*Manilkara zapota*), is the fruit of an evergreen tree native to central America and the Caribbean, also known as the chicle tree since the sap—*chicle*—is the raw material of chewing gum. The fruit itself, a round yellow-skinned berry covered in brown fuzz, is about the size of a plum; when cut, the flesh looks grainy, like a pear, and ripens to a sunny apricot or pinkish color, with large, flat, black seeds.

Considered one of the most delicious of the continent's native fruits, the naseberry has a delicate fragrance—jasmine, honey, lily of the valley—and soft, juicy flesh of an intense sweetness, like brown sugar. It is usually eaten raw and ripe (some people like it overripe). To eat raw, cut it in half, flip out the smooth seeds, and eat it with a spoon, with a squeeze of orange juice to counteract the sweetness; in the West Indies, it is boiled down into a syrup for later dilution.

The white sapote or zapote blanco (Mexico), matasano (elsewhere in South America) and Mexican orange (*Casimiroa edulis*) is a native of Mexico that has never really been popular anywhere else. The small round fruit is a member of the citrus family (Rutaceae) and has an orange skin, the characteristic citrus interior, and a mild pearlike flavor. Its last name—*matasano* or kill-health—is a reference to suspected soporific properties.

Black sapote or *zapote negro, zapote prieto,* or *sapodillo* (*Diospyros ebenaster*) is a winter fruit that ripens on the branch after the leaves have fallen, and looks rather like a slightly flattened tomato. A member of the persimmon family, it is about the size of a large tangerine with a thin, greenish skin and soft, sweet, almost black flesh, with small seeds.

Star-apple or *cainito* (*Chrysophillum cainito*) is an ancient Central American cultivar, probably native to the West Indies. A soft-fleshed fruit about the size of a small apple, the star-apple is pointed at the flower end, with a thin skin and a star-shaped, jelly-like heart in which are buried flat brown seeds. The fruit needs to ripen on the tree, making it difficult to export. When mature, the flesh is a soft ivory (*cainito blanco*) or a deep purple (*cainito morado*). It is usually eaten fresh, but is also made into jam.

Consumption warning

The skins and seeds of all these winter fruits are often toxic. Take no risks: when eating raw, use a spoon to scoop out the soft pulp, and skin and core carefully.

Sorbete de lucuma

(Sapote sorbet)
Makes about 1 quart

Peru's favorite ice cream. The lucuma gives it a creamy texture and a maple syrup/vanilla flavor. In Chile as well as Peru, the pulp and juice can conveniently be bought canned—ready for a smoothie or a sorbet.

1 can (12 ounces) evaporated milk
4 egg yolks
2¹/₂ cups sapote pulp

Make a custard with the milk and egg yolks: put both in a bowl set over simmering water (or in a double boiler), and whisk until it thickens to a custard that will coat the back of a spoon.

Let the custard cool. Stir in the pulped sapote. Freeze as usual—easier if you have an ice cream machine. If all you have is the freezer, you will have to freeze the sorbet until it is nearly solid and then remove it, and beat it thoroughly to incorporate as much air as possible, and pop it back in the freezer. Move it from the freezer into the refrigerator half an hour before you are ready to eat. Serve with crunchy cookies flavored with cinnamon and cloves called *revolución caliente*, a political reference to the struggle for independence.

Matrimonia

Serves 2—of course

A marriage of two juices, Jamaican-style, one smooth and flowery, the other sharp and citrus.

1¹/₄ cups sapote juice
1¹/₄ cups orange juice

Mix the two juices and pour over ice. Sit under a palm tree and sip it in the sun.

Matrimonia

index

Author's acknowledgments

First and foremost, I owe a deep debt of gratitude to Francine Lawrence, not only for her skills as a photographer but for her foresight in abandoning the editorship of *Country Living* to explore some of the lesser known corners of what is, after all, a dauntingly vast, ethnically diverse, and sometimes inaccessible continent. Without her collaboration—no other word will do—along with the sparkling styling of Susi Hoyle and the help of Brent Darby and Jon Day on long days spent between camera and stove, this book might never have blossomed. My thanks are also due to Helen Woodhall, Caroline Taggart, Esme West, and the meticulous Robina Pelham Burn for unflagging support and patient editing from first bud to final fruit, and to designer Geoff Hayes for creating order out of chaos. And to Kyle Cathie for proposing and piloting the project, Michael Bateman for confirming her choice, and my beloved agent Abner Stein for making the whole thing happen.

Among sources consulted during the course of research, I have sought both inspiration and information from the work of Diana Kennedy, Elisabeth Lambert Ortiz, Nitza Villapol, Michelle O. Fried, Alan Davidson, Jessica B. Harris, Sophie Coe, Heidi Cusick, Cristine Mackie, Christopher Idone, Antonio Montana, Himilice Novas and Rosemary Silva, Michael Bateman, Maricel Presilla, Marlena Spieler, Lourdes Nichols, and contributors to the small but brilliant Petits Propos Culinaires.

The author, publishers, and photographer would like to thank the following for their contributions to the book:

Fired Earth Ltd,
Twyford Mill,Oxford Road, Oxon OX17 3HP, England
Telephone: 01295 814 300

The Spice Shop
Spices, herbs from all over the world
1 Blenheim Crescent, London W11, England
Telephone: 020 7221 4448

Sean Miller
Colorful ovenproof and dishwasher-safe pottery
108 Dewsbury Road, London NW10 1EP, England
Telephone: 0208 208 0148

Ceramica Blue
Brightly colored plates and bowls
10 Blenheim Crescent, London W11, England
Telephone: 020 7727 0288

Fired Earth
Tiles from Mexico and South America
117 Fulham Road, London SW3, England
Telephone: 0207 589 0489

The Denby Pottery Company Ltd
Denby, Derby DE5 8MX, England
Telephone: 01773 740700

Photographic acknowledgments

Key: GPL—Garden Picture Library; SAP—South American Pictures; APA – Andes Press Agency; RH—Robert Harding; TI—Travel Ink; ICL—Impact Colour Library; FY—Francesca Yorke; (t)—top; (m)—middle; (b)—bottom; (l)—left; (r)—right

All photographs by Francine Lawrence except the following pages:
1 ICL/Adrian Sherratt; 2–3 SAP/Marion Morrison; 6 FY; 9 FY; 10 ICL/Rhonda Klevansky; 11 APA/Anna Gordon; 12 TI/David Forman; 14 SAP/Robert Francis; 15 SAP/Jason P Howe; 16–17 FY; 18–19 FY; 20 ICL/Robert Gibbs; 24 ICL/Peter Menzel; 26 SAP/Robert Francis; 28 TI/Abbie Enock; 32 GPL/Gary Rogers; 34 SAP/Tony Morrison; 38 APA/Carlos Reyes-Manzo; 40 RH/Robert Frerck; 42 GPL/Brigitte Thomas; 44 FY; 47 APA/Carlos Reyes-Manzo; 48–9 SAP/Charlotte Lipson; 50 (l) Holt Studios International/Willem Harinck; 51 SAP/Charlotte Lipson; 56–7 SAP/Tony Morrison; 58 SAP/Tony Morrison; 60(m) ICL/Nancy Bravo; 60(b) APA/John Curtis; 62 ICL/Susan Campbell; 64 APA/Carlos Reyes-Manzo; 65 TI/Grazyna Bonati; 66 ICL/Rachel Morton; 72(t) FY; 72(b) Julie Dixon; 74 SAP/Tony Morrison; 78 ICL/Piers Cavendish; 80 APA/Carlos Reyes-Manzo; 84 SAP/Robert Francis; 88 TI/Dennis Stone; 94 APA/Carlos Reyes-Manzo; SAP/Marion Morrison; 100–1 SAP/Tony Morrison; 102 ICL/Rhonda Klevansky; 104 ICL/Charles Coates; 106 RH/Charles Bowman; 108 SAP/Tony Morrison; 110–1 APA/Carlos Reyes-Manzo; 112 TI/Abbie Enock; 114 TI/Brian Garrett; 118 ICL/Robert Gibbs; 120 SAP/Robert Francis; 123 SAP/Tony Morrison; 126 SAP/Tony Morrison; 128 ICL/Rhonda Klevansky; 130–1 ICL/Neil Morrison; 134 SAP/Chris Sharp; 136 FY; 140 ICL/Simon Shepheard; 142 ICL/Robert Gibbs; 144 ICL/Robert Gibbs; 146 SAP/Jason P. Howe; 148 SAP/Chris Sharp; 150 ICL/Sergio Dorantes; 156(b) SAP/Mike Harding; 160 SAP/Jason P. Howe; 162–3 SAP/Tony Morrison; 166(b) FY; 168 APA/Carlos Reyes-Manzo; 170 SAP/Chris Sharp; 172 SAP/Mike Harding; 174 ICL/Christopher Pillittz; 176 ICL/Charles Coates; 180 APA/Carlos Reyes-Manzo; 182(t) SAP/Tony Morrison; 184 SAP/Chris Sharp; 186 SAP/Tony Morrison; 190(br) APA/Carlos Reyes-Manzo; 192 SAP/Chris Sharp; 194(l) SAP/Tony Morrison; 196 Sally Maltby; 197 ICL/Sally Fean; 200–1 TI/Brian Garrett; 202 FY; 204 ICL/Alain le Garsmeur; 206 ICL/Cristina Pawel); 208 SAP/Tony Morrison; 210 APA/Carlos Reyes-Manzo; 212 APA/Carlos Reyes-Manzo; 214(bl) SAP/Mike Harding; 216 TI/Brian Garrett; 218(t) SAP/Mike Harding; 218(b) SAP/Tony Morrison; 220 APA/Carlos Reyes-Manzo; 220 GPL/Lamontagne; 224(m) APA/Carlos Reyes-Manzo; 224(b) ICL/Michael Mirecki; 226 SAP/Rolando Pujol; 228 APA/Carlos Reyes-Manzo